CROSS-CULTURAL TEAM BUILDING

Latest titles in the McGraw-Hill Training Series

Details of these and other titles in the series are available from:

The Product Manager, Professional Books, McGraw-Hill Publishing Company,
Shoppenhangers Road, Maidenhead, Berkshire SL6 2QL, United Kingdom
Tel: 01628 23432 Fax: 01628 770224

Cross-cultural team building

Guidelines for more effective communication and negotiation

Mel Berger

The McGraw-Hill Companies

London · New York · St Louis · San Francisco · Auckland
Bogotá · Caracas · Lisbon · Madrid · Mexico · Milan
Montreal · New Delhi · Panama · Paris · San Juan · São Paulo
Singapore · Sydney · Tokyo · Toronto

Published by
McGRAW-HILL Publishing Company
Shoppenhangers Road, Maidenhead, Berkshire SL6 2QL, England
Telephone: 01628 23432
Fax: 01628 770224

British Library Cataloguing in Publication Data
Berger, Mel
    Cross-cultural team buliding: guidelines for more
    effective comunication and negotiation. – (McGraw-Hill
    training series)
    1. Work groups – Cross-cultural studies 2. Personnel
    management
    I. Title
    658.4′02

    ISBN 0-07-707919-1

Library of Congress Cataloging-in-Publication Data
Cross-cultural team building: guidelines for more effective
    communication and negotiation / Mel Berger.
        p. cm. – (McGraw-Hill training series)
    Includes index.
    ISBN 0-07-707919-1 (pbk.: alk. paper)
    1. Work groups. 2. Intercultural communication. 3. Corporate
culture. I. Berger, Mel. II. Series.
    HD66.C764   1996
    658.4′02—dc20   96-19791
                                                                    CIP

McGraw-Hill

A Division of The **McGraw·Hill** Companies

12345 CUP 99876

Typeset by BookEns Limited, Royston, Herts.
and printed and bound in Great Britain at the University Press, Cambridge

Printed on permanent paper in compliance with ISO Standard 9706.

This book is dedicated to my cross-cultural loved ones:
wife, Pam
son, Josh
daughter, Monica
my parents

Contents

Series preface

Training and development are now firmly centre stage in most, if not all, organizations. Nothing unusual in that—for some organizations. They have always seen training and development as part of the heart of their businesses—but more and more must see it that same way.

The demographic trends through the 1990s will inject into the marketplace severe competition for good people who will need good training. Young people without conventional qualifications, skilled workers in redundant crafts, people out of work, women wishing to return to work—all will require excellent training to fit them to meet the job demands of the 1990s and beyond.

But excellent training does not spring from what we have done well in the past. T&D specialists are in a new ball game. 'Maintenance' training—training to keep up skill levels to do what we have always done—will be less in demand. Rather, organization, work and market change training are now much more important and will remain so for some time. Changing organizations and people is no easy task, requiring special skills and expertise which, sadly, many T&D specialists do not possess.

To work as a 'change' specialist requires us to get to centre stage—to the heart of the company's business. This means we have to ask about future goals and strategies, and even be involved in their development, at least as far as T&D policies are concerned.

This demands excellent communication skills, political expertise, negotiating ability, diagnostic skills—indeed, all the skills a good internal consultant requires.

The implications for T&D specialists are considerable. It is not enough merely to be skilled in the basics of training, we must also begin to act like business people and to think in business terms and talk the language of business. We must be able to resource training not just from within but by using the vast array of external resources. We must be able to manage our activities as well as any other manager. We must share in the creation and communication of the company's vision. We must never let the goals of the company out of our sight.

In short, we may have to grow and change with the business. It will be hard. We shall have to demonstrate not only relevance but also value for money and achievement of results. We shall be our own boss, as accountable for results as any other line manager, and we shall have to deal with fewer internal resources.

The challenge is on, as many T&D specialists have demonstrated to me over the past few years. We need to be capable of meeting that challenge. This is why McGraw-Hill Publishing Company have planned and launched this major new training series—to help us meet that challenge.

The series covers all aspects of T&D and provides the knowledge base from which we can develop plans to meet the challenge. They are practical books for the professional person. They are a starting point for planning our journey into the twenty-first century.

Use them well. Don't just read them. Highlight key ideas, thoughts, action pointers or whatever, and have a go at doing something with them. Through experimentation we evolve; through stagnation we die.

I know that all the authors in the McGraw-Hill Training Series would want me to wish you good luck. Have a great journey into the twenty-first century.

ROGER BENNETT
Series Editor

About the series editor

Roger Bennett has over 20 years' experience in training, management education, research and consulting. He has long been involved with trainer training and trainer effectiveness. He has carried out research into trainer effectiveness, and conducted workshops, seminars, and conferences on the subject around the world. He has written extensively on the subject including the book *Improving Trainer Effectiveness*, Gower. His work has taken him all over the world and has involved directors of companies as well as managers and trainers.

Dr Bennett has worked in engineering, several business schools (including the International Management Centre, where he launched the UK's first master's degree in T&D), and has been a board director of two companies. He is the editor of the *Journal of European Industrial Training* and was series editor of the ITD's *Get In There* workbook and video package for the managers of training departments. He now runs his own business called The Management Development Consultancy.

About the authors

Editor **Mel Berger**

Mel Berger is the business group manager of the Human Resource Development team of the GEC Management College, near Rugby in the UK. He is a very experienced trainer and consultant, with a reputation for developing innovative approaches to learning and organizational development.

An American by birth, where he received an MBA from the University of California at Los Angeles, he has lived in Britain for over 25 years. During the past five years he has specialized in cross-cultural training and team building. He has carried out major assignments for European, American and Asian managers. Additionally, he has developed and implemented approaches to building interdepartmental collaboration.

He has written over 20 articles and is currently on the editorial board of three professional journals.

Contributors **John W. Bing**

President and founder of ITAP International, John Bing was educated at Harvard College and received his EdD from the Center for International Education, University of Massachusetts. His firm, located in Princeton, New Jersey, USA, provides a global consulting, training and information service to the pharmaceutical, telecommunications and consumer industries, as well as to the United Nations. ITAP International is now involved in a two-year, global team-training project with the lead scientists of a Swiss-based pharmaceutical firm. John was a recent winner of the American Society for Training and Development's International Practitioner's Award.

Raymond B. Cadwell

Dr Raymond B. Cadwell, PhD, is an Irish practitioner who has been in the organization development and training field for over 25 years. He currently directs an international consulting and training practice which covers the USA, Belgium, Sweden, Germany and the Netherlands. He speaks fluent German and Dutch.

Some current projects include:

1 Introducing more self-directed teams in two manufacturing companies.
2 Implementing a programme called 'working together to create a quality world' for a health care company.
3 Carrying out a culture assessment for a large life assurance company and developing an OD programme.
4 Reducing prejudice between managers and workers in a company in the food industry.

He has just completed a book entitled *Leading on Equality* for McGraw-Hill which describes his work on changing attitudes in British, Irish and US companies. He has also written a manual on coaching.

His organization structure design workshop is part of his ongoing commitment to developing rapid change capability within organizations. This enables managers to restructure their organizations within a short period and develop buy-in at the same time.

Raymond is the Irish co-ordinator for the International Organisation Development Association.

Sue Canney Davison

In the early 1980s Sue Canney Davison, PhD, spent six years as part of an international team running a charitable institution in the Himalayas. During that time she acted as an informal adviser to an Indo-Canadian hydroelectric project, witnessing the rewards and disasters that spanned the cross-cultural divide. She returned to the UK in 1986 and began facilitating cross-cultural programmes with Shell. Clients have included Ford Motor Company, Citibank, BP, Grand Metropolitan, Daimler Benz, ICI, Shell, Wellcome, British Gas, Exxon Chemicals, Fiat, Kone, Management Centre Europe, business schools and universities.

During 1993/4 Sue was part of a team of four that conducted a large research project into transnational teams for International Consortium for Educational Development and Research, Lexington, Massachusetts, (ICEDR), a consortium of 30 multinationals and 20 business schools, including Ford, Daimler Benz, Fiat and many others. Through interviews and surveys of over 50 teams, this research highlighted the strategic contributions, the human resource implications and effective best practices of transnational teams. By combining research with her practical consulting with real teams, a life-cycle model of best practices for high performing international teams has evolved.

In recent years, Sue has travelled the world running executive programmes and talking at conferences in order to promote diversity and share best practice in effective international teams and management. She currently spends her time between homes in London and Nairobi.

Dennis Clackworthy

Dennis Clackworthy holds the position of consultant, intercultural relations for Siemens AG, Munich. He commenced his working life in human resources with a postgraduate Diploma in Personnel Management from Manchester University, after studying psychology and sociology at Rhodes University in South Africa. He then gained human resource management (HRM) experience in London, Pretoria and Johannesburg, where he headed up the HR function for Siemens in South Africa for seven years. Married with two children, he was transferred to Germany 20 years ago and has concentrated on intercultural management issues since 1982. After pioneering the bicultural interaction training described in Chapter 6, his main interest is now multicultural team training.

Sergio Gardelliano

Sergio Gardelliano is chief of the staff development and training section, personnel services division within the United Nations Industrial Development Organization (UNIDO) at the Vienna International Centre in Austria. He has co-facilitated many of UNIDO's team-building programmes with John Bing.

Abraham Kaplan

Abraham Kaplan, PhD, was professor emeritus of philosophy and of sociology at the University of Haifa. He taught for some years at the University of California at Los Angeles in philosophy and at the Graduate School of Management; and at the University of Michigan. He has lived and worked in many parts of the world. He has published and lectured extensively on social ethics, human resources, decision making and creativity. Sadly, Abe Kaplan passed away in 1994, shortly after completing his chapter, Chapter 3.

Paul J. Kingston

Paul Kingston, PhD, is an international human resources development professional specializing in mergers, acquisitions and joint ventures. Currently head of group education and learning for the NatWest Group, he was previously director of management education and training for Cable and Wireless in the telecommunications industry. He also spent over three years as training and development manager for GEC ALSTHOM, world leader in power generation, rail transport and power distribution. The company was formed by a merger in 1989 and encompasses 70 000 people worldwide. Bilingual in French and English, Paul has acted as a consultant on intercultural integration issues and process reconfiguration for international companies from different sectors.

Imre Lövey

Imre Lövey, PhD, is a management consultant and senior partner of

Concordia Limited and the president of the Hungarian Organization Development Society. He is one of the pioneers of OD and experiential training in the management field in Hungary. Since the changes in central-eastern Europe, he works more and more with joint venture and multinational companies, helping them with cross-cultural issues, with the aim of creating win–win situations where the investors, the foreign service employees and the local people can benefit together. He has carried out assignments for such companies as Ford Motor Company, Marlin Gerin Vertsez, GE-Tungsram, Levi Strauss and United Technology.

Dr Lövey is a regular visiting professor of Anderson Graduate School of Management at the University of California, Los Angeles and a member of the National Training Laboratories of Applied Behavioural Science.

Helen Price

Helen has in-depth experience of Asia Pacific human resource management based on 17 years of working and living in the region. As general manager, people development in Jardine Pacific, she successfully created and implemented a people development strategy for the group. Her work included co-ordinating teams of faculty to deliver senior programmes and working with directors to develop their international strategic and leadership skills. Prior to this she worked with Cathay Pacific Airways and the Central Electricity Generating Board, UK.

She is now a consultant in Europe and Asia, helping companies to design and implement development programmes for international managers, and helping human resource teams to develop strategies for diverse and decentralized organizations. Helen is a senior fellow with the Warwick Manufacturing Group, University of Warwick. Her research interests include how technical companies penetrate regional markets, and approaches to developing the business and general management skills of engineers and technical specialists.

Ronny Vansteenkiste

Ronny Vansteenkiste is the European training and development director for Seagram Spirits and Wine Group, one of the largest beverage companies in the world. He has overall responsibility for the development and implementation of the European training and development strategy aimed at progressing the careers of international managers. He is also largely involved in organizational development and change management initiatives across Seagram's various businesses. He has recently become the lead internal consultant for the corporation's worldwide change management process and leadership development linked to Seagram's global re-engineering effort.

Ronny's career includes extensive industrial and management education experience. He was programme director for human resource programmes at Management Centre Europe (MCE), the leading management training company in Europe. He remains a speaker and facilitator on a variety of MCE's programmes and also lectures in the International Institute for Management Development's (IMD) Programme for Executive Development and at the European Institute of Business Administration (INSEAD) and Escuela Superior de Administración y Dirección de Empresas (ESADE) (Barcelona).

He is a founding member and director of the European Learning Alliance (© ELA-N), an alliance of leading management and organization development practitioners in Europe.

David Wigglesworth

David C. Wigglesworth, PhD, has been president of DCW Research Associates International in Foster City, California, USA since 1967. His primary areas of interest include: the cultural determinants of international technology transfer; effective multicultural management for safety, productivity and profits; and international/intercultural team building. He was the recipient of the American Society for Training and Development's 1988 International Practitioner of the Year Award. He serves as a member of the advisory panel of the International Cultural Ergonomic Initiative (ICEI). He has been a frequent speaker at national and international conferences.

Acknowledgements

Chapter 2

I am indebted to Fons Trompenaars in the writing of this chapter which has largely come about as a result of the many seminars on cross-cultural management we have organized together, plus various early drafts of articles Fons has shared with me. Although the chapter attempts to summarize the essential lessons of Fons's books, it is by no means a summary of the wealth of insights that can be found in them.

Ronny Vansteenkiste

Chapter 7

The original design work on the project described in this chapter was provided by Andrea C. Zintz; Carina Stern facilitated several of these programmes.

John Bing and Sergio Gardelliano

Chapter 11

Thanks to Susan Schneider of INSEAD, Elizabeth Marks of NBS and Andrew Mayo, Director of Human Resources in ICL for constructive and helpful comments in the editing of this chapter.

Sue Canney Davison

1 Introduction to cross-cultural team building

Mel Berger

The barriers are up, each side prepares its case explaining why it is right and the other party is wrong. Stereotypes quickly develop, face-to-face contact reduces, communication is misinterpreted, blame is debated, and so on. This classical 'inter-group' phenomenon is very familiar between departments in the same company and becomes amplified when we add the dimensions of nationality, region, race, class and gender.

Imagine a situation in which a British salesperson, 28 years old, is meeting with a 50-year-old French engineer. Their ways of thinking and assessing problems will be strongly influenced by the education system, work attitudes and organizational values of two different generations, cultures, disciplines and languages. How would the situation be further affected if the Frenchman were of a higher organizational level and the British salesperson was a woman?

The challenge is to break through these 'culturally-reinforced' barriers to evolve collaborative, 'win—win' solutions. Practical questions as to how this breakthrough may be achieved immediately arise: how to increase awareness and tolerance of 'the other side'; how to work together in mixed culture teams; how to respect the values of others while maintaining one's own integrity.

The purpose of this book is to offer practical insights and techniques for developing cross-cultural understanding and team work. The book will explore the psychology of stereotyping and mistrust and examine methods for breaking down attitudinal barriers. It will describe case studies where people from different cultural backgrounds have learned to appreciate one another and work collaboratively.

Intercultural learning

The book is organized so as to guide the reader through a learning process, what Clackworthy (see Chapter 6) calls the 'intercultural learning curve'.

Intercultural learning can be viewed as following a process. The starting point, level one, is a state of unawareness—a state of not recognizing that cultural differences exist. It is an attitude of 'our way is the only way' or 'everyone is like us'. The more narrow the confines of one's experience, the more strongly this attitude will be maintained. For example, a culture that has been isolated from the rest of the world is likely to be unreceptive to different approaches. If anyone does appear different, they are labelled social deviants, obviously 'not brought up correctly to fit into the way people do things around here.'

Through intercultural contact, communication and observation, people can move to level two, a state of being aware of the differences. This is an attitude of 'other people have different ways of doing things from us'.

From awareness comes level three, tolerance. This is the attitude of 'they are different from us', but without attaching any judgement of better or best. The typical barriers which can form are based on the conclusion 'we are better than you', which implies that if you smarten up you will conform to our way or that it is in everyone's interest that we should manage or control you. The opposite conclusion is 'you are better than us' and, therefore, we will obey you; at the extreme, someone from another culture may be seen as a god.

When an individual is transplanted into a new culture for whatever reason, they are likely to experience a culture shock, which can be an intensely frustrating situation. Ultimately, the individual is faced with three basic choices: tolerating and adapting to the new culture, remaining but with a negative attitude towards the host culture or returning to the home culture.

From tolerance of differences, the final level—four—is possible. This is a state of using our differences positively to achieve team work and the attitude is one of 'let us work together in an integrated manner'. If the cultural differences are too great, the person may conclude that they respect the differences but cannot bridge them. For example, adapting may go beyond our cultural or personal ethics or beyond our behavioural capabilities. In this circumstance people may find ways to work at a distance or to use intermediaries. They may conclude that while it is possible to adapt, it could take years to do so and, therefore, is an unrealistic option.

The roots of cultural differences

Cultural differences evolve because given groups of people develop different values and basic concepts for understanding the world around them and for guiding their action. The starting point is to appreciate the human dynamics which can result in intercultural barriers to effective relationships. These differences can become barriers between cultures because of four human factors. First, the psychological processes and defence mechanisms of the individual can result in suspicion and distrust. Second, barriers are often reinforced by group dynamics, that is, the predisposition of groups to close ranks against and stereotype other groups. Third, barriers may be erected as a result of the competitive nature of business. All parties are not going to get everything they want, so they must either fight, compete or find collaborative forms of working together. Finally, problems of language can make understanding difficult, generate frustration and lead to misinterpretation of important communication. From these discussions, hopefully the reader will appreciate that the obstacles to intercultural team work are deeply embedded in the human psyche and that building positive relationships requires time, careful planning and ongoing support.

The remaining sections of this introductory chapter define in more detail what is meant by culture and values, explore the human processes which result in cross-cultural barriers and outline the structure of the book.

Defining culture

Culture will be defined, following Hofstede (1980), as 'the collective programming of the mind which distinguishes the members of one group or society from those of another'. The programme starts from babyhood, when parents tell children what to do and not do, what is good and what is bad. Programming continues from teachers, friends and eventually from organizations. The more narrow the individual's experience, the more uniform and powerful the programme. Eventually these programmes are applied to other people—this person is clever, another one is lazy and still others are not to be trusted.

Where these positive and negative labels are applied to groups of people, stereotyping and prejudice begins. It is possible to be aware of cultural differences without holding prejudice. Prejudice says, 'I am better, smarter and more able than another. And if I think I am better than you, this gives me the right to control you or even to exploit you.' Prejudice is undoubtedly as old as Cain and Abel, and ancient tribal rivalries and wars.

National culture can be broken down into different subcultures, such as regional, class, generational and professional, as illustrated by the case of the British salesperson and the French engineer. Building effective teams across different cultures within the same country is subject to the same issues of understanding and trust as when the teams span national boundaries. For example, the previously referred to French engineer may find fewer barriers to understanding between himself and a German engineer, aged 48, than with either a British or a French sales manager.

The individual   It is often debated whether human beings are inherently caring and loving or whether they are competitive and power seeking. Regardless of one's belief, the careful observer will see people who fit both categories. This suggests that in many situations the 'hawks' and 'doves' will argue their perspective when dealing with other groups or cultures. Part of the argument is whether the 'others' are hawks or doves. If they appear to be doves, is that appearance to be trusted? Is the olive branch genuine or a trick? If you believe that the other is genuine and respond with openness, you are taking the risk of being deceived. So you may choose to make a show of strength, in response to which the other will probably put up a defensive barrier or put on a similar show. This results in the well-known 'self-fulfilling prophecy' in which both sides conclude that the other is intending to take advantage, to win or even to destroy them. When an individual oppresses another or when one group opposes another, positive sounding rationales are always given, such as 'we know better than them' or 'they would threaten us if we didn't get the upper hand quickly'.

It is generally believed that where people are similar and appear similar, trust will be easier or quicker to develop. The greater the differences, the greater the caution. Caution is not necessarily negative, rather it means that relationship building will take longer and more patience will be required in the search to find the 'common ground'.

From the perspective of individual psychology, Robin Skynner (1993) describes the conditioning process of growing up in any culture. He says that babies are given 'sealed orders' as to how to behave and, additionally, are given three rules which reinforce the orders. The first rule tells us not to examine or discuss these orders. In other words, the rules should stay in the unconscious mind. Fear of being found out and guilt can reinforce the attitude of not wanting to know. The second rule defines the orders—family rules, religious beliefs and moral imperatives—as both healthy and better than those of other families or groups. So, in individual terms, we all grow up to believe ourselves blessed to have been born to the best family, belong to the best religion and live in the best city of the best country—we should each count our blessings! The third rule is that we should avoid contact with people with other beliefs, that is, 'stick to your own kind ... or else! People from other backgrounds are not to be trusted, believe me, I have experience'.

Skynner goes on to explain that to escape our 'orders' we must find ways to re-evaluate the relevance and objectivity of our given rules. Central to this is making contact with people who subscribe to other sets of rules, and to try to understand what they do, think and value. This can be done most fully by living among people from another culture and living another set of 'orders'. Of course, there are limits to our ability to adapt. For a Briton to live in the US is a relatively small step compared, say, to Japan or the Middle East. This is because in the latter case, the way of life differs much more and the language will be much more difficult to learn. Without understanding the language of the other, it is difficult to understand how the other sees their world.

Studies have shown that people who grow up exposed to different cultures are much more likely to develop an openness and adaptability to different ways of life. Therefore, these people tend to adapt positively to international assignments.

Inter-group dynamics

Schein (1969) describes typical causes of intergroup problems and how they may be overcome. If you split people into two groups, restrict their communication, and given them an inter-linking task, they will usually quickly form negative stereotypes and will engage in competitive, non-co-operative behaviour. In this state, communication becomes restricted and formal. Distrust of one another's motives will colour the interaction, resulting in mis-communication, blame and conflict. The competitive, win–lose, situation can become lose–lose as both parties prepare to give up their potential gains to block the other.

Gemmill and Elmes (1993) graphically describe the human tendency for 'an in-group to perceive itself in only exaggerated positive terms (and) the out-group (to be) depicted only in exaggerated negative terms'. These reinforcing perceptions enable a group to avoid internal conflict, to feel 'good' about itself and foster loyalty based on élitism. The way in which this negative spiral can be broken is through the introduction of 'win–win' goals, the establishment of mixed-membership task forces and the use of mutually trusted third parties. Schein's work reinforces the difficulty of achieving collaboration but does offer positive solutions which revolve around finding avenues for communication and identifying common goals.

Inter-organization behaviour

When two or more companies do business there is usually a competitive element to the outcome: 'I want to maximize my company's income'. Concessions of even small percentages can have a big effect on the overall profit margin. With the best will in the world, the results of a negotiation can mean a company's survival and the negotiator getting a bonus for a job well done! Where the companies are in a joint venture, competition can take the form of which side's management systems and procedures are implemented, who gets how much money for developing new products, who fills the senior positions, which people and departments are made redundant and who makes the key decisions.

In addition to the competitive side of inter-organizational dealings, there are straightforward business preferences. For example, how people like to negotiate will differ between companies and they naturally feel more confident when using what is familiar. Even the meaning of 'contract' has a cultural context. In the Far East, for instance, a contract means a statement of policy, the satisfactory implementation of which depends on the goodwill and trust among all parties. This is why, in many countries, developing a personal trust is the essential prerequisite to any serious discussion of business. In contrast, the Anglo countries take a legalistic view of a 'contract'; for them, the contract is meant to be followed to the letter and without deviation. This is why they invest much time and effort in spelling out contractual conditions covering every eventuality.

Language

The designated business language is English, for which most Anglos can breathe a sigh of relief. Was English chosen because it is the most universally spoken language, the basic common denominator? Or was it chosen out of compassion, in recognition of the Anglos's absence of language skill? Regardless of the reason, the use of English creates its own dynamics, most specifically in meeting situations where there are very considerable differences in the levels of skill in English. For example, French managers who regularly negotiate in English say that working in English is not a problem when dealing with Swedes, Spaniards and Japanese. However, they find it extremely difficult to communicate with Americans and the British!

Let us explore potential language barriers in more depth. If we imagine that Mr X, a native English speaker, is having an important discussion with Sr Y from Spain, for whom English is the second language, what can go wrong? The most obvious source of difficulty will be vocabulary. Mr X will know perhaps twice as many words as Sr Y. Additionally, and more importantly Mr X will be familiar with perhaps twice as many different meanings for each word. Potentially, this is a bigger problem because Sr Y may well think he understands Mr X, whereas they may each be defining the same words differently. Words such as manipulate, flexible, fabricate and exercise are but a few examples of this difficulty. Many arguments between the British and French have their root in the use of the word 'delay' which means lateness to the former and delivery date to the latter.

Even where the two parties are working to the same vocabulary, Y will take longer to understand X because he may be having to translate from English into Spanish to understand and back again to respond. Additionally, X will naturally use idiomatic expressions and jargon which could be unknown and baffling to Y, such as 'You kick off the discussion'. Even when Americans meet with British, they may be surprised at how many words carry different meanings, many of which may not be apparent at the time of the meeting.

At the level of pronunciation, other communication blocks can occur. Accents often vary between regions and sometimes between different social strata. Some people speak quietly or do not articulate their words clearly; others may speak quickly, with hardly a pause for breath. All of these factors can exacerbate communication difficulties.

Finally, cultural values can influence the meaning of what we think are universal terms. Debate and analysis to reach the 'ideal' solution is valued by the French whereas the British may prefer 'to split the difference' in order to negotiate a quick result. Therefore, to compromise is a sign of weakness to the French while being a measure of decisiveness to the British. There is no word for negotiation in Japanese, therefore, a mutual understanding of the concept is likely to be difficult to achieve. For an effective business relationship, a workable understanding must be found.

Structure of the book

Chapters 2 and 3 will define the basic elements of culture and their impact on human interaction. Ronny Vansteenkiste, in Chapter 2, examines the elements of cultural differences, drawing on the research of Fons Trompenaars. Culture is looked upon as a way to solve problems of day-to-day living in three areas. The solutions take the form of acceptable and unacceptable behaviour. The first area is the nature of human relationships which includes the degree of emotional involvement, the adherence to personal as against group goals, and the legitimacy of power and status. The second area is the relationship people have to nature, specifically whether they try to control it or to adapt to the world around them. The third area is the attitude towards time, which concerns the emphasis given to past history and tradition, present needs and inclinations, or future achievement. The unique solutions of a given culture will clearly impact on business behaviour as well as on daily life.

Abe Kaplan, in Chapter 3, describes the structure of a culture as 'metaphysics'—the basic shared assumptions, sets of rules, values and beliefs that are rewarded or expected by the society or group. To behave in contradictory ways may result in isolation, banishment, imprisonment or even death. The metaphysics of a culture is often unconscious and only becomes overt when it is violated or when you visit a culture which has a different set of notions of what is acceptable. In fact, the strictness of enforcing 'acceptable behaviour' is an important element of culture. In the sphere of business, for example, we assume that our 'business ethics' are 'logical' and 'right and proper'. When another party does not follow that ethic, we call them unethical! But, seen through the spectacles of culture, 'unethical' may simply mean 'a different set of ethics'. If you can accept and adapt to the ethics of the other, then it is possible to do business; alternatively the other may not adapt, then no deal is possible.

When conducting business with a culture which is markedly different from your own it is particularly important to understand that what we take for granted as a 'universal' truth is, in reality, the conventions to which we have tacitly agreed—that is, the rules of the game. When relating cultural differences to team building, the critical perspective is to recognize that different cultures will give different meanings to the same behaviour, therefore, they play by different rules. What is natural for one may be abnormal and offensive for others. Individual creativity to one culture is destructive disobedience to another culture. Different cultures will have different attitudes and practices surrounding work, problem solving, technology, organizational structure and decision taking. Only when your mind has been thoroughly scrambled about the relativity of what is right and wrong are you ready to proceed with the rest of the book!

The next five chapters present case examples of team building between different cultures. In each case, the intention is first to describe the impact of cultural differences on communication and team work. Typical misunderstandings and preconceptions will be highlighted. Second, the team building events will be described, within the context of a company-wide strategy. Specific practical designs, techniques and exercises will be outlined.

Chapter 4, by Paul Kingston, describes how a large multinational company, recently formed by the merger of a British and a French company, built teams and business networks across several national boundaries. He also discusses the importance of language learning and how communication difficulties can arise when people have different levels of language proficiency.

Chapter 5, by Imre Lövey, describes the changing culture of Hungary, including problems and opportunities. Two cases are given of building management teams, including one with an American multinational and another which resulted from a Hungarian–Franco joint venture.

Chapter 6, by Dennis Clackworthy, describes communication difficulties between German and American teams, particularly with regard to how they resolve conflicts. He also describes a general strategy for developing cultural awareness and tolerance. Chapter 7, by John Bing and Sergio Gardelliano, describes a major team-building initiative in a branch of the United Nations. Following a major restructuring, their work aimed to train managers to work efficiently in teams. Chapter 8, by Helen Price, describes some key characteristics of the Asian culture and how team building can be used to strengthen the bonds between Asian and Western managers.

The next two chapters focus on team building between diverse national cultures of the same organization. In Chapter 9, David Wigglesworth discusses the principles of diversity training within the American context. Chapter 10, by Raymond Cadwell, provides a detailed case example of team building between management and unions in the

Republic of Ireland. He also discussed aspects of prejudice and stereotyping and how they can be overcome.

The final two chapters are focused specifically on the insights and competences needed by facilitators to conduct team-building events. Chapter 11, by Sue Canney Davison, focuses on team factors which impact on performance. She identifies eight cultural and organizational factors which must be understood before designing a team-building event or intervention. Examples of these factors include:

- levels of fluency in the common language;
- cultural preferences in leadership styles;
- similarities or differences between functional or professional 'cultures'.

These factors are plotted against the phases of the group's life, from forming to disbanding. Guidelines are offered as to how these phases can be managed in order for the group to achieve 'interactive synergy'.

Emphasis is given to the importances of patient preparation including the establishment of trust, agreement to an agenda, and objectives. The underlying message is the need for 'extra 3 × 1 preparation', which means that the prudent facilitator will allow three times longer to plan a cross-cultural event, as compared to a single cultural one.

The final chapter, by Mel Berger, concentrates on the facilitator's role in conducting a cross-cultural event. Three general types of intervention are described and illustrated. First, the facilitator can model the type of communication he or she is trying to foster, such as openness. Second, short inputs/lectures to highlight important issues of culture or team work can be offered. Third, the facilitator can offer feedback and coaching to individuals or the group as a whole. Chapter 12 also discusses the benefits of a multicultural training team.

For a multicultural training team to work synergistically there must be an agreement on the learning methods that will underpin the design. For example, experiential learning and lecture-based learning are two fundamentally different approaches, both of which reflect cultural preferences. Unless the training team can evolve an agreed method of working, delegates will be pulled in conflicting directions, resulting in confusion and the reinforcement of cultural stereotypes rather than breaking them down.

How to use this book

This book has been designed as a reference book for trainers, consultants, facilitators and any managers faced with building collaborative cross-cultural relationships. As such, it can be read cover to cover (monochronistically) or scanned for specific ideas and techniques as and when required (polychronistically).

Working in a cross-cultural setting can be a fascinating learning experience but will require more preparation and patience than usual— and more than may be comfortable. The process takes time to move from the level one unawareness of differences to the level four attitude of using differences in creative ways. To help others to broaden their tolerance and skill, you will have to broaden yourself. Good luck!

References

Gemmill, G. and M. Elmes (1993) 'Mirror, Mask and Shadow: Psychodynamic Aspects of Intergroup Relations', *Journal of Management Inquiry*, 2 (1), 43–51.

Hofstede, G. (1980) *Culture's Consequences*, Sage Publications, London.

Schein, E. (1969) *Process Consultation*, Addison-Wesley, Reading, Mass. pp. 99–102.

Skynner, R. and J. Cleese (1993) *Life and How to Survive It*, Methuen, London.

Introduction to Chapter 2

'The business of culture and the culture of business', by Ronny Vansteenkist, describes and illustrates the building blocks of culture. To manage internationally, it is important to understand the impact of culture on the acceptability of different management methods and practices. From understanding should follow respect for differences and the will to adapt to find common ground. Culture provides people with guidance for day-to-day living. As culture is often unconscious, recognizing potential problems in an international setting can be difficult. The starting point for overcoming these difficulties is to be clear about one's own culturally-determined behaviour and how it is likely to differ from that of others.

Trompenaars's seven dimensions of culture provide a powerful framework for understanding culturally-determined behaviour. This chapter describes them, including examples of how they may be manifested in business and interpersonal situations. The first five dimensions focus on human relationships, the sixth dimension is based on the relationship to nature and the seventh dimension relates to time. These dimensions are listed below.

1 Universalism–particularism: reliance on a fixed set of rules or a contract versus reliance on friendship, trust and circumstance.
2 Individualism–collectivism: emphasis on personal freedom and inner direction versus stress on group loyalty and mutual support.
3 Display of emotion: feelings expressed openly versus neutrally represented or hidden emotions.
4 Specific–diffuse: preference for relationships that can easily be made and broken depending on circumstance versus those developed over a long time and based on trust.
5 Respect and position: status based on achievement versus ascription, for example, on age, class, gender or education.
6 Internal–external orientation: belief that people can control their environment and other people, like machines, versus the opinion that people need to be flexible and adapt according to circumstances.
7 Time: decision-making has a time orientation. It may be based on the past or tradition, the present or the future.

A questionnaire is described which helps people to identify their own cultural preferences and to compare themselves to others. The strong conclusion is that cultural differences are inevitable and they cannot be changed. The challenge, therefore, is to recognize and utilize the differences to achieve harmony or even synergy.

2 The business of culture and the culture of business

Ronny Vansteenkiste

'As business gets more globalised, the competitive advantages of multinational teams increase. Any single-nationality corporate culture will run into problems as soon as it aims to integrate larger operations from other countries.'

(Percy Barnevik, 1994)

The business of culture

The increasing internationalization of business over the last five years has brought about an explosion of business books and journal articles on such themes as globalization and transnational companies. Each of them propagates its own model of the various stages a multinational company passes through on its international journey (see Bartlett and Ghoshal, 1989; Adler and Bartholomew, 1992, to name only a few). This trend in academic research has revived, be it to a lesser extent, the interest in the concept of culture, particularly from a geographical point of view. The number of consultants and articles commenting upon cultural differences and their impact on international business relationships has seen a similar exponential increase so that, indeed, we can speak of a real business coming about that thrives on 'culture'. Ever since the pioneering work of Hofstede (1980), there has been considerable interest in the influence of culture on the way in which management methods and practices are applied across countries, companies, functions, genders, etc. Until recently we were lacking up-to-date research and a real practical model, not only to understand the concept of culture but also, and more importantly, to help managers deal with its impact in their day to day reality. Trompenaars (1993) and Hampden-Turner and Trompenaars (1993) provide a welcome change to this. This chapter is largely indebted to their work.

... and the culture of business

Many traditional analyses of management practices have based themselves on the objective characteristics of the organization. When you choose the subjective human being as the point of departure you quickly discover that a single 'best way' of organizing does not exist. In fact, different people with different cultural backgrounds look at and react differently to the same objective structuring methods and practices. In the emerging 'business of culture' best sellers, we are often led to believe that the world is gradually becoming a smaller global village where some universal principles of being an effective manager apply. However, within this global village, there still appear to be as many different approaches to business as there are national cultures. For example 'management by objectives (MBO)' is regarded as a sound management practice in many cultures, but is seen as 'losing face' in others. The social aspects focus on the need to direct and stimulate the motivation of the ones who are being managed. But to do so, you not only need to understand how fundamentally different other cultures are, but also you need to act differently once you have acknowledged differences and respect them. For a business to succeed in a multicultural or international environment, it has to be able to identify and quantify the values, beliefs, expectations and ways of doing business of everybody involved. Responding to the complexity, diversity and ambiguity of cultures becomes a crucial task of management and training alike.

Overview of the chapter

Largely inspired by Trompenaars's work, this chapter will first introduce the concept of culture and its dimensions as he defined it in his research, going on to illustrate how those dimensions apply when doing business in different countries. After the summary of the seven dimensions of culture model the chapter will describe some techniques and tools which use those dimensions to find ways to reconcile differences. They can easily be integrated into cross-cultural training and have proven to be effective ways to help people overcome the differences in international team-building sessions. Trompenaars's work taps into the most up-to-date and, at present, still ongoing research in this field, using a dedicated questionnaire that has been administered to some 15 000 senior and middle managers in over 50 countries. The model has been used with hundreds of managers across Europe and it has been judged as extremely practical by them. Of interest for trainers is that the approach is being supported by a comprehensive train-the-trainer package and workshop.

It starts with yourself

In the field of cross-cultural training you are often led to believe that by attending a seminar you will become a better American, French or Japanese than they are themselves. This starting point is not taken here since such promises are Utopian and largely unrealizable. The first fundamental requirement for any international manager who wants to survive in the global business landscape is to identify and understand his or her own cultural values, style of communication and organizational concepts. It is only by understanding your own origins and heritage that you can start to make meaningful comparisons and truly enter into the world of the other cultures. A large part of the road towards reconciling cultural differences is being aware of where and how you started your journey on that road. Self-awareness is the key to happiness in working with international teams. The issue is not how to become an American, Japanese or Brazilian but rather to discover the bit of American, Japanese or Brazilian in you!

The same holds true for international teams

Many international companies have discovered, for better or worse, that their global success depends largely on their international teams achieving high performance standards. This has been revealed also in the, undoubtedly, largest and most comprehensive research study on transnational teams to date, funded by the International Consortium for Executive Development and Research (ICEDR) (see Snow et al. 1993 and Chapter 11 in this volume). This research has examined the strategic context, leadership roles, human resource policies and team skills needed to achieve that performance. The conclusions offered show that this is not achieved by using standard formulas based on cultural stereotypes. Indeed, findings from three data sources (interviews, questionnaires and videotapes) indicate substantially different degrees to which the national culture of team members influences their thinking, language use and behaviour. This presents a major challenge to team leaders who must assess the impact of cultural differences on the functioning of the team. Teams need first to understand the key factors dictating their interaction. The research indicates that four international team skills are then needed actively to mould the interaction to fit the specific task:

- negotiating a workable group process
- surfacing and reweaving cultural similarities and differences
- using culturally-sensitive feedback and reviews to improve the interaction
- working effectively across geographical distances

Team leaders in particular need the courage and skills to risk tackling cultural differences in the team as ignoring them is likely to result in an under-effective, if not failed, team effort.

Trompenaars's culture model (Trompenaars, 1993) offers a highly practical way to help international team members develop mutual understanding of, and a common vocabulary to handle, the differences that may tend to push the factors that govern their performance in different directions.

The concept of culture

The key to this puzzle lies in a practical definition of the word 'culture', to which individuals working in an international context can relate in simple and experiential terms. Modern dictionaries and academic literature often are of little help, variously describing culture as an intellectual or moral discipline and training, a state of intellectual and artistic development or an historically transmitted pattern of meanings. Such definitions are quite meaningless when set in the practical context of international business life.

Culture has also been described as a set of rules, values and beliefs— good or bad—which a community adopts as its norm. It is said to give its constituents a sense of who they are, of belonging, of how they should behave and what they should be doing. Shared culture gives a sense of group identity, especially in terms of behaviour and values to be encouraged or rejected. It is made up of customs, traditions, beliefs, attitudes, concepts, hierarchies, roles, special needs, and verbal and non-verbal communication. A culture also makes it difficult to identify things which that culture takes for granted, as they have become unconscious to the active mind. It is ultimately based on a set of questions which are no longer asked within its entity.

For a full understanding of the concept of culture we need to go back to the original meaning of the ancient Greek word 'kultura': 'to act upon nature'. It implies that people had to organize themselves to cope with the problems nature and their environment were presenting them with. This acting upon nature—in fact, this continuous problem-solving for survival—is the source of culture. As soon as a solution has been found, a new environment comes into being which presents another set of problems. It is from the confrontation with repetitive problems that culture get its unconscious problems. We can illustrate this with the fact that we take it for granted that we go and lie down for sleeping. But in fact, this is a real survival problem (caused by the laws of gravity) for which we have developed a regular system for solving and it has slipped out of our consciousness. In the same way, we do not give much conscious thought to the same laws of gravity that keep us on the ground when we stand or walk.

Definition The concept of culture may be defined as follows: *implicit culture* which determines the meaning of life and can be said to be the *basic assumptions*—the accumulations of solutions to survival problems which have become habitual and are passed down from generation to generation. Our basic assumptions define the meaning we assign to things around us. They produce norms and values which then show in the manifestations and visible artefacts (the *explicit culture*) such as music, architecture, food, language, dress, etc. (see Fig. 2.1). These visible manifestations are very often the source of culture shock to people who move abroad to cultures with which they are not familiar.

An illustration Let us illustrate this concept with an example of how meaning comes about in organizations. A focus on planning systems, organizing work

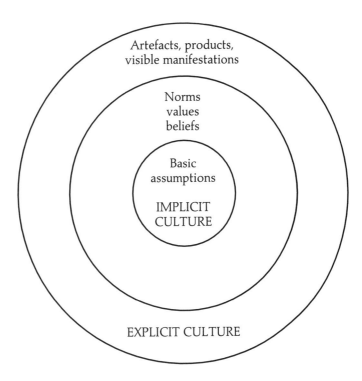

Figure 2.1 *A model of culture* (© F. Trompenaars, 1993)

according to deadlines and short-term results are visible manifestations and artefacts of behaviours and management practices of the 'explicit culture' of an organization. When you ask people in such an organization what underlies these practices you are likely to find that the declared organizational norm and preference is expressed in the typical 'time is money'. It may be more difficult to obtain a clear statement about the basic assumption such a norm is based upon, which seems to be the fundamental presupposition that time is limited. Often this is taken for granted—unconsciously accepted.

You will discover that another organization is characterized by management practices with a more flexible use of time and investment in long-term strategies. Such an organization values the belief and preference that time offers its stakeholders a space for relating with each other. People, therefore, appear to be organized in such a company according to the basic assumption that there is plenty of time.

Basic assumptions   We have to bear in mind that the basic assumptions of our own culture are not shared around the world. Other groups experienced different problems due to peculiarities of the environment in which their survival struggle took place. Their adaptation processes have taken different paths. People adopt their own cultural set of assumptions so wholeheartedly that, over time, they forget there were any survival problems in the first place. As a consequence, the solutions of people in other cultures have become just as unconscious as ours. Take, for example, the meaning assigned to many premium brands of whisky. In some cultures such a whisky is a precious gift item you would buy for somebody else but could not afford for yourself. In American high society it is a typical social drink that shows your status and class. In many Far East cultures, Hong Kong and Japan in particular, good whisky is a drink you have with lots of ice and water during a meal in a restaurant with friends, instead of a bottle of wine.

Seven dimensions of culture

Because these assumptions are unconscious, the meeting between cultures creates confusion. In order to come to grips with these subtle, unconscious differences we need to go back to the source of culture and the basic problems of humanity. There are at least three universally-shared problem areas: our relationships with other people, our relationship with nature and our relationship with time. From the different solutions that various cultures have chosen to these three universal problems, we can further identify seven fundamental dimensions of culture. First, five orientations in the area of human relationships that define our way of approaching dilemmas in the human arena are distinguished (see Dilemmas 1–5). Next, we will look at our relationship with nature (Dilemma 6) and finally, we will consider the problems created by our relationship with time (Dilemma 7).

Dilemma 1: universalism versus particularism

Each society develops its own standards and values when dealing with a conflict between societal and personal obligations. Universalist societies (USA, Australia, Sweden, Switzerland, the Netherlands, many northern Europeans and Germans, etc.) tend to feel that general rules and obligations are a strong source of moral reference. Universalists tend to follow the rules of society even when friends are involved and look for 'the one best way' of dealing equally and fairly with all cases. They assume that the standards they hold dear are the 'right' ones and will attempt to change the views of others to match. You are dealing with a universalist culture when the community shares a predominant belief that the rights of the society or organization prevail over the rights of a specific individual. Universalists focus more on rules that apply equally to everybody than on relationships. For them there is only one truth or reality: that agreed upon by the culture in which they live. Typically, their behaviour will be rule based and they will resist exceptions that might weaken those rules. They like legal contracts in business and will consider a person trustworthy when he or she honours the contract: a deal is a deal.

However, other societies like Russia, Venezuela, China, Korea, India and many Latin cultures solve dilemmas with a particularist approach. In those societies particular circumstances are much more important than the rules. Bonds of particular relationships, such as family and friendship, are stronger than any abstract rule. Their behaviour in and response to situations may change according to circumstances and the people involved. In a predominantly particularist society, the rights of a friend are taken to be more important than the rights of the larger community. This does not mean that a particularist society has no general or formal rules and laws; it only means that they are likely to be broken for the sake of friendship, even to the detriment of 'order' within society. Particularists focus more on personal respect. For them, there are several perspectives on reality relative to each person. This person is not 'a citizen' but 'my friend, brother, husband, child or person of unique importance to me as an individual' with special claims on my love or my hatred. Consequently, in the particularist society people may sustain or protect another person no matter what the rules dictate. A trustworthy person is, therefore, the one who honours changing circumstances.

Management application

The problems arise when an universalist society tries to impose its solutions on a particularist society or vice versa. In Western countries which are highly universalist, head office tends to hold the keys to global strategies, global marketing, global production and corporate financial control. A good example is the way in which HR policies are drafted and how training programmes are developed. Written at head office, with the basic assumptions inherent in the head office's culture, the policies often take the form of a rule book (policy manual) which describes right and wrong behaviours. Training programmes, for example, are then developed to support these policies. Yet, policies and programmes developed at head office are not necessarily transferable to all field locations and very often fail to shape local ways of operating. What may appear to be employees breaking company rules in a particular location may simply be the standard way in which work gets done in that culture. Different groups develop their own local standards which then become the basis of their solidarity and resistance to centralized edicts.

Reconciling universalism and particularism

International managers are often caught in the dilemma of the universal truth and the particular or local circumstances. Trompenaars (1993) suggests a way of reconciling these two extremes to avoid pathological excesses. Awareness of the differences is a good start but is not enough. On the one hand, we need to listen to the universalities of headquarters and apply rules and procedures to ensure equity and consistency. Going overboard on this may lead an organization to degenerate into rigidity and bureaucracy; to avoid this, we need to encourage flexibility by adapting to local situations. However, since we neither want to drown in chaos or lose our sense of central direction we must now and then rely on those rules and procedures that ensure stability. Intuitively, international managers go through this cycle—through which the middle ground can be achieved—using their talent to strike a balance between central guidelines and local adaptations.

Dilemma 2: individualism versus collectivism

The dilemma between what each of us wants as an individual and the interests of the group we belong to is the second of the five orientations with respect to human relationships. In individualist societies people are expected to make their own decisions and to take care only of themselves and their close family. The quality of life for society in general is assumed to result from the personal freedom and individual development of its members. In the USA, the UK and many European countries people will put individual freedom first and assert that individual freedom will lead to an improved society.

In collectivist cultures such as Japan, Brazil, France and Nigeria people say 'We will serve society first because then society can serve me better'. Members of such societies are firmly integrated into groups which provide help and protection in exchange for a strong sense of loyalty. Here, the quality of life for the individual is regarded as improving according to the extent to which individuals take care of their fellows.

Management application

Again, there will be many consequences of this dilemma in business. A typical example will be business visits and international business negotiations. Many Western societies herald the mystique of the 'lone ranger'—the individual who gets the job done on his or her own and who does not need to rely on anyone or anything. They praise the self-sufficiency of this person. However, when this lone ranger goes on 'lonely business rides' to countries like Japan or Thailand, the collectivist business people will think: 'Can this person be powerful since he is all alone? There is no one to carry his bags? Can we negotiate with an individual? There is no one to show his status? How insulting that such a powerless person comes to do business with us.'

Another typical example is pay for performance. Commission pay plans for sales people can work beautifully in individualist cultures because people believe that their individual success will result in the company's ultimate success. Yet they can fail miserably in collectivist cultures. This dilemma needs to be considered very carefully when organizations set up incentive schemes for their transnational teams.

These two orientations will also differ strikingly in the decision-making process. Individualist cultures usually have a short decision-making process. Decisions are made on the spot by individual representatives in a few seconds or there is a vote to have all noses pointing in the same direction. On the surface, this orientation seems to make for quicker deliberations, but it is often followed by significant delays due to implementation problems. Collectivist decision making typically takes much longer and is likely to frustrate individualist managers who do not understand that people cannot decide on the spot but always seem to need to refer decisions back to the organization. Collectivist managers will frequently ask for a time out in negotiations so they can go through the famous loop necessary for reaching consensus.

A sales training course which is predominantly geared to individual selling takes more than language and custom translation when it is taken to an international audience. It requires a deeper understanding that individual selling is the kiss of death in many cultures and only through team selling will success be achieved.

Additionally, the participative style of conducting training programmes in individualist cultures—where the instructor asks questions and involves individual participants directly—can flounder horribly in collectivist cultures. It is far better in collectivist cultures to design group and team projects as part of the training so that no one individual is put on the spot.

Reconciling individualism and collectivism

International managers can increase their effectiveness if they try to see the issue of individual versus group as essentially circular with 'two starting positions'. The individualist culture sees the individual as 'the end' and improvements to collective arrangements as the means to achieve it. The collectivist culture sees the group as its end and improvements to individual capacities as a means to that end. Yet, if the relationship is truly circular, the decision to label one element as an end and the other as a means is arbitrary. Every 'end' becomes also a means to another goal. The effective international manager is convinced that individualism finds its fulfilment in service to the group, while group goals are of demonstrable value to individuals only if those individuals are consulted and participate in the process of developing them.

Dilemma 3: do we display emotions?—neutral versus affective relationships

This third human relations dimension relates to the question about the expression of emotions. This dilemma points to how much emotion is allowed to be revealed in day-to-day discourse or to what extent the displaying of emotion is sanctioned by the society. In relationships between people, reason and emotion both play a role. Which of these dominates will depend upon whether we are affective—i.e. show our emotions, in which case we probably get an emotional response in return—or whether we are emotionally neutral in our approach. Latin Europeans and North Americans prefer to show how they feel spontaneously and act accordingly. The Japanese call these societies 'transparent cultures' because these societies show emotions about everything they feel, believe and think. Neutral cultures, like the Japanese and the British, often see affective cultures as somewhat childlike and irrational, full of generalized enthusiasm and superficial sloganeering. Affective cultures often see neutral cultures as secretive and difficult to read and believe. As a consequence, this difference in displaying emotions can lead to scepticism, a lack of trust and, ultimately, to hostility.

Management application

These different orientations are often observed when a meeting of a transnational group of managers is in progress. They have different styles of discussion. For the Anglo Saxons, when person A stops talking, person B starts. It is not polite to interrupt. The more verbal Latins interrupt slightly more. Person B will frequently interrupt person A and vice versa to show how interested they are in what the other is saying. While for Italians, for example, this is a sign of growing interest in what the other person says, and they will emphasize this with abundant gestures, for British and German people it may come across as a sign of lack of respect for the other person, since, in their perception, the Italians do not take the time to process the information before talking themselves.

Some areas of personnel policies and training programmes deal with job satisfaction and employee morale. Values which place importance on satisfaction, morale and loyalty are essentially emotional in content and they are given more attention in affective cultures than in neutral ones. It is important to note that if you go to a neutral culture with a training programme geared to improve morale and you are looking for evidence of that improvement, you are likely to have a long wait.

Dilemma 4: specific versus diffuse cultures

The fourth value orientation with respect to relationships with people has to do with the degree of involvement in a relationship. This is probably the most complex and consequently the most misunderstood dimension in working across cultures. Therefore, it is undoubtedly one of the most important explanations of cultural differences. A person with a *specific* orientation easily makes close contact with others because this type of person knows quite well what kinds of contact he or she wants to establish, what to share and what not to share with others. This enables them to be flexible when dealing with different people. Specific cultures, like that of Americans, have a very small intimate or private core which is well separated from the larger public layers and people mostly live as if their life were a large, public arena. They easily share possessions and do not think of them as all that private. Their personalities are easily accessible but they get to know other people for limited or specific purposes only. On the other hand, most Southern Europeans and Orientals will not allow another person to enter their large private domain. This area is so large that it needs protection. You will only be allowed to enter this domain when you have spent a long time building a personal relationship. Once you have been admitted through to their private arenas, there are few secrets. They are *diffuse* cultures with a tiny public veneer which covers a huge private care.

Specific cultures, like the USA and Australia, start from the foundation of nearly everything being public. With a small private core or self, privacy is not involved in relationships; therefore, relationships are easily made and broken. Specific-oriented managers segregate out the task relationship they have with a colleague and insulate this from other dealings. Diffuse cultures start from a foundation of great privacy. With a large private side, the only way to penetrate this privacy is by building trust over time. Relationships are slow to develop, but once you are in, you are fully in—and you are usually in for life. Someone with a diffuse orientation is less explicit in what he or she expects from relationships. Sharing some things expands to sharing many others as well; hence, he or she prefers to be choosy about sharing at all. It is harder to make contact, but once this has been achieved, it is more likely to involve the entire person than it is when dealing with a specific-oriented person. Because of the reluctance to get close to others, diffuse-oriented people are less likely to become socially flexible.

Management application　In doing business, people from specific cultures are very direct and get straight to the point and to the objective aspects of the business deal. They have a very clear purpose in relating with others. Doing business with people more diffuse than yourself will appear very time consuming because they are extremely indirect, circuitous and have seemingly aimless forms of relating. This may be particularly frustrating in international meetings. The directness of specific-oriented people may cause diffuse people to lose face, i.e. making public what is perceived as being private—and we know how important it is to maintain face in countries like Japan and Spain.

In South America, the upfront investment in building relationships is as important, if not more so, as the actual business deal. It is important to take this into consideration when timing a business trip. A well-thought-out presentation that demonstrates the superiority of your product is definitely the wrong way to enter into a business relationship in these countries.

Consider also the use of titles in business. In specific cultures, if you have a PhD you are known as Dr So-and-so within the university where you teach or the professional societies with whom you are associated. The moment you are outside of these environments you are known as Mr So-and-so or just as Bob or Sue. This is not the case in Germany or in Italy. In Germany you are Herr Doctor both inside and outside the university or company; in fact, your wife becomes Frau Doctor. 'Herr Doctor' is not a specific label, it is 'you' and defines your identity. Think also about how work is assigned in your organization. In specific cultures like the USA, work is assigned on the basis of tasks to be performed. You hire a person with the specific skills to do the job and compensate the person based on the job, regardless of the person's needs. In diffuse cultures, however, you hire the person first, initiate him or her into the organization, and then shape a job around his or her skills and knowledge. Compensation is based on the person's needs, not on the job itself. Specific-oriented societies are characterized by a higher mobility and turnover of staff than diffuse cultures which tend to have lower turnover and employee mobility because of the importance of loyalty and the multiplicity of human bonds.

Reconciling specific and diffuse cultures

This is perhaps the area in which balance is most crucial, from both a personal and a corporate point of view. The specific extreme—to keep business separated from the rest of life—may lead to superficiality. So we must recognize that the integration of different aspects of one's personality can deepen the relationship. Yet, we need to retain perspective in order not to compromise privacy and business. The effective international manager must avoid collision between the two at all costs and realize that business is business but that stable and deep relationships mean strong affiliations.

Dilemma 5: achievement versus ascription

The fifth and final human relations dimension relates to how a person gets respect and status. All societies give certain members higher status than others but not in similar ways. Some societies accord status to people on the basis of their *achievements*; others *ascribe* it to them by virtue of age, class, gender, education, etc.

When we introduce ourselves to other people we typically position ourselves in terms of status and in terms of our role in society. In North America, people talk a lot about what they do because Western society is an achievement-oriented culture ('doing'). In ascription-oriented cultures ('being') like Spain, Turkey, Poland and France you actually are what you are even if you do not get things done. In the latter societies you will introduce yourself by describing attributes of ascribed status which are given by birth or by society's notions of personhood. This is the opposite of status which is achieved through activities or accomplishments after birth.

In the last decade we have been able to witness a tragic example of achievement versus ascription orientation to human relationships as the American push to compete against the Japanese. Americans see the Japanese as a major competitive threat and try to mobilize forces to beat the Japanese in this major economic competition. The Japanese, on the other hand, being an ascription-oriented culture, do not see this as a competition; high quality is an end in and of itself in their view. It is beneath their dignity, literally a disgrace, to create anything less than perfect. The fact that quality translates into success in the marketplace is a natural outcome of this cultural belief.

Management application

In achievement-oriented cultures we assume that people in authority positions will feel a sense of accountability for the organization's accomplishments. If someone is the boss, he or she must be there because they have earned the title and position. In many cultures, though, positions of authority are natural consequences of having gone to the right schools, having been born into the right class or sex, or having seniority. So the fact that someone is in a position of authority does not necessarily mean that he or she will need to achieve, or be motivated to achieve, organizational objectives to remain worthy of the position.

You may observe the same in international negotiations. Sending young 'eager beavers' to deal with ascriptive people who are 10 to 20 years their senior often insults those of the ascriptive culture. The status and job title will also reinforce ascribed status.

You can also imagine how this dimension can impact on personal career development if you need to rely on the managers in remote locations to prepare the groundwork for your efforts and to follow-up after training is delivered. In some ascribed cultures, it simply will not work because the managers are not in their positions based on their achievements, as we would define it in Western society. And yet, you cannot just replace them with managers who do have a proven track record of accomplishments, as any such new management would be viewed by employees who value ascribed status as having no status or credible authority. What may look comprehensible in a Western culture—for example, appointing an intelligent, female, postgraduate manager with an excellent track record to work in Turkey—will require an appropriate cultural adjustment if you do not want your project to fail and to ruin the career of this 'high potential' woman.

Reconciling achievement and ascription

People who are achievement-oriented are convinced that they need to appreciate and reward what people do and achieve on the basis of their skills and knowledge. But valuing the last performance only can lead to insecurity and instability. Hence, they should try to understand the conviction of ascription-oriented cultures who respect people on the basis of their experience and past record. But ascription-oriented cultures should also understand that most companies cannot afford to hinder their achievements by not challenging the status quo and should, therefore, reward people on the basis of what they do as well as on their experience. The common ground that the international manager should try to hold is to respect people for what they are so that better advantage can be made of what they do.

The discussion now turns to the last two dimensions of culture, starting with our relationship to nature.

Dilemma 6: internal versus external orientation

This dimension concerns the role people assign to their natural environment. Different cultures have perceived nature differently throughout human history. Prior to the Renaissance, nature was seen as an organism. People believed that their environment determined what human beings needed to do. In their view, the environment controls us. The Renaissance turned this organismic view of nature into a mechanistic one. If you picture nature as a machine, as Leonardo da Vinci did, you start realizing that if you push here you can cause a reaction there. In this view, nature is pictured as a machine and can be controlled. These views of nature are reflected in the management literature, beginning with Rousseau and Voltaire who saw society as a natural phenomenon. Over time, management theorists have moved gradually towards the American MBA mode of thinking which is that you can control everything and towards the new wave of cybernetic management theory which stipulates that management is about the art of steering and not of controlling.

Today, language ability is highly related to locus of control. Inner-directed cultures try to control the environment and expect the environment to adapt to their language (no other languages). Americans or Britons are unlikely to speak Japanese, for example. But the Japanese, who are outer-directed and thus feel that they should adapt, will try hard to speak other languages. Our Western contention that Asians steal our ideas is shaped by our notion that what comes from inside us is, therefore, 'ours'. Asians regard Western technologies as part of the environment, like fruit on a tree, which wise people pick and incorporate into themselves. To take something from the external environment and then refine or improve it is not copying but celebrating that environment. Similarly, many Westerners still have not realized that the Japanese word for 'copying' is 'learning'—internalizing what is given to you from the outside.

Management application

Very often Westerners go into other societies and try to put control mechanisms on everything. Typically inner-directed management systems are job descriptions and job grading systems to control staffing, budgeting to control finance, pay-for-performance to control compensation and staff appraisal to control performance. Yet many of these systems lead to corporate rain dancing since they do not work in outer-directed cultures. Customer service and TQM programmes are typical of Western organizations. They think they can control the customer and quality and, therefore, act accordingly. The Japanese hold the opposite point of view: 'How can you talk about quality? It is the basic thing of life.' From their perspective, a society would have to be seriously sick if it needs to talk constantly about quality.

Reconciling inner- and outer-directedness

Deming's (1988) quality work comes closest to a good example of the harmony balancing internal and external control. Deming points to systems, not performance, as the key to quality. Inherent in this viewpoint is an acknowledgement of the power of nature and business's need to work within nature, not try to control it. Japan's post-war success in using Deming's strategies gives a good idea of the strength of this approach when applied in an appropriate cultural context.

Again, effective international managers will seek reconciliation. They know that they should focus on things they are good at and persuade their environment to accept them. This is known as technology-push. But they also know that there needs to be a market for what they produce and that they need to respond to the environment and the needs of the customer. This is known as market-pull. Effective international managers realize that they do not want to be at the mercy of the forces around them but to lead them.

We now turn to the final cross-cultural dimension and consider different implications of time.

Dilemma 7: relationship to time   To co-ordinate our business activities, we require some kind of shared expectations about time. The time agreed for a meeting may be approximate or precise. The time allocated to complete a task may be vitally important or merely a guide. The notion of time also expresses the importance cultures assign to the past, present and future, and will influence peoples' lifestyles and future aspirations. Some people will say, 'I love this meeting because it is just like the meeting in Paris back in '90. Now that was a great meeting.' Others will say, 'I love this meeting because it is so enjoyable just being here, seeing old friends and meeting new people. This is the best group I know.' The meeting means different things to each person because each person relates differently to time. Time often becomes an expression of a relationship between people. A past-oriented culture, e.g. Europe, bases its future on past events. Everything will be viewed in the context of tradition, heritage or history; change will have to be introduced as a continuity of the past. A culture oriented towards the future, however, such as the USA does not care about past events and views the present only as a first step towards the future.

The other aspect of our relationship to time has to do with how we structure our thinking in the present. If people's view of time is sequential or monochronic, they see time as a series of passing events. Typically they will do one thing at a time because they view time as a narrow line consisting of discrete, consecutive portions. Time is tangible and divisible in this view. Monochronic people like planning and keeping to plans and schedules once they are made. Time commitments are taken seriously. Alternatively, if your view of time is synchronic or polychronic you will usually do several things at the same time. Time is viewed here as a wide ribbon, allowing many things to take place simultaneously; time is flexible and intangible. Time commitments are seen as desirable rather than as absolute. Polychronic people change plans easily and place more value on the satisfactory completion of interactions with others. To them, being 'prompt' will depend on the specific relationship with the person who urges them to be prompt and, as a consequence, will often be not as 'prompt' as the monochronic person but rather subject to other things they feel a need to accomplish simultaneously.

Management application   It is clear that different perceptions of time have implications for running meetings with international groups. Sequential people are likely to upset synchronic people when they insist on running such meetings like clockwork. Synchronic people will frustrate sequential people when they seem unable to stay focused on the single, specific issue at hand.

Let us consider also the problems that arise when you are faced with the task of introducing strategic planning or goal-setting or management-by-objectives into cultures that are not future-oriented. Cultures like Spain and Venezuela could not care less about planning for the future because the future has little or no bearing on the present. Any planning they do is little more than reflecting on what might happen, based on what they know from the past.

Another interesting element of time surfaces when we consider when, according to different cultures, the future starts and ends. According to many American business managers, the future starts tomorrow and ends with the next financial report. This reveals one of the problems of the US economy: it does not invite long-term thinking. You will hear this observation very often among employees of US organizations in Europe. Americans have short-term jobs and short-term bonuses. They like to talk about the future, as long as this does not stretch beyond three months.

The time dimension may explain one of the basic underlying tensions between sales and marketing groups. Planning for anything longer than the sales cycle is seen as waste of precious selling time by many sales departments; in contrast, the marketing department is very future-oriented and will spend half its time planning. Since it believes there will be a significant future, its planning consists of devising new paths and possibilities.

Reconciling time orientations   Once again we find that differences in time orientation are not truly alternatives but are capable of being used in conjunction. Future-oriented cultures will get the present into focus by relating it to a desired future. But visions need to be realistic. So, cultures that are past- or present-oriented will build the present of their business upon the learning of the past. But it is quite clear that we should not simply repeat the past but relate the present to a desired future. The wise cross-cultural manager will hold the middle ground by developing clear plans which lead from current competences to a new vision.

Applications in training and development

Three ways in which the preceding conceptual model can be used in practical training and development sessions will now be shown. The other chapters in this book will each familiarize the reader with specific case studies on how to build teams across cultures. As stated at the beginning of this chapter, the focus here is primarily on self-awareness as the start of all effective cross-cultural dealings. The following techniques can help you to apply the seven dimensions of culture to your own cultural background, to discover why you differ from other members in your (international) team.

Cross-cultural mapping

Scoring Fons Trompenaars's cross-cultural questionnaire[1] you will obtain your own cross-cultural profile expressed on the seven dimensions described above. The questionnaire is based on dilemmas that occur typically in cross-cultural encounters. Consider the following dilemma:

'You are riding in a car driven by a close friend, and your friend hits a pedestrian. You know your friend was going at least 35 miles an hour in an area of the city where the maximum speed limit is 20 miles an hour. There are no witnesses. The lawyer of your friend said that if you testify under oath that the speed was only 20 miles an hour, it may save him from serious consequences. What right has your friend to expect you to protect him?

(a) my friend has a definite right to expect me to testify to the lower figure
(b) he has some right as a friend to expect me to testify to the lower figure
(c) he has no right as a friend to expect me to testify to the lower figure

Would you help your friend in view of the obligations you feel you have for society?

(d) yes
(e) no   (Trompenaars, 1993, p.34)

This story was created by Stouffer and Toby (Americans) and serves as an exercise in cross-cultural workshops. It focuses participants on taking decisions that probe for underlying cultural beliefs in the form of a dilemma which requires either a universalist or a particularist response.

The 'cross-cultural snowflake'

Once each team member has scored his or her profile, it can be fun to carry out the exercise of building a 'cross-cultural snowflake' (see Fig. 2.2). First, each team member transfers his or her cross-cultural profile, as scored from the diskette, onto a transparency. These are then laid over each other, providing a picture of the whole team's profile. This is a good team building exercise to let the team members find out on which dimensions they overlap—and, therefore, will have little problems in accepting each other's perception—and where they differ in their perceptions. In the latter case, misunderstandings are likely to occur unless the individuals are made aware of their differences. The 'snowflake' exercise helps them to discover and discuss the potential danger zones in their communication.

Critical incidents

Another helpful way to increase the awareness of participants in cross-cultural training sessions, using the seven dimensions of culture, are critical incidents—short stores of encounters that demonstrate misunderstandings that typically occur when one individual is not aware of the other individual's different basic assumptions.

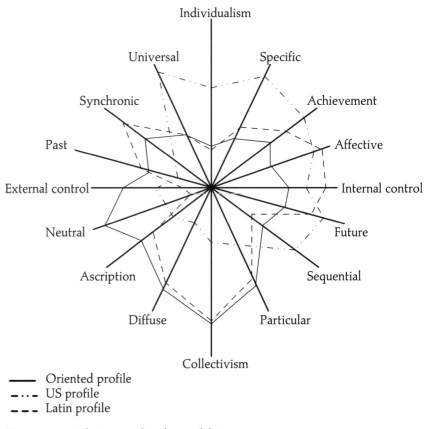

Figure 2.2 *The 'cross-cultural snowflake'*

Consider the following critical incident:

'I do not understand the Americans' was the conclusion of a French human resource manager who had been seconded for six months to the American headquarters in Pennsylvania. 'Two weeks before I came back, my American boss, the head of corporate HR, organized a big weekend party at home and invited all senior executives and the entire HR staff including spouses. If this happens in France and you are invited, you know that nothing can go wrong with your career, you are made. But you know what happened the next Monday after that party: one of the first things my boss did was to fire his corporate compensation man since he had not been happy with the latter's performance. And yet, the compensation director had been at the party with his wife. I do not understand this.'

If you listen to experienced cross-cultural managers you will readily pick up similar stories. This story can be used to discuss the difference between specific relationships cultivated by Americans (a relationship is something that happens at a specific place and time) and diffuse relationships that involve the total personality and which make more sense to the French.

Here is another story:

A newly-hired vice-president of marketing of a Swedish affiliate of a US multinational company went on his first trip to corporate headquarters somewhere on the west cost of California. Being an extremely disciplined and conscientious executive, he sent over in advance a carefully worded 15-page report of market projections for Scandinavia for the coming year. Not being aware of the common use of executive summaries in the USA, when it was his time to present the projections at the meeting he realized with horror that not one of his American colleagues had read his report. Noting his unease, the American President turned to him and said, 'Mr Olavson, why do you not summarize your findings in a few words?' Olavson had spent weeks in analysing and carefully putting his findings together in his report. Quite taken aback, he responded, 'But it is quite impossible to summarize all my findings in a few words.' Whereupon the American President smilingly replied, 'Mr Olavson, if it cannot be summarized in a few words, it is possibly not worth considering. Let us move on to the next item on the agenda.'

A third example is based on a real life case:

The corporate HR function of a big multinational company had had difficulties with the application of its global job evaluation scheme in France. The international compensation director had been sent to Paris to present an adapted set of implementation guidelines to local management. These adapted guidelines included more personal elements in the approach (integration of 'job' and 'person') and the introduction of benchmark jobs for specific positions. They also cancelled the requirement of setting up job descriptions for the sake of job evaluation. The director was pleased with the presentation and the French managers seemed to accept this flexible policy. Yet, over lunch, the French country manager asked the compensation director if he wanted to know how they evaluate their people in France. 'Of course', he said, upon which he heard the country manager tell him the following: 'It is basically the manager and the management team who decide who is up for promotion. When we decide favourably about a candidate, we go and tell him or her and congratulate him or her upon the promotion. And then we ask them to go to personnel to get a new job description and the new grade.' The compensation director became quite upset about this and the country manager did not understand. 'After all,' he said 'we are not doing it fundamentally different to the way you do it.'

Conclusion: implications for training and development

The growing trend toward globalization does not appear to reduce the differences with which managers working across cultures are being faced. We have to acknowledge that every form of management is culture-bound and that there is no such thing as 'the one best way' of management. The myth of a strong, unifying corporate culture does not resolve the issue of differences which are inherent in every organization. We must realize that most of our management and training tools are largely influenced by American business schools, have been developed in a period of rapid economic growth and are focused on the homogeneous work environment found in the USA. Yet, as we have seen, management and training techniques or philosophies that are appropriate in one culture are not necessarily appropriate in another. Let us face it: the world does not even agree on what 'work' is. Some cultures say work is the performance of a task, others say work is the expression of who you are. Work as performance of a task is a profoundly Western concept that has only been around for a few hundred years. Most of the world still operates on the assumption that work is an expression of our being, of who we are.

For years we have been teaching 'universal' principles for good management and successful selling. We need to move away from these so-called universal laws and organizational requirements which are designed to guide all organizational behaviour. We need to move towards a general set of principles, strict in philosophy but loose in application. This entails sharing information and plans, giving rough general ideas of the plans but allowing for enough variance to meet the unique situations which the organization will confront. Most importantly, we need to become aware of how our individual and collective cultural norms and values influence our organizational processes. Forget trying to homogenize the mixture of cultures—it will only lead to frustration in cross-cultural teams. You will have much greater success by cultivating the differences in the team, creating synergies and benefiting from the vast opportunities of cultural variation. We hope that this chapter has provided you with a framework that will allow you to recognize and discuss those differences in your team.

Note

1 The questionnaire is available on a self-scoring diskette and can be obtained from: Intercultural Management Publishers, Laan van Kronenburg 14, NL 1183 AS Amstelveen (The Netherlands), Telefax: + 31 20 640 31 51. The diskette comes with a practical *Better Business Guide to International Management* which summarizes all dimensions.

References

Adler, Nancy and Susan Bartholomew (1992) 'Managing Globally Competent People' *The Executive*, VI (3), pp. 52–65.

Barnevik, Percy (1994) 'Making local heroes international', *Financial Times*, 17 January, p. 8.

Bartlett, Christopher and Sumantra Ghoshal (1989) *Managing across Borders. The Transnational Solution*, Harvard Business Press, Boston.

Deming, W.E. (1988) *Out of the Crisis*, Cambridge University Press, Cambridge.

Hampden-Turner, Charles and Fons Trompenaars (1993) *The Seven Cultures of Capitalism*, Doubleday, New York.

Hofstede, Geert (1980) 'Motivation, Leadership and Organization: Do American Theories Apply Abroad?', *Organisational Dynamics*, Summer, pp. 42–63.

Snow, C., S. Canney Davison, D. Hambrick and S. Snell (1993) 'Transnational Teams—a Learning Resources Guide', unpublished paper by The International Consortium for Executive Development Research.

Trompenaars, Fons, (1993) *Riding the Waves of Culture. Understanding Cultural Diversity in Business*, The Economist Books, London.

Introduction to Chapter 3

'Management and the structure of culture', by Abe Kaplan, explores in depth some key aspects of culture and commonly experienced cultural differences from a sociological perspective. The structure of a culture he calls metaphysics, which refers to the commonalities of a culture to which people conform and through which they perceive the world. The 'metaphysics' of a culture is seldom spelled out and is often unconscious. It defines what is acceptable to say and do, and what is considered deviant and unacceptable. Therefore, it is often easier for the experienced world traveller to identify the deeply-held metaphysic of a culture than for those who have always lived in it.

This chapter outlines and discusses four primary aspects of a culture:

- orientation to time, that is, whether people focus on the past, present or future (this is similar to Trompenaars's dimension described in Chapter 2)
- personal space and physical closeness
- strictness in enforcing cultural norms, including status and procedures
- causality, that is, whether people believe they should influence events and nature or whether they should react and adapt (this is similar to Tompenaars's 'internal–external orientation' dimension described in Chapter 2)

Because these aspects are so basic it is easy for violations to be misinterpreted as rude or having a negative intent. In an international encounter, lack of awareness of these fundamental ways of being and relating can abruptly stop the potential for any business or personal relationship. When this happens, neither party may even be aware of the transgression, especially as it may be publicly, and politely, attributed to something which is socially acceptable.

Predicting when these cultural differences may arise and consciously controlling potentially offensive behaviour is a critical cross-cultural skill. In relationship to the four primary aspects of culture, the following questions can highlight the type of differences to expect.

The first element is *time* and the following questions should be asked:

- How important is strict time management? What is considered too early, too late and on time?
- Are activities fixed to specific times or are they undertaken when the time 'feels right'?
- Are activities undertaken one at a time (serial or monochronic) or concurrently (polychronic)?
- To what extent do people make decisions based on expected future benefits versus immediate outcomes versus tradition or history?
- How do people set priorities between getting down to business immediately versus building trust and developing a relationship before discussing commercial matters?

The second element is *space* and the following questions should be asked:

- How physically 'close' do people like to be with others?
- How much 'touching' is acceptable?
- To what extent do people believe that doors and space should allow easy access to others (i.e. 'my door is always open') versus the belief that privacy behind closed doors should be maintained?

The third element is *strictness* in rule enforcement and the following questions should be asked:

- How rigidly, or legalistically are rules and procedures followed?
- What is fixed and strictly applied and what is negotiable?
- How important is it to acknowledge people's formal title or status directly?
- Are people open and direct or polite and concerned about maintaining 'face'?

The fourth element is the interpretation of *cause and effect* and the following questions should be asked:

- Do people consciously strive to control or manipulate nature, including other people, or to respond and adapt?
- Are there hidden powers, usually assigned to religion or magic, which are believed to cause events to happen?
- Is every occurrence believed to be the result of someone's actions and, therefore, someone must be held responsible?

This chapter delves below the surface of cultural differences and, thus, sets the scene for understanding the depth of issues to be overcome in team building.

3 Management and the structure of culture

Abraham Kaplan

What happens in management is related to what happens in many other kinds of enterprise, such as politics, religion and human relations. A manager is also a citizen, a church-goer, a spouse and performer in many other roles. There may be tension and even conflicts among a person's roles; but this does not necessarily fragment the personality. Society not only defines roles but also defines patterns of interaction between them which allow for the maintenance of a more or less integrated personality. It is expected, for instance, that evenings and weekends 'normally' belong to the family, not the corporation.

Integration is seldom achieved simply by drawing boundaries within which each of the roles is declared to be sovereign. Even where there are such boundaries, unless the personality is pathologically split there is always some infiltration. Moral principles, for instance, might lead one to resign from a company just as economic interest can lead one to compromise moral principles.

Each kind of activity has its own aims and methods, but there are also commonalities. In each society, entrepreneur and jurist, soldier and statesman, priest and prophet, for all their differences and disagreements, can understand and accept one another on some basic level. Where this is no longer true, the society is on the verge of collapse. These underlying commonalities make up the structure or metaphysics of the culture. Because the metaphysics are so fundamental and pervasive they are hard to identify. If you want to know the philosophy of a people, do not look at what they have written but at what they do not write. The metaphysics of a culture is seldom made explicit. It is embodied in the institutions and practices characteristic of the society.

Norms guide to behaviour

Norms are the building blocks of the metaphysics. Norms are the generally implicit guidelines which expected or socially acceptable behaviour follows. Statutory law does not presuppose a written constitution; not every profession publishes a code of ethics, nor do published codes embody the norms actually at work. Company policy is not necessarily articulated in a manual of standard operating procedures. There is a difference between unthinking conformity to norms and conscious obedience to explicitly formulated rules. It is the difference between speaking grammatically, which native speakers do without awareness, and obeying the rules of grammarians, which only school children do. A culture does not obey its metaphysics but conforms to it.

Perceiving other cultures

Our metaphysics structures our perception of the world and of our place in it. Since the metaphysics provides the categories in which we think, alternatives to it are virtually unthinkable. It is hard to understand another culture; because its metaphysics is different, it just does not seem to make sense. If it does make sense, members of the culture do not even mean what they seem to be saying. A Japanese who responds to a request with, 'I will do my best' or 'Let me think about it' is saying, 'No'; a Middle Easterner who breaks off bargaining with, 'Be well!' is saying, 'Drop dead!'

Once we leave home we feel that we are surrounded by foreigners; it is we ourselves who are the foreigners. Nowadays we can go everywhere, but we cannot go outside ourselves. The modern world is adeptly described as a global village. We carry our parochialism with us: the global village is populated by strangers. We are all of us strangers in a strange land.

Another reason why it is so hard to recognize the metaphysics of even our own culture is that individuals live more and more in their own little worlds, speaking in their own jargon, doing their own thing. The division of labour is increasingly refined; ours is an age of specialization, and specialists are notoriously poor at communicating with outsiders.

Historical perspective of culture

The metaphysics of a culture integrates the special domains of the culture. The same fundamental categories appear in diverse areas of concern—religion, science, technology, economics, politics and art. In a given society these all look at the world, more or less, in the same way; as a result it is the same world for all of them.

Europe in the eighteenth century, for example, was largely mechanistic in outlook. Everywhere it saw orderly systems, composed of separable parts interlocking to form unified and harmonious wholes. This is why it was the Age of Reason, the world within mirroring the order, unity and harmony to be found everywhere in the external world. The distinctive theology of the period was deism, the belief in a creator of the world who designed it, established its laws, set it going, and thereafter did not interfere with its workings. The medieval conception of God as the architect of the universe was given new life, finding expression in William Blake's memorable etching, *The Ancient of Days*, showing the bearded deity bending over the world with a pair of engineer's compasses in his hands (though for Blake himself, anti-establishment and mystic, the picture was meant to symbolize the destructive power of reason).

Astronomers elaborated Newtonian physics into a cosmic system, displaying the planets and their moons moving like clockwork in orderly progression. Indeed, their motions were in fact displayed on clocks. The clock was the epitome of eighteenth-century technology; in the public squares of Berne, Strasbourg and countless other European cities, the doings of both animals and humans were simulated by the motions of clockwork figures.

Adam Smith's economics and the *laissez-faire* philosophy saw the economy as a similar system, working well if only it is kept clean and oiled and is not tampered with. The economy is governed by market forces, not by managerial decisions. It is ruled by the invisible hand of competition, in accord with the inexorable law of supply and demand and similar principles, deriving from our intrinsic human nature rather than from managerial policy.

The world-view characteristic of the period found expression in art and music as well. The capricious frivolity of rococo and the convoluted fantasies of the baroque both gave way to neo-classicism, with its emphasis on harmony, proportion and rationality. The passionate subjectivity of Bach was replaced by the objective clarity and simplicity of Haydn and Mozart. Art and music were experienced as intelligible systems, like all else in the metaphysics of that culture.

Other world-views characterize other periods. In the nineteenth century unities were seen, not as mechanisms consisting of separable interlocking parts but as organized wholes engaged in the transformation of energy. Thermodynamics was the paradigmatic physical science and biology flourished. The epitome of technology was not the clock but the steam engine. Social institutions were thought to grow and evolve or else to decline and become extinct. Progress could be maintained, it was held, only as a dynamic, ever-changing equilibrium—a delicate balance of power.

In the twentieth century it is the computer which is central, not only to technology but also to the metaphysics in which the technology is embedded. Neither matter nor energy is the basic category but information. The significant flow of phenomena does not run like clockwork and is not the transformation of energy; it is the processing of data. Nature is neither mechanistically determined nor organically evolving but a random succession, into which we ourselves must put meaning.

In a different world-view, management too views itself differently. Many responsibilities which it once assumed, like maintaining an appropriate inventory, it now assigns to computers. The task of management today is not to preserve a given order of things, whether mechanistic or organic, but to make decisions in uncertain conditions, to take calculated risks, to minimize losses and, above all, to manage crisis and cope with chaos. The manager who played his part according to classical economic theory alone would be quite bewildered in this new world.

Culture and conformity

What belongs to the metaphysics of a culture is revealed in other ways than by the commonalities of diverse domains of the culture. The metaphysics is not merely descriptive, defining reality for the culture; it is also prescriptive, defining what the culture endorses as the appropriate response to reality. The norms implied in the metaphysics are enforced by sanctions of ridicule, suspicion, hostility and ostracism or worse. Deviant behaviour is condemned as unnatural, barbaric, antisocial or even inhuman.

A more tolerant attitude may perceive the deviant as simply stupid or irrational, more to be pitied than censured. The deviant behaviour might make sense if the world were other than all right thinking people know it to be. The deviant, poor soul, lives in a private world which is all askew; we must put him or her straight.

Putting someone straight is a matter of behaviour modification, not of explanation—especially not explanation of the metaphysics. The metaphysics is either outside awareness or is self-evident, serving to explain everything else without itself needing explanation. It is axiomatic, always a premise and never a conclusion. It provides justifications without ever needing justification; its normative force is the ground of value. If a metaphysics is questioned, the question can only be begged.

Culture and subcultures

To speak of 'the' metaphysics of a culture can be misleading. Every society is more or less heterogeneous, comprising different subcultures. Every corporation has its own culture. Generalizations about corporations belonging to the 'same' society are as hazardous as generalizations about different societies; at best they are only hypotheses. Stereotypes of societies and 'national characters' are prejudicial, not because they impute differences, but because the imputation so often is literally a prejudgment, a preconception, not an empirically grounded generalization. Empirical evidence inevitably points to statistical variations within each culture.

The Japanese culture, for instance, has in it characteristics both of the

Zen Samurai and the Shinto peasant. Traditional Chinese culture was embodied both in the cultivated Confucian and in the unsophisticated Taoist. Typically East-Indian in the nineteenth century were both the luxury-loving maharajah and the ascetic sannyasin. Seventeenth-century England had both self-indulgent Cavaliers and self denying Roundheads, a heterogeneity going far beyond dress and manners and culminating in the Puritan revolution.

External differences are not necessarily only superficial: at meetings of the Hawaii Chamber of Commerce one can see both flowered silk and pin-striped flannels, not as stereotypical gender differences in clothing, but according to significant differences in corporate cultures of the men and women wearing the garments. Changes in dance-styles in America—from group dances like square-dances and the Virginia Reel, through couples dances like the foxtrot and jitterbug, to the present-day 'touch-me-not' style—may be more than superficial; the changing fashions may reflect the change from a collective to an individualist culture in the course of the last century. On the other hand, external differences in cultures may really be no more than superficial. Americans are put off by the Israeli clerk's impersonality, as Israelis are by the American clerk's cheery, 'Have a nice day!', but the one is not necessarily rude nor is the other necessarily hypocritical. The stylized warmth of Japanese and Arabic treatment of strangers is not necessarily more genuinely friendly than British standoffishness. Metaphysics and manners are two different things, though the latter may provide useful data if read aright.

Key cultural differences: the meaning of time

One of the most significant differences among cultures is the degree of importance they attach to time. One portion of time is not the same as another; the continuous stream of time divides itself into segments of differing content. Where the segmentation is not thrust upon us, it is culturally defined. What is called a year varies with its significance in the culture. There is a fiscal year and an academic year, a religious year and a secular one. All may be rooted in the cycle of seasons. Other segmentations are more cultural than astronomical. The week in some cultures is as short as three days and in others as long fifteen, determined, say, by the period between market days.

The hour is altogether culturally defined. Japan, until 1873, divided the day and the night each into six hours, as a result of which a summer daytime hour could be more than twice as long as a night-time hour. Ancient China divided into one hundred parts, making each 'hour' about fifteen minutes long. Hours may vary not only in length but also in content, by which they are identified. Western countries have the academic hour, the psychoanalytic hour, the cocktail hour and the still long 'happy hour'. The Israeli forenoon and afternoon are not before and after 12 o'clock but before and after the midday meal, usually eaten around 2 o'clock. Therefore the afternoon extends well into what elsewhere would be called the evening.

Time, in short, has quality; even if segments are equal in length they may be far from equal in significance. Virtually every culture has its propitious and inauspicious times. In China, years differ from one another not just in date but in intrinsic character, symbolized by the animal, such as horse or rat, by which it is named.

Importance of time

In most cultures, time is a quantified commodity, very often treated as a scarce resource and correspondingly valuable. Status is marked by who waits for whom and how long. 'Please hold', requested during a telephone call, may be used as a reminder of a status difference; how long a wait there is for an answer to a communication is a similar indication.

That time is a commodity with a value of its own was already noted in the Book of Exodus, which legislates compensation for an inflicted loss of time. Related themes are elaborated throughout Exodus and elsewhere in Scripture. Similar injunctions are familiar from *Poor Richard's Almanac* to contemporary conventional wisdom: 'Time is money', 'Use time or time will use you' and the like. In cultures with that metaphysics, managers are likely to come to work earlier and stay later than their subordinates.

In many places work has been put on nearly a wartime footing. Continuous operation is treated not as a matter of optimal use of plant and equipment but as a matter of life and death for the company. It is as though the only alternative to full speed ahead is shutting down altogether. In such management there is a breathless urgency, a perspective of permanent crisis. This outlook is not the result of the press of competition but has deeper roots. It is as marked in the monopolistic public sector as in the competitive private sector.

The time clock

The abstract concept of time as a commodity is concretized in the time clock. The measurement of time has normative force, enjoining appropriate action. In many cultures, the clock has been from the outset a handmaiden of religion. The Scriptural injunction is to talk of God's work 'when you lie down and when rise up'; in most religions this vagueness is replaced by more precise time specifications.

The Talmud begins with the question of when is the proper time for morning prayers and later deals, at length, with when the Sabbath begins and ends. In Israel to this day the exact time of sunset, which marks the beginning of the Sabbath, is published for each major city, lest the time be off by a minute or two. For Christianity, the first detailed time discipline was the Rule of St Benedict, in AD 530. It specified seven services, designated by clock hours—the canonical hours. To pray is to 'recite the hours', as today one might say that to go to work is to 'punch the clock'. The factory whistle and the school buzzer are the descendants of monastery bells and the muezzin summoning the faithful to prayer.

Religious obedience to time implies punctuality. Opposition to Hassidim, as to Quakers, often focused on their refusal to be bound to fixed times of prayer rather than waiting till the spirit moved them. In secular society, being late risks missing the plane, an examination, a deadline, a meal, a television programme, the game or a party. Swiss and German punctuality are well known. In contrast, the Japanese begin ceremonial dances and other activities 'when the time is right'. The language of the Sioux has no word for waiting or for being late.

Polychronic and serial time

Two events can occur at the same time, but some events must take place one after the other. On this basis Edward Hall (1959) distinguishes between polychronic and serial time (Hall's presentation of what he calls 'the hidden dimension' provides a number of the illustrations given here). North European cultures usually treat time as serial, while the Mediterranean cultures take it to be polychronic.

In Israel a clerk will wait on several people at a time rather than in turn. An Israeli contractor will promise to meet the respective deadlines for several constructions at once, but it is understood that work on each will be only intermittent, so as to be fair to all. Cultures with a metaphysics of serial time must decide on priorities. This may be on the basis of status, suitably defined, or by seniority, or by a principle such as first come, first served. In the USA delicatessens, butchers shops, bakeries and other crowded markets provide a numbered card on entry, fixing the order of being served.

Cultural significance of time

The flow of time differentiates past, present and future. A culture may attach relative importance or unimportance to each or all of them. Exclusive preoccupation with the past is unlikely to be successful. It was said of the Bourbons that they forgot nothing and learned nothing. Being guided by past experience is one thing; it is quite another to ignore new circumstances. Exclusive preoccupation with the future characterizes the visionary, who can provide a goal but cannot tell how to get there from here. Infantilism knows only the present; the infant wants *what* it wants *when* it wants it. The conditions and consequences of satisfying the wants remain outside its purview.

Often a metaphysics emphasizes two of the three stages of timeflow. Conservatives find value in the past and work so as to conserve the value in the present. Visionaries are often associated with men of action who move the present toward the envisioned future—pairings like

Jesus and Paul, Marx and Lenin, and Ghandi and Nehru. Revolutionaries turn their backs on the past altogether, even introducing a new calender in which the revolution marks the 'year one'. Both past and future may be emphasized, as in the romanticist notion of a golden age that once was and will yet be again—a paradise lost and to be regained. This is the perspective of communism, fascism and religious fundamentalism.

Living in the past   Emphasis on the past is expressed in various ways. It may be the careful preservation of mementos and souvenirs, dwelling on memorabilia, attending class reunions—in short, living in the past. An organization, too, can live in the past, remaining, in Emerson's phrase, the 'lengthened shadow of its founder', sticking to its established products, methods and markets, and managing through the 'old boy' network. Regions within a country may cherish tradition; in the USA, for example, New England and the Old South maintain links with their past, in contrast to Southern California.

Tradition can be self-consciously preserved—in chronicles and monuments, and what has been called the ritual perpetuation of the past. A sense of history turns to the past to give meaning to the present. In Israel, names of people, places and institutions often reach into the distant past: Boulevard Father Abraham and the Samson Cement Works. Chinese ancestor worship, the Mormon focus on genealogy and the Black search for roots are other expressions of a sense of history.

Living in the future   Quite different from a sense of history is a historical sense, which finds meaning in the present by way of the future. Insurance policies and retirement plans, college funds and savings clubs all express a historical sense. It is expressed, too, by the importance attached to preparations, as in the Hopi culture, and in many Western cultures to planning—for a career, a corporation or a country.

A distant time-horizon, as in long-range planning, is less common in the USA than in some other cultures, perhaps because of its history of rapid and unforeseen changes. Israeli appointments are often unilaterally cancelled or postponed and neither party feels that the appointment was broken—it was made, not as a commitment to the future, but as an expression of a present intention.

In the nineteenth century the historical sense, expressed as the idea of progress, had a powerful impact. The idea was that the standard of living will steadily rise; children will be better off then their parents; our problems will gradually be solved without the solutions bringing new problems; the present will inevitably bring us to a better future. Tradition must not and will not stand in the way of progress.

Living in the present   Several time-perspectives share the view that what does not happen in the present never happens. On this view, the present is the locus of all fulfilments and all frustrations: the past can longer satisfy or disappoint and the future can only promise or threaten. The principle is crystallized in Hillel's aphorism, 'If not now, when?' What we do when we get around to it, when we can find the time, when the time is right, we never do. A company which always reinvests all its earnings never declares a dividend.

For realism, present decisions are guided both by past experience and by expected future outcomes. Infantilism ignores both past and future; its actions are the rituals of a cult of immediacy. Those who embraced the culture a few decades ago call themselves 'the New Generation'; it was a generation of instant learning, instant intimacy, fast foods, instant weight-loss and solutions *now* for long-enduring problems.

Postdating cheques, instalment buying (as distinct from lay-away plans), high-interest borrowing, discounting for cash are practised by people of all ages in many Western countries. In the nineteenth century, Navajos would willingly accept small immediate payments rather than much larger ones at a later time. American high-pressure selling techniques ('Buy now!') contrast with the French slow build-up of personal relationships, perhaps extending even to more than one generation.

Time, pressure and patience

A common modern response to time pressure is to live by deadlines and schedules, a lifestyle which only increases the pressure. The style has only the virtue of diligence: its devotees keep 'busy' even though nothing is being accomplished. Centuries ago the clock was a liberation, freeing people from schedules imposed by religious authorities or by king and nobles. Today, for many the clock is a curse; what is liberating is to ignore the clock. Many people have leisure time in their 'busy' lives but use it in a far from leisurely way, lacking altogether the Italian *dolce far niente*, Puerto Rican *serenidad* and Druze unhurried dignity. Such people spend not only their working hours but their leisure hours, too, watching the clock.

Patience or its absence may be cultural trait, not a purely personal one. American 'getting down to business' is very different from the Bedouin or Chinese politely gradual approach. In decision making, many American Indian cultures are quite willing to take as long as is necessary to attain consensus. Concerts in India often seem interminable to Western ears, though the Indians themselves— including even the children—listen with unmoving attention. Buddhist monks studying in Western universities have been known to submit study plans requiring 20 years or more to complete, explaining that they have 'all the time there is'. Israelis, on the other hand, are continually demanding of one another, *Savlanut!*', 'Patience', which none of them has.

Key cultural differences: the meaning of space

The second major category of the metaphysics of culture is space. Distances in cultural space can embody important attitudes. 'Close' can imply intimacy, as in 'close friend' (though not necessarily in 'a close relative'); friends can 'drift apart'; a mere acquaintance can have a 'distant manner'. In nineteenth-century America neighbours may be physically distant yet be 'neighbourly'; in England and France, on the other hand, living near one another does not in itself raise expectations of friendliness.

The boundary between people

The study of body-space, which Hall (1959) calls 'proxemics', is revealing of cultural differences. The boundaries of one's body-space do not necessarily coincide with the skin. In cultures where they do, touching people is not an invasion of their privacy. There are people to whom touching is quite acceptable, like Jews of East European descent and Hispanics, and others who recoil from it, like Germans and the English. For Italians the boundary is close to the skin; both vehicles and pedestrians move in ways which elsewhere would be perceived as infringing on someone else's lane.

Hispanics stand or sit close to their interlocutors, about half as far apart as Britons do and significantly closer than Americans, who misread closeness as either a hostile stance or one inviting intimacy. In a cross-cultural negotiation, one person might feel put off by the continuing effort to increase the distance between the two parties, while the other feels threatened by the continuing effort to come closer. Status differences call for a 'respectful distance' which is culturally defined, determining how near one approaches someone's desk, for instance, ranging from barely close enough to remove the need to shout, to leaning over the desk. There are likely to be unfortunate misinterpretations if the 'respectful distance' is differently defined by the two parties.

To exclude anyone runs counter to American equalitarianism. This is applied to spatial exclusion as well as to group membership. The American managers declares, 'My door is always open!' The implication is that he is accessible to all; everyone can be an insider. Moreover, his open door proclaims that he has nothing to hide; he is 'open and above-board', as one can see in his 'frank and open' face. An open door may also be a sign of hospitality: the doors to the tents of Abraham were kept open for guests and Job's tent had four doors so as to welcome travellers from every direction. Generosity is 'open-handed' and acceptance extends 'open arms'.

Germans regard an open door as unbusinesslike, relaxed and informal. They, like the Dutch, often have double doors, to shut out sound as well as people who have no good reason to enter. To Americans, the closed door is suspect, because it excludes.

Key cultural differences: strictness in rule enforcement

An important component of the metaphysics of a culture is how its norms are perceived. Cultures differ in the strictness with which their norms are followed. The respectability of the *noblesse oblige* subcultures of England and France, and German respect for authority contrast with Polish disregard and even defiance of authority. Switzerland and Singapore impose fines for dropping cigarette stubs, while Israelis freely litter public places with the shells of sunflower seeds and Americans deposit their chewing gum wherever convenient.

Bureaucratic power

A measure of the strictness of society is the extent and power of its bureaucracies. The essence of a bureaucracy is applying abstract and general rules to concrete and particular cases. A bureaucrat is not authorized to make exceptions. The bureaucratic ideal is to anticipate all grounds for departure from the rules and incorporate them in new rules, so that circumstances will no longer call for exceptions. The aim is to ensure that no one will be treated exceptionally and to free the bureaucrat from exercising judgement.

In some cultures norms rest lightly on the citizenry—not that laws are readily broken but that they are bent to suit individual urgencies. Israeli bureaucracy is tempered by *protekzia*, special treatment accorded to close friends, distant relatives, connections of all sorts and people of status in some respect or other, like professionals to whom colleagues extend professional courtesy. *Protekzia* is not downright criminal, not 'protection' in the American sense of payment extorted by an implied threat. It is objectionable, but is accepted as 'the way things are'.

The application of general rules to particular cases unavoidably calls for judgement. In American towns near the border with Mexico there are sizeable Hispanic populations. Acculturated Americans interpret speed limits, for instance, as allowing a margin of five to ten miles an hour but expect norms of judicial proceedings to be strictly observed; Hispanics, on the other hand, are strict in their interpretation of the law but expect to be treated leniently when judgement is rendered by friends, relatives or other connections.

Conflicts of interest such those between buyer and seller may be resolved, not by predetermined norms strictly applied, like fixed prices, but by negotiation, as in Middle Eastern bargaining. The pattern can be widespread in a culture. Israeli conduct, not only in the marketplace, is governed by three principles: every right is transformed into a privilege; every privilege is denied; every denial is negotiable. What another culture might take to be a binding commitment is, in Israeli society, a point of departure for further negotiation. Politicians everywhere violate campaign promises, but few openly explain, as did one Israeli prime minister, 'I didn't promise to keep my promises'.

Importance of status differences

Social norms reflect the social structure; if this embodies inequalities, so will the norms. In traditional Japan, when two people meet formally they bow; how many times they bow, how low and who bows last all depends on status differences. In Western cultures, who looks directly at whom depends on actual or perceived status differences such as those between an employer and employee, a supervisor and subordinate, an older person and younger, or a man and a woman. For the person of lower status to stare at the other would be felt to be aggressive or hostile.

Inequalities are often embodied in titles, which are subject to varying norms. In Israeli universities academic titles are used far more often and more carefully than in American universities. The German 'Herr Doktor Professor' is used even in informal circumstances ('Will Herr Doktor Professor have another cup of tea?'). Titles of clergy and modes of addressing them are specified in detail in some religions and not at all in others.

In Russia and India students rise when the professor enters; were this to happen in America it might be thought to signal a student rebellion.

Interpersonal relations differ widely in other respects, too. The British think it proper for people to deal with their problems by themselves and they respect privacy. Israelis, on the other hand, have no hesitation in sharing many of their problems and in inviting or offering help; surprisingly, this pattern is less marked in the kibbutzim, for all their socialist idealogy. Israeli clerks, secretaries and minor bureaucrats seldom do for themselves what they can get others, co-workers or even clients, to do for them.

In some cultures, efficiency can give way to a division of labour in which workers perform their allotted tasks even if circumstances make the allocation far from optimal. In India, differences of caste and rank are strictly respected; a technician will have an unskilled worker carry his tools even when he needs only one or two and a chauffeur will be accompanied by a subordinate to keep the car clean. In Hindu metaphysics these allocations are a matter of karma, fruits of one's actions in this life or a previous one. In Western cultures, similar allocations are unbending provisions of union contracts meant to protect jobs, without regard to the loss in productivity from such protective devices.

Japanese perspectives emphasize collective effort rather than the duties of individual workers. The work day or night begins with group exercise, as in America a football team or military unit might do. Japanese workers on the same project take their breaks together, eat together, are likely to live near one another and might very well vacation together, accompanied by their families. Their managers may share offices with one another so as to facilitate consensus.

Leadership based on status or performance

The difference between cultures that emphasize status and those that emphasize performance is embodied in a corresponding difference between structural (positional) and functional (task) leadership. The functions of a leader are not necessarily performed by those formally designated as having the appropriate authority. A functional pattern, however, cannot effectively be imposed on a group with structural metaphysics. Japanese prisoners of war, for example, refused to accept the leadership of other prisoners appointed to this task without regard to their civilian status. They no longer objected when formal authority was assigned to status figures, even while the functions of leadership were actually being performed by the original appointees. Israeli military effectiveness is partly due to a pattern of functional leadership, everyone in a unit being capable of assuming command if need be; in armies from status-oriented cultures, however, the entire unit is incapacitated if its commanding officer becomes a casualty.

Manners, politeness and face

An important set of norms serve as social lubricants, minimizing the friction inevitable when many individuals are going their own ways. Such norms make up the manners of a culture. These can have more than a superficial significance: they define what will be accepted as civilized behaviour. Foreigners and natives typically see one another as barbarians, and so view one another with suspicion and distrust.

A Japanese cabbie, asked if he knows how to get to a certain address, will always answer affirmatively, since admission of ignorance would be a loss of face. Japanese students asked if a certain point in the lecture was understood will also always answer affirmatively, since otherwise the professor would lose face for having failed to provide intelligible explanations. Dishonesty is no more involved here than in an American's asking, 'How are you today?', as if he or she wanted to know, or in an airline stewardess's apparently eager friendliness, as though she longed for the passenger's companionship.

What is often perceived as Israeli rudeness is the expression of a metaphysics in which action fills a power vacuum. Israelis push until a reaction shows that a boundary has been reached; if I am infringing on your domain, it is for you to let me know. Rudeness has nothing to do with it.

The importance of family

An individual reacts not only with other individuals but also with institutions, perhaps with the society as a whole. To cushion these unequal encounters cultures provide mediating structures, protective subgroups such as the tribe, the clan and the caste. Most basic is the family, especially the enlarged family, like the Jewish *mishpacha* and the Arabic *chamoulah*.

Such structures are not always perceived as mediating; they may even become the chief targets of resistance to social pressure. Confucian thought took the family as the key metaphor of its ethics and politics;

for Americans today the family often provides metaphor for unwanted control, like 'paternalism' and 'Big Brother'. When asked, 'What do you do to be alone?' Italian, British and Black American mothers answer, 'Get away from the family'; Puerto Rican mothers answer, 'Get away from strangers and from public places'.

Norms and values

Associated with every normative system is a set of values. Customary ways of doing things become matters of morality, evoking a sense of obligation. In our time the most common bases of values are religious (as, say, in Iran), political (as, say, in China), or humanistic, more or less empirical theories of human needs and fulfillments (as, say, in Holland or Sweden). Managerial values and the decisions to which they lead may have a personal basis, something internal, like a leader's vision; they may have an ideological basis, something external and abstract, like a policy handed down to an administrator; or they may have a situational basis, something external and concrete, like the circumstances which determine an executive's operations.

Differences in values are as marked as differences in their bases. The two sorts of difference do not necessarily correspond. People may offer different justifications for the same value, opposing abortion, for instance, on religious or on medical grounds. The same justification may be offered for contrary values, as in the case of members of the same religion disagreeing about contraception.

What is valuable, and why, depends on who is doing the valuing. This does not make values subjective but only relative. That one person's meat is another's poison does not imply that biochemistry is a matter of opinion. What it does imply is that it would be folly to serve the same dish to both people.

Differences which seem trivial to one culture may be significant to another and have a different significance to still another culture. Names and candidates for office were colour-coded blue and red by the government administrator, the intention being simply to help the voter distinguish the names; but to the Navajo blue is a propitious colour and red a threatening one. Apropos of colour significance, Chinese wear black at weddings and white at funerals. Differences in values are especially confusing when we are not even aware of their existence.

Values in heterogeneous societies

In heterogeneous societies, important values become public issues. Matters relating to marriage and the family are controversial in many Western societies—divorce, abortion, homosexuality and the status of women. Increasingly pressing are differences concerning the use of violence—weapons of mass destruction, capital punishment, terrorism, police power and forcible intervention in affairs of other nations.

Issues relating to the economy provide other examples: nationalization and privatization; market and planned economics; taxation based on ability to pay and on benefits received; what constitutes a just distribution of goods and services, a fair wage and equitable profit. Other issues concern the work ethic: in some cultures manual labour is felt to be degrading; in others all work is thought to be at best a necessary evil; in still others the so-called Protestant ethic makes work a religious duty and industriousness a moral virtue.

A classic instance of bad management because of unawareness of culture differences concerns an American admiral charged with rapidly building airstrips on a chain of Pacific islands, using local labour. The construction proceeded slowly, because, he was told, workers spent only four days a week on the job 'Double their wages!' he ordered. As a result, they worked only two days. To say that the utility of money is not a linear function of the amount does not solve the problem but only formulates it.

Key cultural differences: action, cause and effect

The final component of the metaphysics of culture considered here is the standard it sets for acceptable explanations, for understanding the world and acting reasonably in it. Every culture has its own conception of why things happen as they do. The search for the meaning of events is universal. The universal aim is to know which actions will most effectively lead to our goals. The metaphysics of a culture defines the culture's conception of causality.

Every culture has a technology, often better suited to the circumstances and values of the culture than people from other cultures, with their ethnocentrism, readily appreciate. Human beings can be savage and primitive in their behaviour but there is no such thing as a 'primitive culture' or a 'savage mentality'. Survival does not define truth, but what works must have an element of truth in it, a close approximation to the truth in a limited domain to give its practitioners a hold on the external world.

The Hebrew word for wisdom, *chochma*, originally meant craftsmanship or technical capability. The wise men first identified as such in the Scripture, Bezalel and Hiram of Tyre, are described as skilled in the working of metals, stone and wood. Only later did wisdom become the province of priest and prophet, as in India, and of scholarly élites, as in Greece and China.

In some cultures technology is thought of mechanistically. As applied to human behaviour, mechanistic conceptions are illustrated by human engineering, behaviour modification, and the activities of propagandists, advertisers, unprincipled evangelists and others engaged in manipulating people. In other cultures efficacy is thought of in organic terms, not a manipulation but a cultivation. Indonesian farmers, for example, resisted using fertilizers 'to make the soil more productive', but readily accepted the use of fertilizers when this was presented as 'feeding the soil'.

Symbolic causation: religion and magic

Different from both mechanistic and organic conceptions of causality is the idea of symbolic causation, in which efficacy attaches to the utterance of certain words, invocations of particular names, performance of specific gestures—in short, the use of certain symbols. Mechanistic and organic conceptions are perspectives of technology; symbolic causation, usually assigned to religion and magic, relates to what is perceived as lying beyond human powers (which may include assuring the success of the technology).

Many cultures view events as manifestations of hidden cosmic order, impinging on human affairs as enactments of the decrees of destiny. This underlying order, so far as it bears on human endeavours, was known to ancient Greeds as *moira*, to Hindus as karma, to Muslims as kismet and to Jews as *goral*. The belief is not to be confused with fatalism, which is a denial of causality altogether, since it holds that destiny will overtake you no matter what you do. Instead, the belief attributes events to higher powers which can be bent to human ends, not by action but by communication. We invoke the powers by their names, and they reveal to us the constraints imposed by the cosmic order. This linkage constitutes symbolic causation.

Discerning the hidden order is appropriately called divination. The order comes to be known by signs, which typically are apparently random events. Among them are dreams; the flight of birds; configurations of the lines on the hand or of the entrails of fowls; the fall of sticks; patterns of tea-leaves and coffee grounds; and, until very recent times, the appearance of comets.

Attributing such events to chance does not deprive them of significance in the metaphysics of symbolic causation, for which 'chance' is but another name of the goddess Fortuna or, her modern avatar, Lady Luck. The charge of superstition is construed as mistaking the failure to understand for the absence of a meaning to be understood. Here relation is very much to the point—what is superstition in one culture is the true faith in another.

Symbolic causation: bureaucracy and magic

Magic is the implementation of symbolic causation; hocus-pocus is its very essence. Magic is thought both to strengthen technology and to provide a substitute for technology, an open sesame. Because the promise of its powers counters anxiety, magic has a recognizable role in religion. Not so readily recognized is the role of magic in management, especially bureaucratic management.

The stock-in-trade of every bureaucracy, its raw material and its final product, is nothing but documents; bureaucracy demands of its clients, 'Show me your papers' and 'Fill out these forms'. In return it gives clients only another document. As with all magic, exactitude is essential. If one word is wrong, all is for nought; if the right words are in the right places, all is well. For the bureaucrat, the most important function of the piece of paper is to provide him or her with protective cover. For the client, the piece of paper is full of promise. Both obtain reassurance in the encounter; they are bound together, like all else in the bureaucratic world, by red tape.

In the secular version of the will of the gods, the role of the cosmic order is played by company policy, expressed in the rules for filling out the forms and for reacting to the result. 'It is our policy' is taken to be the necessary and sufficient condition for the bureaucrat's decisions. To question whether it should be the policy is to challenge the divine order.

The bureaucracy defines reality. What does not appear in its files does not exist; what does appear is beyond dispute. A visiting professor at a university which shall be nameless, trying to find out why he had not received his pay cheque, was told by the clerk examining the files, not that there was an omission or error somewhere, but simply, 'You don't work here'. All is formless and unreal until it is structured by a bureaucratic formula. Whatever preserves the formula is permitted— and nothing else.

Formulas become more significant than what they structure; the symbol becomes its own reality. The Wizard of Oz understood that the cowardly lion lacked only a medal to be courageous; the Scarecrow whose head was stuffed with straw needed only a diploma to be intelligent; and the hollow Tin Woodman needed only a heart fixed to his sleeve to be sensitive and caring. Oz can be found anywhere. Bezalel was picked to build the Temple, not because of his technical skill, but because he knew how to combine the letters by which heaven and earth were created. In many modern societies that would qualify him for a high managerial post.

A sophisticated variant of symbolic causation purports to explain and predict events by reference to abstractions. These are conceived as if they were concrete things capable of serving as causal agents. This might be called 'ideological causation', after a familiar kind of reified abstractions. 'History', 'class', 'nation' and 'state' are used to delineate a hidden order underlying events. The managerial style which relies on abstractions invokes such symbols as 'policy', 'market forces', 'the economy' and a variety of 'theories' and 'models'.

Individual accountability

Congenial to the personal style of management is a conception of a personal causation, which views all events as outcomes of deliberate choices. Everything that happens is someone's achievement or someone's fault. If it is not people who are responsible, it is personalized 'higher powers'. Magical words become the names of spirits, angels and demons; in late medieval times, even 'Hocus' and 'Pocus' were construed as proper names. In modern times, magical power is ascribed to the words of the 'great leader', which provide reassurance and guidance merely by being quoted.

From this perspective, managers are not only magicians exploiting powers by which they shape the course of events. Whatever happens during their tenure of office is the result of what they have chosen to do. There are no impersonal forces to be taken into account and no unanticipated or unintended consequences. The manager is personally responsible for everything. The perception of such powers is what gives their possessors charisma. The greater the power, the greater the responsibility.

Management with this perspective focuses on the future. It seeks, not explanations for what has already happened, but forecasts of what is going to happen. It sees itself as realistic and pragmatic, dismissing 'theories' as pointless speculation and turning to statistics and computer technology to find trends in the data on the basis of which forecasts can be made. Its ideal manager is one who sees what is coming, sees further and more clearly than others and sees it sooner.

Cultural styles of thinking

At the root of ethnocentrism with regard to norms of explanation is the notion that there is only one set of standards of rationality, one way of coming to know the world, one logic—and that, of course, is the thinker's own. There are significant differences, not only among cultures but even from person to person, in cognitive style, in how people learn, how they think, how they solve problems. It is hard to believe that only one style is effective or better than all others in all circumstances.

There are cultures like that of ancient Greece, which look to abstractions, reasons and theories. Other cultures, like that of ancient Rome, prefer the concrete and look to experience and the data it provides. France in the Age of Reason aspired to clarity and exactness of thought, in contrast to the rich metaphors of Taoist China. There are linear thinkers like Aristotle, moving unswervingly from premise to conclusion; and radial thinkers like Plato, circling around the subject yet eventually bringing its various facets to a focus. Generalists and specialists, theoreticians and experimentalists, those who cultivate intuition and those who refine observations—all, in their own ways, have contributed to an understanding of the world.

The relativity of logic

The same premises can lead people to different conclusions and the same conclusions can be reached from different premises. Both Maimonides and Philo of Alexandria defended the Judaic dietary laws. Philo argued that the prohibited foods provide pleasures of the flesh unsuited to a people devoted to the spiritual life, while Maimonides supported the prohibitions on grounds of hygiene. Both defend the taboos, either because the foods are too good for the Jews or because they are unfit for human consumption.

Reaching different conclusions from the same basic premises is illustrated by the reasoning behind the Hindu and Parsi ways of disposing of the dead. Both religions regard fire and water as sacred. Hindus, 'therefore', burn corpses or throw them into the Ganges. Parsis do not allow either fire or water to be defiled and, 'therefore', expose the corpse to be devoured by vultures (burial is excluded because for Parsis earth is also sacred). One religion sees the sacred as purifying the profane and so brings them together, while the other religion sees the profane as polluting the sacred and so keeps them apart.

Illogicalities are not limited to any culture, nor is the unwillingness to give a fair hearing to what appears to be illogical. The closed mind takes its stand on a rock of certitude. Its logic is that of the incorrigible premise, a belief which it takes to be absolutely and undoubtably true. Whatever follows from the incorrigible premise is taken to be equally certain and beyond dispute. This is the logic of absolutists in all times and places. It is the logic which underlies non-negotiable positions, uncompromising 'all or nothing' demands and the conviction that to kill those who reject the premise is a moral obligation.

The importance of open-mindedness

Open-mindedness is a feature of the Jain logic of ancient India. Its teaching is called *syadvada*, the partly-so, maybe-so doctrine. Jain is the source of the story of the seven blind men and the elephant (i.e., it is a wall, a snake, a tree-trunk, a rope . . .). What we know, says *syadvada*, is at best only a partial truth, and perhaps no more than a likely story. To probabilism *syadvada* adds fallibilism, the awareness that beliefs, however plausible, may in the end prove to be wide of the mark.

Pluralism is especially evident in India with regard to religion, though in recent times encompassing absolutisms are having an effect. Religion permeates the Indian culture, but the traditional view is that there is no one true faith. Turbans are wound differently in different regions; unwound, Indians say, they are all of the same cloth. There are many paths up the mountain and all lead to the same summit. That we all live in one world has become a commonplace; not so common is the recognition that there are many ways to look at the world. No perspective is absolutely right and all others absolutely wrong. A virtue tragically lacking in modern times is humility.

The so-called cultural imperialism of our time is less an imperialist conquest than an eager borrowing by former colonials; indeed, it is by no means limited to the Third World. There are pizza parlours in Tokyo, sushi bars in Los Angeles and dispensers of fast food hamburgers in Moscow; blue jeans, amplified guitars and rock music can be seen and heard everywhere. To be sure, nourishment and growth depend on what we take in, but only if it is suited to our digestion. Perhaps the Japanese managerial style is effective only in Japanese culture; the same may be true of the American, German and any other style in its own setting—and religion, art and other dimensions of culture as well as management.

The importance of understanding

Understanding other styles does not entail abandoning our own nor is recognizing differences only a preparation for obliterating them. The encounter with another culture need not be confrontation, in which one either surrenders one's own identity or sets about destroying the other's. Nor need it be an intermingling which produces a homogenized, vapid, characterless society, achieving only the neo-nothing style so marked in modern cities worldwide.

Understanding may lead instead to appreciating better both self and other, and accepting both for what they are. Living with others in genuine coexistence, whether as members of a regional community or of the human family, means respecting their otherness, recognizing that community is not uniformity. It is in this perspective that one's identity is enriched. To understand differences is to transcend them.

Reference

Hall, E.T. (1959) *The Silent Language*, Anchor Books, Doubleday, New York.

Introduction to Chapter 4

'Bridging the language gap through international networking', by Paul Kingston, describes how a large, predominantly Anglo-French multinational company of 80 000 employees developed and implemented a strategy for improving cross-cultural, cross-functional, cross-product networking. The starting point was to recognize the potential and actual problems of communication which derived from a rich mix of languages and cultures. Many of these difficulties had the effect of reinforcing intercultural separation and stereotypes.

The company recognized the importance of language learning in the achievement of international communication. Unfortunately, they discovered that initial expectations of a 'quick fix' language injection were unrealistic. This was particularly the case for the British, whose school system gives less encouragement to language learning than that of the French.

Some simple but powerful guidelines for communication among people with differing levels of language facility are offered:

1 Slow down your communication rate and remove idiomatic expressions from the message.
2 Verify understanding through questions and reformulations of key points.
3 Have patience and remember that the best ideas may come from people whose language skills are poor.

Two key elements of the strategy for building a truly international company ethos were participation in a cross-cultural senior management training programme and establishment by senior directors of criteria for promotion to senior positions which emphasized cross-cultural experience.

The Senior Executive Programme was composed of managers drawn from the top 250 senior managers in the company and from different countries. A key objective of the programme was to develop international communication skills. This goal was tackled directly by establishing cross-cultural project teams which had to work together in tackling real business problems. To carry out their project they needed to find communication channels among themselves without relying on professional interpreters. During Part One of the programme the teams were formed, projects were allocated and implementation plans developed. After Part One, they returned to their work units and were given 3 months to carry out the projects. The projects were completed and presented during Part Two of the programme. Through this enforced team situation they learned how to communicate across language barriers and developed a strong international business network. At the beginning of the programme, people talked about a company 'management style' and by the final session they had changed the emphasis towards 'exploiting diversity'.

The second aspect of the strategy was to introduce criteria for promotion to senior posts which emphasized cross-cultural experience. These included the necessity of speaking more than one language, working in more than one country, and having responsibility for managing people of nationalities different from their own in more than one assignment.

This case study is particularly illustrative of an approach that can be introduced at director level and which can drive the achievement of cross-cultural team work. The case also provides an example of breaking down the negative intergroup stereotypes by creating mixed membership task forces with win–win goals and by rewarding people for successful international assignments.

4 Bridging the language gap through international networking

Paul Kingston

Introduction Successful business depends on effective communication. To be successful in international business demands even greater recognition of the central role of communication with others, whose cultural and, therefore, behavioural framework/points of reference are essentially different from one's own. This chapter will not seek to emphasize differences. It will, however, demonstrate that recognizing differences leads one to discovering what is common between different parties and, much more importantly in the business context, how one can exploit diversity to improve bottom line performance.

We shall look at issues commonly identified as relating to 'language and international business'. Next, we shall move quickly from abstract discussions to concrete examples derived from the fascinating, but not well-known, case of GEC ALSTHOM. This Anglo-French company was formed by merger in 1989 and is a world leader in power generation, power distribution and rail transport. With 80 000 people worldwide, GEC ALSTHOM offers an excellent example of the simple truth, known by those involved in international joint ventures/mergers, that you need to communicate to consolidate and then communicate more to accumulate.

We shall explore the evolution of this company from the point of view of communication issues and management, as well as organizational development, which were consciously interwoven to achieve corporate objectives. At the end of this analysis, we shall draw together the main lessons that can be derived from the GEC ALSTHOM case and see in what way aspects of this specific example can be identified as being of more general relevance to the whole debate on effective communication in international business.

Language and meaning in international business

We have all suffered, even in our own native language, from the gap which sometimes exists between the message we intend to deliver and the message which is received by the person to whom we are speaking. We sometimes believe that this failure to understand correctly is due to the lack of willingness on the part of the other to listen carefully or that he or she is wilfully misinterpreting a message which is crystal clear as far as we are concerned. On other occasions, we recognize that our choice of words may not have been as helpful as it could have been, with ambiguity and confusion creeping in where none was intended. Keeping this distinction between intended and received message in mind, let us think back to when we first started to learn a foreign language and the frustration we experienced in not having what the experts call 'an appropriate lexical range' (sufficient vocabulary in the foreign language) to enable us to encapsulate the idea we wanted to convey. Not merely did we have insufficient knowledge of nouns in the target language, but we also faced the difficulty of navigating successfully through the 'rapids' of grammar and syntax. No further excuse was needed for us to revert, exhausted, to our own language which, in the case of English, is supposed to be the international business language. We then spend many hours/months/years musing on the apparent canniness, duplicity, perversity and obstructionist behaviour of other nationalities whose professional conduct seems, in our eyes, to be not measuring up to our own.

In face-to-face exchanges with English-speaking colleagues from other countries we believe that we are communicating effectively. We have certain doubts when speaking over the telephone to the same colleagues that they have 'quite' understood what we wanted to say. And when it comes to written communication, what a surprise! The minutes of the meeting we attended do not coincide with what we had perceived to have been the discussions held and conclusions drawn. The tone and register of documents sent to us by foreign colleagues, sometimes in incomprehensible English, make us despair of 'international/offshore' English. What of the circus which we engage in, quite expertly we believe, at meetings with other nationalities when we wish to hold the floor or, indeed, claim our turn to speak. What patience we need to demonstrate with others in this international business arena in order to build professional relationships! Will 'understanding come to the one who waits'? And just how long does one have to wait when one is used to proceeding at 'awesome velocity' in wrapping up business deals?

Those readers currently involved in international business will recognize among the litany of issues cited above some which are of greater relevance to them than others. Those entering into international business for the first time will need to suspend disbelief until such time as they can live these realities themselves! The purpose of this chapter, and of the GEC ALSTHOM example, is to identify actions which may assist those currently working internationally and those about to engage in this adventure.

Company background

GEC ALSTHOM was the product of a decision by a UK shareholder, GEC, and a French shareholder, ALCATEL ALSTHOM. For market and technology reasons the 'marriage' between the power generation, power transmission distribution and transport businesses belonging to these two substantial companies was enacted in 1989. Neither partner held overall control with a 50/50 shareholding arrangement being agreed. Some thought had been given to the human resources issues involved in merging what was essentially a British/ex-Commonwealth company with a strongly French company. However, the urgent need to create the new company, GEC ALSTHOM, with predatory competitors hovering, meant that the niceties of human resources planning and the supposedly softer issues of international team building were placed much lower on the agenda than the establishing of a sound financial reporting system and coherent technological base. A decentralized business with, at first, nine divisions and then, later, seven divisions was formed.

The challenges of language learning

Each division focused on a product area or areas, with manufacturing locations in a number of different countries. Parallel management structures were maintained at the outset, but soon the need to integrate and, indeed, rationalize became apparent. This gave rise to situations in which the senior management in a division were either English or French and the other senior colleagues were normally of a variety of different nationalities. The knee-jerk reaction to this situation was the rush towards language learning on both sides of the Channel, with GEC ALSTHOM SA devoting 20 per cent of its training budget to English language learning and GEC ALSTHOM Ltd also spending substantial sums in an attempt to bring its management and other relevant staff up to reasonable levels of proficiency in the French language.

Attempts were made to learn the foreign language in all four skill areas: listening, speaking, writing and reading. The needs analysis undertaken by external providers of language training did not prioritize sufficiently, at first, the importance of listening skills in the business context. To understand what your counterpart is saying is the pivotal requirement for eventual effective communicaiton. Competence in listening skills, therefore, needed to prefigure, but be closely aligned to, the ability to express albeit in simpler (sometimes simplistic) form one's own ideas in the foreign language. Aural competence contrasts with the fact that one can read a document slowly, with the assistance of other linguists and with prompts from dictionaries, effectively 'off-line' from direct interaction with another person. Reading skills are very important in a foreign language. The primacy of the spoken word in business interaction, however, requires that reading underpins aural and oral competence rather than allowing it to be considered to be on the same level.

Substantial debate exists in the language learning community about the relative importance of written skills in a foreign language. To gauge just how important the ability to write in a foreign language is, one needs first to question why thoughts should be committed to paper in the business context. Written business communications can take the form of a record of agreements and meetings, a contract, a specification, and so on. In all instances cited, clarity and accuracy are of the utmost importance. Normally, there is a need to be precise. Approximation or conveying the gist is much less likely in written form than in the spoken exchange of messages or information. Accordingly, and significantly, many international businesses have elected to place minimal emphasis on written skills in foreign language learning. The debate on this issue (both in spoken and written form!) will no doubt continue.

As already noted, hundreds of managers in GEC ALSTHOM Ltd attempted to remedy the substantial deficiencies in the UK school system's method of helping pupils to learn a foreign language. In France, much faster progress was made by French engineers whose English language studies had continued into higher education rather than being abandoned, as in the majority of cases with British colleagues, during their secondary school careers. After a brief honeymoon period lasting approximately six months, UK colleagues discovered that language learning is not a 'quick fix', and that operational performance was not going to be improved dramatically over a short period. This disillusionment translated itself into a fall-off in attendance at language learning courses and an abdication of responsibility for effective communication to French colleagues, who were increasingly asked to communicate in English. Having shown their willingness to attempt to learn French, many British colleagues were disappointed when some of their French counterparts continued to speak among themselves in French at meetings, with the 'clear intention' (as some maintained) of putting non-French-speaking colleagues at a disadvantage. Even more frustrating for the reluctant British linguists was the fact that they now had to listen not to what was being said or written but to what was 'meant' or 'intended' by their French counterparts expressing themselves in English. An extreme example—but *not* a parody—of this gap between message sent and message received could be the following:

One of the problems to which we are facing actually and since the fusion of our societies, is the important differences in delays between productions in France and the UK. We can hardly make an interesting performance for this exercise.

Such a 'message sent' causes, at best, confusion and, at worst, bewilderment. A possible translation of the two sentences above could read:

One of the issues we are now tackling and have had to tackle since the merger of our companies is that there are significant differences in production run-times between France and the UK. We shall have difficulty in recording a profit at the end of this financial year.

The critical words in the original statement were: 'actually', 'fusion', 'societies', 'delays', 'hardly', 'interesting' and 'exercise'. Francophones will recognize that 'actually' means 'currently'; 'fusion' means 'merger'; 'societies' means 'companies'; 'delays' means 'lead time'; 'hardly' is confused here, and by many French people, with the adjective 'hard/difficult'; 'interesting' in a financial sense relates to 'profitability'; and 'exercise' is a direct translation from the French *exercice* meaning 'financial year/period'. If we believe that people convey a message as to who they really are through what they communicate, ambivalent communication can easily lead to distrust. Both sets of colleagues discovered that language and identity are intrinsically linked. They found out that a shift in behaviour is possible, but not always perceived as essential by those who feel threatened in a merger situation— particularly one in which a 50/50 shareholder interest gave no clear answer as to who had taken over whom.

Training in cross-cultural business skills

The Paris head office of GEC ALSTHOM was sensitive to those attitudes and designed, along with the GEC Management College in Dunchurch, an international management development programme to seek to understand better the differences in perception and approach which foreign language competency demanded in the area of presentation and negotiation skills. With many nationalities being present in such a seminar it was possible to note the substantial variance in what different colleagues felt to be the purpose of business processes as well as their views on 'appropriate' behaviour associated with such actions as presentation and negotiation.

This seminar engendered a number of ideas on how to break through the apparently opaque glass wall between French and British colleagues in GEC ALSTHOM. The first was that, in the negotiation process, language was clearly seen as a vehicle for carrying values, beliefs in the purpose of the business process, a tool for discovering the intentions of the other party and as a means of gaining competitive advantage. Language was also seen as part of the need to develop a lasting relationship with the other party, which meant that an understanding— *common to both parties*— of the constraints and environment in which both had to work was an essential prerequisite for doing business together.

The seminar also demonstrated the need for facilitation to be used to bring out attitudes/prejudices which were based on perceptions rather than on reality. In addition, the individuals attending the seminar needed to confront the image others had of *them*, before being able to understand why others behaved in the way they did. Slowly but surely language issues were being placed in a cultural and behavioural context through the interaction of participants in this seminar, which purported solely to improve presentation and negotiation skills. The focus on business skills was an excellent reason for bringing people of different national and corporate cultures together:

1 To take a look in the mirror at themselves.
2 To ask others how they saw them.
3 To question others on the reasons for a specific behaviour/ procedure.
4 To seek to find common ground in improving their own performance by aligning their performance with that of their foreign colleagues.

Although originally intended for colleagues working in commercial functions, this seminar soon became the most popular management development event in GEC ALSTHOM, and its benefit was seen to be of direct relevance to effective interaction throughout all functions and parts of the Group.

Building a corporate identity: The Senior Executive Programme

At the time of the merger, GEC ALSTHOM's most senior managers felt very strongly attached to their 'base' companies and national cultures. Their loyalty lay with their business unit and, to a lesser degree, with their division. To exploit the huge potential benefits which could be gained from an interchange of expertise, experience and market intelligence, the chief executive officer (CEO), Pierre Bilger, together with the corporate human resources department and divisional directors, defined an event which would eventually be labelled the 'Senior Executive Programme' to create a new corporate identity among the top 250 senior executives in the Group. At the same time, a corporate language policy was established, which, in general terms, noted that English would be the 'corporate language', i.e. in exchanges between the divisions and the corporate head office. Additionally, divisions would be asked to communicate between themselves in English as well. This 'ideal' was not achieved, but the statement in itself was of substantial importance and appeared to deal a mortal blow to the idea that GEC ALSTHOM wanted to be a French company active on the world scene. By now the CEO had underlined the fact that he wanted the Group to aspire to being 'a European company in international markets'. Ironically, the language policy also had a negative effect on British colleagues, the majority of whom felt substantially relieved at the thought that they would no longer have to learn French and could spend their time addressing 'more important issues' than that of communications. French colleagues, on the other hand, noted the opportunities that English language proficiency would give them in terms of career advancement, and were further motivated by the language policy statement to maintain and develop their expertise in English.

The Senior Executive Programme was timed to coincide with an appreciation of the commercial damage caused by intercultural difficulties and linguistic confusions, as well as an appreciation of the need for synergy across the organization if the Group were not merely to survive, but to make use of its rich diversity of national and corporate cultures. Any earlier and the programme would have been perceived as unnecessary or contrary to its objectives. In fact, the first Senior Executive Programme seminar was launched in December 1991, over two years after the pre-merger discussions had begun. It was also considered essential that the Senior Executive Programme should avoid the 'hothouse' effect of a number of senior management programes held in international companies. (In other words, creating an artificial environment for the growth of unrealistic ideas and aspirations which 'wilt' rapidly when transposed to the harsher climate and exigencies of the workplace.) It should be strongly anchored in business realities and with tangible outcomes, which could be measured by the Group and owned and implemented by the participants.

Programme objectives   The objectives of the Senior Executive Programmes were stated as follows:

- To encourage managers to work effectively in a multicultural, international business environment, developing useful GEC ALSTHOM networks and enhancing the identity, strength and performance of GEC ALSTHOM and their sense of belonging.
- To explore the rapidly changing global business environment and to enable the participants to consider the implications for themselves and their businesses, and to make plans to exploit opportunities and potential.
- To encourage managers to look upwards and outwards, to be receptive to new ideas and to take initiatives.
- To strengthen managers' determination to communicate with, to develop and make the most effective use of their people.

The opening of minds, therefore, was considered an essential first step to improving corporate communication and the development of networks which would focus on concrete actions to drive GEC ALSTHOM forward. These objectives could have turned out to be nothing more than words—shells without substance. In fact, they created a new identity for GEC ALSTHOM, a new business reality and, indeed, a new language. To understand how this came about, we need to look closely at the structure and operation of the Senior Executive Programme, not as a management development action, but as a lever for creating effective communication in this international group.

Structure of the Senior Executive Programme

Confronting language barriers

By bringing together colleagues from all around the world and from radically different business sectors, Senior Executive Programme design managers had anticipated linguistic and cultural difficulties in building group identity and understanding in the early parts of the Programme. Two working languages were identified: English and French. Simultaneous interpreting was to be available in all plenary sessions, and it was envisaged that interpreters would move between the working groups to facilitate discussion where colleagues lacked sufficient knowledge of English or French.

After running the first seminar along these lines, the programme management team decided to take a number of risks to improve/ accelerate the development of group identity and, indeed, effective communicaion. The first action was to allow participants on the first day to confront their lack of ability to communicate effectively in English or French in their working groups and to discover coping strategies. This would mean that they would have to take responsibility for their communication needs, rather than looking for an outside interpreter to assist them. In practical terms, this meant that each group identified very quickly those people who in discussion were clearly (a) not able to follow the discussion in English or in French; and (b) were not able to contribute effectively in the other language. A natural process arose through which colleagues of the same nationality, but with different linguistic levels of proficiency in the target language assisted each other through liaison interpreting. When things were still unclear, time was taken by the whole group to explain through diagrams, mime and putting the idea in written form to assist the colleagues who did not understand the meaning of what was being said. What has to be remembered in all of this is that the participants were, in the majority of instances, very senior managers (typically managing directors or functional directors) of units from throughout the world, often used to international travel, and to working at speed and under pressure, whether in their home environment or abroad. They quickly discovered a number of things through the absence of interpreters:

1 They needed to slow down and remove idiomatic expressions from their presentation/exposition of points.
2 They needed to verify understanding through a series of questions to check that their colleagues had received the intended message rather than having interpreted that message wrongly.
3 Lack of linguistic ability is not an indicator of intelligence. In addition, the simplification of language posed a real challenge to the expression of complex, finely-nuanced ideas and to ensuring that they were understood.

Circuitous or involved arguments could not be put forward quickly with any hope of the listener understanding the meaning on the first occasion. Therefore, these senior colleagues had to break down their ideas into constituent parts and select the simplest delivery vehicle for the ideas, using as much visual support as possible to reinforce their meaning.

Although the degree of effort required from all involved was substantial, above all in the first few days of the seminar, the earnestness of this communication activity was more than matched by a strong sense of humour. Peals of laughter echoed around the working rooms and 'glorious misunderstandings' occurred which were recounted at mealtimes and are still remembered to this day. Artistic skills were developed—to an extent beyond all expectations of the majority of colleagues—in order to illustrate a point. That most essential of all venues for any management development action, the bar, resembled a multi-tasking classroom in a language learning institution, with halting English or French questions being posed and simplified answers being framed by two or three colleagues, often using amateur dramatics to make the point more forcibly. For once, the adage that international understanding increases with the number of drinks one has did not hold true. After constant effort throughout the day, over dinner and at the bar, colleagues found that after two or three drinks they felt too tired to explain carefully, slowly and clearly ideas which they were trying to express. This meant that by closing time small clusters of national groups could be located in the bar, occasionally lapsing into 'expository mode for foreigners' quite unconsciously when speaking to people of their own nationality. When this was pointed out, most people recognized that it was not easy to 'turn off' the projection skills they had been developing over several days and that, in fact, these skills were of fundamental benefit in their own language as well.

Use of project teams   At the end of the first week of the Senior Executive Programme colleagues returned to their units, and through a dispersed network focused their energies once more on the priorities of their normal day-to-day environment. They had, however, also to undertake a project which, by definition, had to be international in its terms of reference and in the identity of members of the project set. The project was 'sponsored' by a divisional director or, in a number of instances, by the CEO or one of his two group managing directors. There was, therefore, a need to deliver a product as well as to demonstrate the ability to work across national frontiers and, indeed, business sectors. The project was to analyse a specific issue of corporate interest, explore the scope and dimensions of the issue and put forward recommendations on its implementation where appropriate. Of the 40 or so project sets, only five or six failed to produce the work they had committed to do. In a number of instances this was due to one or more key members of the project set leaving the company, changing business unit or division or, quite simply, failing to prioritize sufficiently well among the day-to-day operational priorities and the requirements of the Senior Executive Programme project.

Building colleague networks

Project sets based in Europe sought out opportunities to meet in colleagues' units to promote a better understanding of how differently processes were managed between countries in addition to working on the project itself. Colleagues from the Indian sub-continent found it difficult to justify to subordinates, as well as to their own board, the investment of any significant amount of time in a corporately-focused project rather than on something of direct relevance to their own unit's performance. Colleagues from South America and South Africa complained of a Eurocentric quality to the seminar, and yet still were proactive in the project area 'in order not to let our colleagues down'. The corporate ideal was not, therefore, what motivated all colleagues. What grew out of the linguistic and cultural differences between colleagues was a sense of team identity, strengthened by their common efforts to overcome 'linguistically adverse situations'. Linguistically adverse situations was an expression used by an American colleague during the programme; it took him 25 minutes to explain what he intended by this to a group of French/South American/Italian colleagues!

After a period of three months undertaking networking and working on projects in a 'dispersed' fashion, the same group of 25–30 colleagues came together again for a second residential phase to the Senior Executive Programme. Two layers of identity were visible: the first that of the wider group, with a strong degree of highly sociable 'friendliness'. At the second level, there was an easy relationship between project set members, whose experience of working with a limited number of other colleagues within both a physical and a conceptual framework which related to their home business units had brought them together. In several instances, we discovered that colleagues who had previously been hostile towards the idea of language learning had, over the three-month period, been sufficiently motivated to return to language learning and were anxious to demonstrate their new-found competence to their foreign counterparts. The rather self-congratulatory atmosphere of the first day of the second residential phase soon changed, however, once participants were back in their working groups (alternating membership from day to day), discussing highly complex issues and recognizing that, although they had made progress in the foreign language, they had still a long way to go.

Developing cultural awareness

In reviewing issues arising from the seminar process itself, participants often made the point that the foreign language was the 'window' that offered a 'view/understanding' of another culture. However, they felt that the Senior Executive Programme had demonstrated to them that variation in business processes and, indeed, varying definitions of the purpose of business itself, were fundamental keys to understanding other nationalities. This assertion has translated itself after the Senior Executive Programme into a spate of cultural awareness events, particularly in the UK and in France. At these events, colleagues at middle and junior management level are given the opportunity to explore the way others do business and what those differences in process and approach are, as well as why these differences exist. A number of units, who have sister units in another country, are now seeking to use the cultural awareness seminars as a first step in international team building—work that has already started to show promising results.

Outcomes of the Senior Executive Programme

The Senior Executive Programme in GEC ALSTHOM was intended to be finite in duration and scope. It lasted some 18 months, from December 1991 to June 1993, and has had a fundamental impact on the organization. Strategically, it has given a sense of ownership and involvement to senior managers in assisting the CEO in defining 'the way forward', demanding of each manager individual actions as well as proposals for corporate-wide actions.

At the outset of the programme participants were talking about a 'GEC ALSTHOM management style'. By the final seminar participants were talking of 'exploiting diversity'. This shift in objective was the consequence of confronting cultural and linguistic diversity as part of a focused effort to achieve corporate synergies and identity among senior managers. GEC ALSTHOM has created for itself a networked organization, still imperfect, but capable of stimulating continuous improvement actions extremely effectively across functional and business divides. One of the major challenges the company now faces is how to integrate an effective mobility policy to strengthen further interchange and understanding between the separate divisions and countries. Mobility is always a substantial issue, with line managers not always willing to release the best performers in their team to enable them to develop for the greater good of the Group. In certain companies, these difficulties have been overcome by starting with a recruitment policy which focuses on international placement as an integral and necessary part of career development in that company, and encourages applicants to believe in and demand international opportunities to prove themselves.

Defining criteria for promotion to senior posts

Changing recruitment policy does not, however, have an impact on the organization until several years later. GEC ALSTHOM recognized this and has adopted a top-down approach by changing the value set and horizons of senior managers through the Senior Executive Programme and by a series of actions relating to promotion. The Chief Executive Officer published criteria for promotion to senior posts within the company. This document noted that no one would be eligible for the most senior posts in GEC ALSTHOM unless they met the following criteria:

- Had worked in more than one function
- Had worked in more than one country
- Had had management responsibility for people of other nationalities
- Were proficient in more than one language

These and other criteria are, of course, presented as being subject to the individual performing satisfactorily in his or her current and future posts.

What this means, however, is that unless British colleagues in GEC ALSTHOM decide to take language learning seriously, offer themselves for international placement and actively seek out opportunities to supervise the work of colleagues from other countries, they will have little hope of securing the most senior posts in the Group. It counterbalances the potentially negative impact of the corporate language policy.

Conclusions

Internationalism has, therefore, been redefined by GEC ALSTHOM along lines similar to that of many other multinationals. To communicate effectively in international business one has to 'look through the language'. Language must be transparent to enable one to understand cultural difference which is both value-based and behavioural. No longer is it merely a question of avoiding phrasal verbs such as: turn in, turn back, turn out, turn up, turn around, turn into, etc., with their numerous literal and figurative meanings. It is much more a matter of first understanding the social, economic and ethical framework within which others work in business and encouraging them to understand the same factors in relation to oneself. Once this platform has been established, the way is open for focusing on specific operational or strategic issues. What occurs most often in both newly-formed and well-established international companies is that priority is accorded to resolving operational issues before a common framework for understanding has been recognized.

We have seen, through the case of GEC ALSTHOM, how fluency is less to do with words and more to do with understanding. Few would argue that putting people and, therefore, communication first, does not make evident sense in international business. Team-building actions are essential, but not sufficient in multinational organizations, where speed of response to meet rapidly evolving customer needs demands the immediate creation of 'virtual' teams drawn from a variety of functions, product/service backgrounds and cultures. Competitive advantage for companies operating currently on a transnational basis, and for those who aspire to be global in their markets and impact, will increasingly depend on the extent of effective internal and external networking. Networking systems do not simply appear, they have to be understood, established, maintained and continually developed. Linguistic and cultural diversity influence, but do not determine the effectiveness of networking; in fact, they can act as catalysts in identifying areas for process change, which can best be addressed through 'virtual team' networking.

Structured international networking, therefore, offers both tools to achieve improved business performance and motivation to improve personal performance through greater foreign language proficiency and cultural awareness.

Further reading

Flynn, P. (1988) *Facilitating Technological Change*, Ballinger, Cambridge (Ma).

Mulholland, J. (1991) *The Language of Negotiation*, Routledge, London.

Walton, R. (1987) *Innovating to Compete*, Jossey-Bass, San Francisco.

Yates, J. (1989) *Control through Communication*, John Hopkins University Press, Baltimore.

Zuboff, S. (1988) *In the Age of the Smart Machine: The Future of Work and Power*, Basic Books, New York.

Introduction to Chapter 5

'Culture change and team building in Hungary' by Imre Lövey begins with a fascinating description of the changing culture of Hungary. Over the past 50 years organizations were operated according to central planning, in a relatively non-competitive environment and under autocratic circumstances. Now the Hungarians are open to change, in varying degrees, towards a more Western style. The differences are most clearly experienced where Hungarian organizations are in joint ventures with, or are owned by, Western companies.

An initial problem of team work between the Hungarians and Western business people is the raised expectations of Hungarians who hoped that the Western standard of living would be instantly available. However, generally the reality is that slightly higher wages are countered with greater work demands. These unmet expectations can quickly turn to frustration and apathy. The two cases presented describe how specific team-building events resulted in greater cross-cultural empathy and collaboration.

In the first case study, a large American multinational set up a subsidiary in Hungary. In order to improve efficiency they introduced currently popular Western methods of developing organizations. The changes included flattening the structure and establishing self-directed teams, approaches which run counter to Hungarian tradition.

The team-building workshop looked at cross-cultural perceptions of different business methods with the aim of reducing stereotypes, examining specific work problems and considering how to improve team work.

The second case involved a French-Hungarian joint venture. In this team-building workshop the focus was on strategic issues, such as developing a company vision, and on improved interpersonal communication.

In both cases, the keys to success were the facilitation of multicultural teams to work together on real business problems, the sharing of perceptions and understanding of one another's culture, and the opening up of communication on both social and work levels.

5 Culture change and team building in Hungary

Imre Lövey

Introduction

Since the fundamental socio-economical changes in Central and Eastern Europe, Hungary has attracted more than half of the Western capital invested in the region. Several multinational companies bought out Hungarian state-owned enterprises or erected their own plants on greenfield sites. Most of these Western companies assigned their own managers to fill the top executive positions, expecting them to turn a traditionally rigid and overstaffed configuration into a high-performing and profitable organization or to create one from scratch. Either way, the Western management had to face at least three basic cross-cultural problems:

1 **General differences in organizational culture.** In Western countries, organizations are designed to operate within a competitive, market-driven economy within a democratic environment. In Central and Eastern Europe, enterprises are used to operating according to central planning, typically within a shortage economy and under autocratic circumstances.
2 **Specific differences in organizational culture.** There are differences based on the unique business culture, policies and practices of the parent company as opposed to the traditions of the local companies.
3 **Cultural differences.** The differences beween the culture of the Western managers and that of the Hungarian employees relative to lifestyles, backgrounds, mentalities, traditions, cultural heritage, etc.

I am a Hungarian management consultant and I have worked and taught in this field for the past 15 years. Having made extensive visits to the West on various professional assignments, I have had the privilege to be actively involved, along with my colleagues, in the organizational transformation and development process with several joint ventures and wholly-owned subsidiaries of multinational companies in Hungary. In addition to the standard organization and management development consultancy, we also provide assistance to our clients in managing cross-cultural issues. We regard our role as a kind of bridge between the West and the East—trying to help create a win–win situation for both sides. In this chapter I would like to share some of our experiences which are part of our ongoing learning process.

Of the three cultural differences listed above, this chapter will primarily focus on the first area: general differences in organizational culture. This topic allows us to take a more general approach to the cross-cultural issues, typical not only of Hungary but also of other former eastern bloc countries.

Local cultural context after the political changes of 1990

In March of 1990, following a 40-year-long period of political and economical oppression, Hungarians for the first time had the chance to freely elect the leaders of their country. As a result of this election the communist regime was overthrown and replaced by a democratic parliament destined to lead Hungary back to the Western world, where it had always wished to belong.

When great expectations meet reality

During these first few euphoric months of political transition, expectations were running high, focused on the impact these changes would have on the quality of life in Hungary. Since Hungary had been a comparatively open country even during the communist era, Hungarians had had the opportunity to travel to the West during the 1980s, where they had seen the bright side of the consumer society: shining shop windows, well-dressed people, nice houses and good cars. They had also learned about the salaries and wages of their Western counterparts. This idealized picture of the West was to become a vision that suddenly seemed to have come within their reach.

Large multinational companies were a manifestation of their dreams come true. People thought that, if they were to work for one of these companies, their lives would almost immediately take a turn for the better. This somewhat naïve approach obviously shows a lack of understanding of the capitalist labour market as opposed to the socialist system, where wages were centrally regulated and unemployment was practically unheard of. They also failed to realize one of the major motivating factors for Western investment in Eastern Europe, namely a well-educated workforce used to low wages.

Inevitably, Hungarians employed by Western companies soon had to face reality and accept the situation. Their newly-found dreams having been shattered, their feelings of disappointment and frustration were quite understandable. Let me illustrate this by a few quotations from Hungarian employees working with state-of-the-art technology at a brand new plant erected by a huge US concern:

- 'We are expected to be the best in the world, beating even the Japanese, but we only get 10–15 per cent higher wages than those Hungarians who are not required to work so hard for the old, ineffective state-owned companies.'

- 'The company's expectations that we should be the best in the world and the compensation system should be linked together. Our wages should be determined by our performance and not by the compensation survey.'

The compensation survey that the company carried out in order to ensure competitive wages for its employees may have backfired, bringing to light an already existing mistrust. Some Hungarians thought that the company had created a cartel with the other enterprises participating in the survey in order to keep the Hungarians' wages low.

- 'The company does not take care of us the same way it takes care of its employees in Western Europe with respect to insurance, social security, vehicle programmes, etc.'
- 'They want us to say *'we'* instead of 'you Americans' and 'us Hungarians', but they have divided us with the compensation system'
- 'If we tell them what we think of the compensation system, their reaction is either: "You don't have to work at this company" or "We pay competitive wages".'

At the same plant, at the same time, the Western managers' perception of the compensation issue is demonstrated by the following comments:

- 'They are basically happy. They have received a very nice increase in salary.'
- I have seen no reactions. I think they were afraid to ask questions about compensation.'
- 'Hungarians want Western wages. They do not understand the labor market.'
- 'Hungarians are overpaid here in comparison with other local companies.'

It is interesting to note that the hourly wages at the plant in Hungary were about 10 per cent of the wages of their counterparts in the USA!

Both these viewpoints represent quite typical perspectives, but I have to emphasize that other opinions, although in a minority, were also voiced. However, these quotations have been reported here to highlight one of the most common sources of cross-cultural conflicts in multinational companies.

The local people need to develop an understanding of the very nature of the capitalist system—with its great emphasis on the market economy—and business principles and practices. This can only be achieved through extensive training and communication, which might prove to be a painful process at first. However, it will eventually help them to adopt a more realistic perspective on the Western world, without which their frustrations would only escalate. This psychological phenomenon of unrealistic expectations followed by frustration and disappointment, even apathy, provides an explanation for the increasing popularity of the social-democratic type of political parties in Central and Eastern Europe.

Double messages transmitted by the Hungarians

This same idealized image of the West was projected into the business world by the Hungarians. They believed that everything was flawless in these companies: the technology, the organization, the management and the work ethic. They were also convinced that all these companies had deep pockets. Based on these false beliefs, they expected the Westerners to tell them exactly what to do and how to do it, so that everything would proceed fast and without any problems. Obviously, no company in the world can live up to these expectations. Here came the second disappointment the Hungarians had to face: doing business Western-style is not as ideal as it was hoped. This is when many Hungarians started to idealize their former workplace and began sending double messages that were very confusing for the foreign service management.

The contradictory signals transmitted by the Hungarians were, understandably, both confused and confusing. On the one hand they demanded absolute leadership from the management, wanting to be told exactly how to do things. At the same time their attitude suggested that they thought they knew better how to do business in Hungary, because they were the ones at home after all. This part of their message came through loud and clear: 'Hey, we know how to make things happen in this country; and if you don't listen to us, you'll never make it'. Indeed, some procedures required by the company made hardly any sense in Hungary. For example, it is a common practice in the West to obtain at least three quotations for material purchase and choose the one that best suits your purposes. However, in Hungary you are often lucky to find one supplier that has something close to what you originally wanted. These double messages are quite a challenge for the management to tackle and come to terms with.

Authoritarianism and rebellion

Another aspect of the Hungarians' cultural heritage was the typically authoritarian style of organizational management under the socialist system. Though not without exception, authoritarian attitudes characterized the most common form of leadership, which very much suited the nature of the political and economical situation at the time. In everyday interaction with their colleagues, the bosses allowed themselves certain ways of communication which in a democratic society would be absolutely unacceptable. The communication channels were typically one-way rather than two-way, so those in top positions were the holders of all the information and behaved accordingly. Of course this situation was frustrating for most of the employees, but they accepted it as an inherent part of the system that could not be changed. At least they did not have to carry responsibility for the boss's questionable decisions. It was also generally understood that many of these top executives were in the position they were, not because of their management skills but because of their connection with the Communist Party. Consequently, they were not always capable of functioning efficiently as directors. In this organizational situation people eventually distanced themselves from what was going on around them. Although it was frustrating for them to see so many unresolved problems due to the incompetent management, they did not feel responsible. This lack of responsibility and empowerment led to a feeling of general apathy and a notoriously complaining attitude of employees in subordinate positions. Blaming the situation without taking any action on their own initiative was a typical reaction of Hungarian employees, simply because they did not think it was their job to resolve the problems—and the management would not listen to them anyway.

It is not hard to imagine why people working in such an organizational climate did not have a sense of ownership or involvement in the company's goals and interests; they simply could not identify with their company. They felt cheated by the system that declared its equality while clearly this was not the case: those who made their way up the Party's ladder got light-years ahead in their careers and living standards. It was a natural reaction to take revenge by exploiting the system. There was a propaganda slogan at that time: 'This is your country; you are building it for yourselves'. Taking this slogan literally, saying, 'Hey, this is mine anyway', people took the liberty of walking off with bits and pieces of property from their workplaces and used company resources for their own private purposes. This was absolutely acceptable and was not regarded as immoral at all, but rather as a silent resistance against the disapproved of regime.

This mentality was imprinted in the employees' minds and would not change overnight just because the company had been privatized. It was a real challenge for the Western managers to deal with this situation, which some of them described as exploitation of the company. At the same time, the Hungarians too felt they were being exploited; they thought the Westerners were trying to take advantage of them, demanding much harder work than they were used to and providing less social benefits than they had enjoyed under the socialist system, such as free or cheap nursery provision, lunch, holidays in the company's cottage or hotel and housing assistance for buying apartments or building houses.

Rebellion is never far distant in the Hungarian nature; their experiences throughout history have taught them well. Until quite recently, the Hungarian nation has been under constant foreign domination for the past 500 years: starting with the Turks, followed by the Habsburgs, the Germans and, most recently, the Soviets. Hungarians have learned how to survive under oppression by pretending to collaborate with the oppressors while, deep down, preserving their national pride.

The lesson from this for us is to realize that Hungarians have double feelings about foreigners in power in their country: on the one hand they look up to them (probably even overly subordinate themselves), but on the other hand they maintain a certain degree of suspicion. This relationship could be characterized from the Hungarians' perspective more like a child–parent relationship, where both the subordinating and the rebelling attitude of a child is apparent.

Expectations of the Westerners

Hungarians may be regarded as being complicated and confusing by some of the foreign service managers. Therefore, it would be important for them to understand the underlying intrapersonal dynamics of a typical Hungarian. Far too often foreigners arrive with no or very little knowledge of the region, its people and its culture. Some of them arrive with a feeling of superiority—although they would not admit it even to themselves. This type of colonial attitude immediately raises a red flag in the minds of local people, putting a major obstacle in the way of open communication, which is always the first step towards a good relationship. One of the main difficulties in handling this conflict is that the managers are unaware of their attitude and its behavioural manifestation. It is so much against their own declared values that it is almost impossible to make them admit their feeling of superiority. By the same token, this lack of awareness is also true for the intrapersonal dynamics of the Hungarians that we have already discussed. Quite a challenging situation for a consultant whose assignment it is to help establish an open, honest and friendly cross-cultural environment!

Double messages sent by the foreign service employees (FSEs)

We earlier touched on the issue of the Hungarians' confusing attitude towards the FSEs. Well, the FSEs transmit their own double messages as well. They invite the employees to come up with creative ideas in order to improve procedures but, when it comes to actually accepting suggestions, all sorts of obstacles arise—most notably from internal company policies. Enthusiastic people will make a couple of attempts and then lose heart and give up, saying: 'Why don't you just tell us what to do and how to do it, and stop fooling around asking for ideas if you aren't going to accept them anyway'.

Power distance

In an organization based on the team concept the issue of power distance is of fundamental significance. From the perspective of the Hungarian employees, almost all the factors appear to strengthen the FSEs' position:

1 They clearly have professional advantage: they are familiar with the technology, the product, and they understand the rules, policies and procedures of the parent company. In contrast, all this information is new to the Hungarians.
2 They know and understand the workings of the market economy, as they were raised and educated in the kind of social-economical environment the Hungarians are just now heading towards.

3 They fill all or most of the key managerial positions, while the local employees are almost without exception subordinates to them.
4 Whenever FSEs are present at a meeting, the language of the parent organization—English is used. This is either the mother tongue of the FSEs or a second language that they speak very well. This clearly provides a communication advantage to the FSEs over the nationals, who may find it harder to express themselves. They sometimes even need interpreters.
5 The FSEs possess most of the status symbols the Hungarians are just dreaming of: nice homes, big cars, good salaries, etc. These all show how much better off they are than their Hungarian colleagues, suggesting a certain superiority.

All these factors are in sharp contrast with the value statements of several companies, which say, in various forms, 'We are all equally important to the company'. In the eyes of the Hungarians it is obvious that they are far from being equal to the FSEs. Research clearly shows that power distance is generally perceived to be smaller from top to bottom than the other way around. This is why this issue is rarely brought up for open discussion: the management, who are supposed to address the problem, does not even identify it as being an issue worthy of discussion.

The language barrier

The language barrier ranks among the top concerns foreign investors have to face in Central and Eastern Europe. During the 40 years of the Soviet regime, Russian was the obligatory language both in elementary and high schools; English, German and French could be studied only as third languages. Although in Hungary the situation is changing rapidly now, generations grew up—among them the now active workforce—who could not speak any Western languages. For the FSEs there is very little motivation to learn this complicated language for those few years they will spend in Hungary, although some of them at least try. Apart from the practical advantages of being able to communicate with the locals, learning their language would also have an important symbolic impact: it would convey a message of appreciation for the people and their culture as well as indicating a long-term commitment.

For the majority of the FSEs the language barrier remains a major source of frustration. One managing director said: 'I would recommend that anyone doing business in a foreign country should learn the language. It is very frustrating for me not to be able to go on the floor or walk around the offices and talk to the Hungarians in their native language. You lose a lot in translation. The Hungarians who have not learnt or are just now learning English have the same difficulties trying to communicate with us.'

The language barrier is a major issue in the hiring process as well. As the interviews are conducted in the language of the foreign company, those people who speak the language well present themselves better, while those with a poor knowledge of the language may appear simple-minded, when in reality they just cannot express themselves properly. Thus, applicants with better language skills are often overvalued.

The language barrier is also responsible for misunderstandings and misinterpretations of certain words and concepts. Some concepts used in the business world, such as 'just-in-time', 'cash-flow', 'empowerment', just do not exist in Hungarian. A simple word-for-word translation will not convey the underlying meaning of the words; the concepts need to be understood first.

Loyalty of the FSEs

During their assignment the FSEs are supposed to represent and serve the interests of the parent company. Their future career depends on how well they do their job. Whenever a conflict of interest occurs between the locals and the foreigners it is obvious which side the FSEs will take, at least at the beginning. However, over time, several of them developed a better understanding of the local situation, which in turn allowed a wider perspective to view the problems. The issue of compensation is almost always the biggest conflict of interest. It is only when FSEs finally realize that a two-salary income of husband and wife working hard on the shopfloor of their company is hardly enough to support a family of four surviving just above poverty level, that they start thinking about what could be done in the interest of a long-term win–win situation.

Working hours

The FSEs are used to working harder, more efficiently and definitely longer hours than an average Hungarian. They did not like to see the Hungarian employees leaving the office promptly at the end of the 8-hour working day. They could not believe how people would dare to leave at 2 p.m. on a Friday afternoon just when the company was planning to lay off some of its employees. But from the Hungarians' point of view, based on their experiences under the old system, personnel-related decisions had little to do with the actual achievement of the individual. Of course, we should not fall into the trap of overgeneralization, since the situation is changing rapidly. Many Hungarians work just as hard as the FSEs, although it must be mentioned that some of them stay longer in the office, unnecessarily, simply to impress the management.

So far we have discussed a few issues, problems and conflicts that may be regarded as typical of a cross-cultural organization in the setting of a former socialist country. Some differences of mentality have been noted in the light of two different backgrounds:

(a) an authoritarian, monolithic society dominated by the communist ideology; and

(b) a democratic, individualistic society in a market-driven, competitive economy.

Next, we are going to introduce some exercises for organization and management development, exercises our clients found most useful in tackling some of the problems in order to build strong and effective cross-cultural teams.

Interventions and exercises for building effective cross-cultural teams

In this section two cases will be cited as examples of the cross-cultural team-building process. Both cases have their own unique characteristics, in spite of the fact that the basic conditions of cultural setting we have been reviewing apply equally.

Case study 1

The first company we will look at is one of the world's largest multinational corporations which established a wholly-owned subsidiary on a greenfield site in Hungary. A US corporation, its practice was to appoint, almost exclusively, North Americans to fill the managerial positions in the new organization. It was not until 4 or 5 years later that they started to promote Hungarians to these posts.

The management of this plant was determined to create a very flat, team-orientated organization. They quite radically put a lot of emphasis on self-directed work teams, employee involvement and empowerment. The cultural setting to support this sort of organizational philosophy was far from being ideal in Hungary, as described above. I had been asked as a consultant to help the process along, right from the beginning, and I would like to share some of the procedures and exercises we used that were instrumental in bringing the two cultures closer together.

Hiring procedure

The management devoted substantial time and energy to developing selection criteria for the people they wished to employ. The criterion of being a team player came before anything, even technical skills and experience. As soon as the first key positions were filled, the new employees were trained and trusted to conduct interviews themselves to select their own would-be colleagues.

Camp meetings

The term 'camp meeting' refers to a special workshop that all the employees in the organization attend. (The name itself originates from the native Americans, who from time to time got together around the camp fire to address major issues, make important decisions and celebrate their accomplishments.) Camp meetings are designed actively to involve everyone as much as possible. They usually last 2–3 days and are held 2–3 times a year. Before each camp meeting an organizational diagnosis is carried out to help identify the burning issues and concerns. The topics and exercises are selected and designed respectively in the light of this diagnosis by a team consisting of the representatives of the organization and the external consultants. Open and honest communication is absolutely essential for the success of the camp meetings. Following are a few exercises that proved to be useful in solving or at least raising awareness about cross-cultural problems.

Coat of arms

This is an ice-breaker exercise—a way of introduction—where the task is to draw, on a large sheet of paper, a coat of arms that characterizes the individual. Then everyone gets a chance verbally to explain their drawing. An interesting result of this exercise was that the Hungarians seemed to be using symbols and abstractions suggesting a world of ideals, while the Americans drew concrete objects referring more to the materialistic aspects of life. We used this exercise as a framework to discuss similarities and differences between the two cultures, as well as to get to know each other.

What is it like to live in Hungary?

Four groups were formed for this exercise: Americans on a short visit to Hungary, Americans on a long-term stay in Hungary, and male and female Hungarian employees. Two lists were to be prepared by each group in answer to the following statements:

- 'Things I like in Hungary' (*Likes*)
- 'Things I don't like in Hungary' (*Frustrations*)

The objectives of the exercise were:

(a) to provide an opportunity for the venting of frustrations;
(b) to remove the taboo of criticizing the other face-to-face and, therefore, to promote open communication;
(c) to learn about the others' values, perceptions and sensitivities;
(d) to learn something implicitly about the others' living standard and lifestyle.

The results of this exercise are given in Table 5.1.

Self-perception and perception of the other

A second task looked more directly at personal characteristics. The task was for both nationalities to prepare four lists according to:

- Situational strengths of the Hungarians
- Situational weaknesses of the Hungarians
- Situational strengths of the FSEs
- Situational weaknesses of the FSEs

The objectives of the exercise were:

Table 5.1 *Results of the 'What is it like to live in Hungary?' exercise*

Group	Likes	Frustrations
1 *Americans on a short visit*	• countryside • cultural heritage • Budapest (without the smog) • business opportunities • food • prices • friendly people • quality of new employees	• bathroom design • wholegrain toilet paper • air pollution in Budapest • language barriers • opportunistic view of Americans • lack of infrastructure (especially telephones) • lack of business ethics • lack of availability of consumer goods
2 *Americans (FSEs) on a long-term stay*	• cultural activities • architectural beauty of Budapest • simpler, less hectic lifestyle • travel opportunities to other European countries • Hungarian cuisine • challenge of the assignment • well-educated, friendly people • good weather • doctors make house calls	• pessimism of Hungarians • language barrier • naïvety of government officials • following a Trabant (pollution) • shopping inconvenience • underdeveloped service industry • traffic/parking • lack of sense of urgency • banking services
3 *Hungarian female employees*	• slow but at least initial changes • national integrity • villages/cities preserving history • friendly, helpful, hospitable people • intelligence of Hungarians	• low living standards • growing unemployment • unstable economic situation • confusing political situation • remains of old bureaucratic system • lack of educational opportunities • lack of self-esteem, confidence • limited travel opportunities • pessimism • unhealthy lifestyles
4 *Hungarian male employees*	• Hungary in progress • Hungary is freer than ever • freedom of speech	• disorganization • simple minded approach • stupid political discussions • low living standard

- sophisticated sense of humour
- ability to survive
- Hungarians' talents
- creativity

- too much work for low wages
- economic crisis
- people are nervous
- relationships with bordering countries
- extremes and extremists
- pessimism

(a) to develop a better understanding of how each culture perceives themselves as well as the others;

(b) to develop empathy towards the others' difficulties.

It is very interesting to notice that both groups perceived a few more weaknesses than strengths in themselves, but that the emphasis was reversed when characterizing the other culture. Compare the lists given in Table 5.2 (the results of this exercise).

Panel discussion on compensation issues   Some members of the US management and a few selected Hungarians representing typical opinions discussed the issue of compensation in front of the entire camp meeting. The rest of the employees were present as passive listeners, but they could later add comments and ask questions. This exercise requires a great deal of courage and openness on both sides, due to the delicate nature of the issue. It takes some self-discipline on the management's part not to get carried away and let the discussion turn into a confrontation. Simply talking about the issue will not solve anything; but it is only the first step towards the solution. The very fact that the issue is being openly addressed is an achievement in itself.

Communication   All sorts of communicational barriers exist in a standard organization, but in a cross-cultural environment the situation is even more complex. This is why one of the camp meetings was dedicated to the issue of communication. In order to facilitate the information flow all across the organization in general, and between the Hungarians and the FSEs in particular, several concepts were introduced and discussed, including:

- The influence of our different socio-economic backgrounds on our communication, and its distorting effects
- The power distance and its negative impact on our communication

Role reversals— developing better mutual understanding   This exercise was intended to respond to the growing concern on both sides that issues had been raised without being listened to. The point of this role play, in which members of the two cultures role played the other culture, was to enable the parties to perceive things from the other's perspective and to think how the other would react to certain issues. The results were enlightening: both sides appeared to be surprisingly aware of the other's concerns but were simply not in the

Table 5.2   *Results of the self-perception and perception of the other exercise*

Group	Strengths	Weaknesses
1 *Americans seen by the Hungarians*	• computer technology • organizational skills • positive attitude • financial background • political background • world market experience • patience • professional skills • optimism • self confidence • business strategies • sense of humour • discussion skills • flexibility • greater responsibility • people oriented • wider horizon	• unfamiliar with local situation/business practices • unable to understand our financial concerns • they are from another planet • looking for America in Hungary • expect American standard of work for Hungarian wages • they are noisy • can't play soccer
2 *Americans seen by themselves*	• experience • resources • enthusiasm • dedication • competitive spirit • teamwork • imagination • optimism • openness	• impatience • Hungarian language • adapting to culture • biases • over-commitment • revert to old practices • impatience • false assumptions • paranoia about past • talk too much • set in our ways
3 *Hungarians seen by the Americans*	• intelligence • willingness to learn • operating within Hungary • strong social ties • resourceful • education • willingness to change • national pride • quick to learn • friendly • genuine	• inexperience • no sense of urgency • unwilling to make decisions • reluctant to lead • pessimism • limited perspective • easily discouraged
4 *Hungarians seen by themselves*	• creative • resourceful • eager to learn • at home in Hungary • skilled • able to work with Americans	• clinging to old practices • pessimistic • not tolerant enough • talkative • cannot listen • constant complaining • lack of self-confidence

- worth ethics
- hard workers

- rigid
- hot tempered
- low living standards
- cannot play American football (but would like to learn!)

position to react to them. The exercise also helped clear some misunderstandings and misinterpretations of the other's standpoints. The exercise had the following objectives:

- To develop a better understanding of one another
- To enhance trust and empathy
- To learn more about one another
- To create better conditions for effective communication
- To develop listening skills

The process consisted of six stages:

1 A Hungarian and an FSE explain why this exercise is important.
2 Short presentation on the importance of listening and how we can improve our listening skills.
3 Preparation for the exercise, Hungarians and FSE briefed separately. The question to the Hungarians was: 'What issues do you think the FSEs are concerned with and what is their attitude towards those issues?' The question was the other way around for the FSEs.
4 Both parties share their opinion in mixed groups, trying to clarify and understand issues.
5 Small groups discuss what they have learned from the exercise.
6 Small groups report out back to the entire group.

Social activities Personal interaction and relations play an important role in the Hungarian culture. Social events and informal gatherings with colleagues are probably more common in Hungary than in the USA. It soon became a tradition to organize a big party after each camp meeting, where the foreign managers danced rock'n'roll with people from the shop floor. Apart from having a good time, this social activity also had a team-building effect, just as important as the formal exercises.

Another example of a social activity was when the Americans taught the Hungarians how to play American football, who in return taught them how to play soccer. Then, matches were played in mixed teams. These memories are an integral part of the company's organizational history and a valuable addition to the team-building process.

Benefits of team building: case study 1 This company put tremendous effort into creating and developing a synergetic cross-cultural organization, and their results clearly prove that it was well worth the time, money and attention they devoted to the human resource side of their organization. Their manufacturing plant was launched ahead of schedule and under-budget and production is now in full swing. According to figures, their plant in Hungary produces less scrap and is more productive than its counterpart in the USA.

Case study 2

The second company I would like to examine is quite different in many respects from the first one. It is a joint venture where a large French multinational firm bought the majority of the shares in a traditional state-owned Hungarian company. There was an equal balance of French and Hungarian representation in the top management team, which consisted of the original Hungarian managers complemented by some French foreign service people, including the managing director. The situation was very complex, more so because there was not one common language that everyone could understand, not even within the management team. Interpreters were used at the meetings, which slowed the process down, not to mention the misunderstandings it generated.

The French managers found their Hungarian colleagues intelligent and technically well-trained but lacking experience in marketing, controlling and team work. They also felt they were expected to perform miracles turning the company into a profitable business overnight, which they attributed to the Hungarians being impatient with a typically short-term attitude to problem solving. The Hungarians thought that the French were democratic and ready to listen to what they had to say; but they also perceived them as being slow decision makers, requiring lots of unnecessary paperwork.

The cross-cultural team building process started with a 3-day off-site programme for the 12-strong management team. This was followed by a large group workshop with the additional participation of the next two layers of the organization—involving about 60 employees altogether. Some of the exercises used at the management off-site meeting, entitled 'Strategic Planning and Team-Building Workshop', are described below.

Self-diagnosis of the team

The team produced a list of characteristics typical of successful and unsuccessful teams, based on their previous experience. These criteria were then used to evaluate their own team, identifying their strengths and weaknesses and where they were on the road to improvement.

Self-caricature of one's culture

The French and the Hungarians were divided into two groups to prepare for a short role play characterizing their own culture in a funny way, e.g. showing a typical communication pattern in a management meeting. It is always easier to make fun of one's own culture than to see others do it! The following two questions were then to be considered:

- What have we observed about the other culture based on our personal experiences?
- How do you think the other culture perceives your culture?

These questions were the prompts for a discussion of cross-cultural issues that had never been brought up before outside their own national groups.

Personal messages to one another

Each person prepared a message to all the other members of the team relative to the following aspects:

(a) Things you do that I personally find very helpful for myself or for our team
(b) Things you do that could be changed/improved so that they would be more helpful for me and for our team

These messages were conveyed personally on a one-to-one basis, providing opportunity to ask for clarification if necessary. This was the last exercise of the workshop and, although the programme had been on schedule up to this point, it took 2 hours for the group to reach an agreement that they were willing to do this exercise. This might be an indication of the amount of anxiety one faces with a cross-cultural situation. However, when they finally decided to do the exercise, they spent three times as much on the one-on-one discussions than originally planned. They evaluated the exercise as being the most useful one of the whole programme in terms of pulling down the walls between them and clarifying issues among themselves.

Strategic planning modules

Although not directly addressing cross-cultural issues, additional modules implicitly contributed to the team-building process by raising business awareness. They also provided an opportunity to clarify strategic issues. These modules were:

- **Environmental overview** (examination of political factors)
- **Stakeholder analyses** (identifying expectations of headquarters, shareholders, customers, suppliers, employees, community, government)
- **Vision statement** (including the desired organizational culture for the company)

Benefits of team building: case study 2

Some of the main benefits of the Strategic Planning and Team-Building Workshop were:

- Brought the French and Hungarian sub-teams closer to each other much faster than would have happened without this programme
- Clarified mutual expectations, helped to get beyond misunderstandings
- Built personal and professional trust among members

- Openly addressed cross-cultural issues, built better understanding of each others' cultural background and increased tolerance and adaptability
- Built trust in the team
- Developed a common understanding of major strategic issues and business terminology.

The role of the consultant in the cross-cultural team-building process

The global aims of all of the exercises described were to help increase awareness of cultural differences, provide a framework for open discussions, and develop a mutual understanding of cultural similarities and differences. Achieving this mutual understanding is crucial in terms of overcoming cultural biases and prejudices. This in turn enables the two cultures to develop empathy with each other, which then motivates them to try to find mutually acceptable solutions to problems. I am not saying that these exercises alone will solve all the problems, but they do provide a solid ground to start dealing with the issues.

We find it extremely useful, whenever possible, to use two consultants in a cross-cultural environment, each representing one of the cultures involved. The main reason for this is the issue of credibility. Here are a few arguments for this point.

1 People from both cultures feel that their uniqueness is represented in the consultant team, which gives them a sense of safety.
2 The consultants' own background provides specific first-hand information and experience about their culture, which is instrumental in planning and facilitating the training programmes.
3 Part of the consultant's job is to survey the organizational climate through a series of interviews with the employees. The employees will be more willing to raise issues and concerns when talking to someone of their own culture and in their first language.
4 A cross-cultural consultancy team will demonstrate a positive pattern for an effective co-operation between people with different cultural heritages.

Whenever a Western management brings in its own Western consultants, they are regarded by the locals as mere tools in the hands of the management, serving only their purposes. On the other hand, if only local consultants are hired, they may find it hard to win acceptance from the Western management. This is due to the widespread belief that people from former communist bloc countries are just not competent enough in the business world by Western standards. As a compromise, if it is not possible to hire consultants from both cultures, a person with cross-cultural experience demonstrating ample knowledge and understanding of both cultures could be considered.

Anyone involved in a corporate cross-cultural environment—employees, managers and consultants alike—carries a certain degree of responsibility to represent their culture in a way that reflects understanding as well as acceptance and appreciation of the other nationalities. Modelling a positive pattern of a synergetic multinational corporation is an important mission for everyone involved in a cross-cultural environment in this part of the world, where the increasing trend of nationalism and chauvinism is one of the biggest threats to all of us.

Note

1   Power distance refers to the degree of closeness and openness between a boss and his or her subordinates. High power distance implies an authoritarian style while low power implies a consultative style. This concept was based on the work of Hofstede (1980).

Further reading

Branyiczkiy, I. and J. Peace (1993) 'Revolutionizing Bureaucracies: Managing Change in Hungarian State-owned Enterprises', *Journal of Organizational Change Management*, 6(2).

Dannemiller Tyson Associates, Inc. (1990) *Interactive Strategic Planning, A Consultant's Guide.* Dannemiller Tyson Associates.

Goffman, E. (1961) *Encounters*, Bobbs-Merrill, New York, pp. 74–134.

Jacobs, W.R. (1993) 'Real Time Strategic Change, A Technology for Unleashing Your Collective Organisation's Knowledge, Skills and Creativity' (working title), Copyright Dannemiller Tyson Associates, Inc.

Lövey, I. (1993) 'Some Issues in the Adaptation of Organization and Management Methods to Contrasting Countries, Cultures and Societies: Reflections from Hungary', in *Advances in Organizational Development*, Vol. 2, Fred Massarik (ed.), Alex Publishing Corporation, Norwood, NJ.

Lövey, I. (1993) 'Measurement of Authoritarian Thinking of Managers and Some Outcomes, A Research Survey', *Journal of Academy of Sciences.*

Pauchant, T. (1993) *In Search of Existence: On the Use of the Existential Tradition in Management and Organization Development*, Vol. 2, Fred Massarik (ed.), Alex Publishing Corporation, Norwood, NJ.

Pearce, J.L. (1991) 'State Directed Profit Motive and Resource Dependence', Working paper, Department of Business Economics, Budapest University of Economic Sciences.

Pearce, J.L., I. Branyicki and G. Biglem (1994) 'The Costs of Organizational Distrust', Western Academy of Management International Meeting, Brisbane, Australia.

Introduction to Chapter 6

'Training Germans and Americans in conflict management' by Dennis Clackworthy, describes how a large German multinational company prepares its managers to work in multicultural teams. The company's overall strategy includes language training, cultural awareness courses, country-specific cross-cultural interaction training and the use of consultants. Using these elements, individuals can be prepared, in a planned way, to adapt quickly to a new culture.

The second half of the chapter describes a specific example in which team-building skills were imparted to key staff involved in joint German–American projects. A basic level course aimed to give knowledge about the cultural differences, hence building understanding. This was followed by an advanced course, described in this chapter, which aimed to help delegates to convert the knowledge into skills. The learning method consisted primarily of involvement in simulated meetings between German and American managers. These meetings were video-taped and rigorously reviewed to draw out key differences in behaviour and underlying assumptions between the two cultures. Delegates soon learned that Germans focus on the facts, that is, the current situation. In contrast, Americans focus on action and vision, that is, the future. Without recognizing the cultural basis of the differences, Germans may perceive Americans as superficial and Americans may see Germans as obsessively bogged down in detail. The end result of the training was that people saw value in both the German and American approaches, and that it is often advantageous to explore issues and problems from both perspectives.

6 Training Germans and Americans in conflict management

Dennis Clackworthy

Overview This chapter will focus on that part of team building dedicated to skill training in cross-cultural conflict resolution, that is, highly important competences needed by cross-cultural team members to cope with tensions and frictions in the team. It adopts a 'culture specific' approach as distinct from a 'culture general' one. This is based on the assumption that conflict resolution skills must be understood and learned in the *context of the specific cultures* represented in the teams to be trained.

It will describe a competency training programme developed by a large multinational concern aimed at pivotal people in German–American project teams. It will focus especially on German–American conflict resolution patterns, by describing a workshop designed to train to achieve the relevant competences.

Central theses The central theses of the programme are:

- We can only manage our conflicts with people from another culture if we know how they manage their conflicts between themselves.
- We need operational insights into the way we handle conflict in our own culture.
- We need to work out together ways and means of meshing the two approaches.
- We need to develop the on-site competency of actually resolving a mixed team's internal tensions and frictions.
- By mapping out this road to constructive conflict resolution we can mould a corporate culture that counteracts destructive outcomes to conflicts.

Company background

The company is a major electronic and electrical engineering concern based in Germany. The main target group are leaders and key staff involved in joint German–US projects. The Americans work from over 70 operating companies in the USA, some of which had been autonomous and mature American entities before being acquired by the new German parent, others having started life as greenfield projects without a previous identity. The majority of the Germans work from one of the 20 business or corporate divisions in Germany.

Trainers

The trainers work either full time or freelance from the corporate office in Germany or from the human resource divisions of the US affiliates. The training architect, and author of this chapter, works from a corporate HRD office in Germany. Due to the size of the concern, the trainers are not close to the everyday life of a project team. They interface with managers and leaders enrolled on central courses or carry out workshops for a business division and its counterpart operating company in the USA. Hence, the full gamut of classical team-building methods is not available to these trainers and has not become part of this competency training package.

History

Ten years ago the corporate executive board decided to introduce cross-cultural training into the company. The main thrust was to be culture specific as distinct from culture general. The first key area was to be the German–American interface, as the company was investing heavily in acquisitions and growth in the USA. Since then employee strength in the USA has grown from 15 000 to over 40 000.

Initially, training was developed for Germans destined for transfer to US assignments, then courses were introduced for Americans going on assignment to Germany. Subsequently the emphasis shifted further, to members of project teams operating from their offices in each country—the 'transatlantic commuters'.

As we gained experience in designing training situations for this widening target group, a five-tier course structure evolved.

Cross-cultural training structure

Language courses

Level 1: Language training provides people who are becoming involved in international activities with an opportunity to improve their language skills. Depending on their level of fluency, they can choose from courses ranging from basic survival language for beginners to specialized classes in such technical subjects as negotiating. As the courses become more advanced, so the proportion of cultural learning is increased: occasional discourses are given on non-verbal patterns, video training is used to improve style and appropriateness of behaviour, role-play situations introduce a greater relevance to the workplace. The trainer's role is, however, basically that of a teacher.

Cultural awareness courses

Level 2: Cultural awareness   courses concentrate on, for instance, a two-day briefing on the USA, which is run for newcomers to the German–US interface. Here the focus is on American values and their related behavioural patterns, with a view to awakening an acceptance of why some things are done differently in the USA. An example is the value pattern labelled 'informality', and the associated practice of greeting in a friendly way, which is demonstrated and explained. It helps for trainers to be American, but it is also important that they have had at least some experience of teaching in Germany, so that they can discuss things with the learners. Their role is that of a country expert.

Intercultural communication courses

Level 3: Intercultural communication   courses give learners the opportunity to practise new skills and receive individual feedback. US trainers demonstrate American behaviour patterns and explain the underlying values, as in the cultural awareness briefings, but in addition, the learning is largely experiential. Films and songs are used to breathe life into the value patterns described. Visiting American 'guests' join in some of the training exercises and role plays. Trainers use video feedback to polish the acquisition of some basic new behaviours, and interact with a clear US profile to give the learners practice in handling US reactions. The trainer's role is to be a coach, and to a certain extent a sparring partner.

Interaction training workshops

Level 4: Interaction training   in workshops with equal numbers of participants from each culture gives people the chance to learn from and with each other, and to learn how to learn together. It is aimed at people with some experience in mixed project teams. The learning material is generated by the learners themselves, during the performance of simulated business tasks, which makes the learning even more relevant to the workplace. Video analysis is used by trainers to sharpen skills in discovering, understanding and describing cultural patterns and cultural differences. By analysing video recordings and carefully selected scenes showing contrasts in behaviour patterns, trainers can elicit very fruitful discussions and develop constructs which can be used as models back at the workplace. By carefully facilitating these discussions, trainers can catalyse learning on how to be open about culture without giving or taking offence.

A German team got into a spirited discussion of a complex issue and, as is their wont, voices were unconsciously raised a little. An American asked the trainer to freeze the video scene and whether he could ask the Germans in the picture (who were sitting next to him in the workshop) a question. 'Go ahead', said the trainer. 'Would you drink a beer with Wilhelm after that discussion,

Heinrich?' asked the American. 'Sure', said Heinrich, 'why not?' And you, Wilhelm, could you go on working with Heinrich after that meeting?' 'Definitely', said Wilhelm, 'he's got good ideas and knows that he's talking about'. The American paused, then turned to the trainer: 'Thank you for this lesson, I've been in Germany for six months now and until today I always thought a strongly worded argument was personal criticism'. The subsequent discussion in the workshop shed a lot of light on a very important difference between German and American meeting behaviour. Germans will 'discuss' objective issues emphatically without including personal characteristics in their argument. In contrast, Americans feel their person to be included if people become emphatic, so they keep the tone 'laid back'. The construct developed was given the title 'hammering out the truth/keeping up the interaction'.

The role of the trainers, who incidentally should be able to understand what participants are thinking and feeling at any point in the workshop, is that of a facilitator and construct author.

On-site consulting

Level 5: Consulting   at the workplace itself constitutes the top tier in cross-cultural training. Trainers meet with key project leaders and/or visit working project teams, observe cultural patterns relevant to the functioning of the teams, and give feedback and make suggestions as to how these patterns can be meshed. Trainers should command consulting skills as well as those needed at the other four levels.

The intercultural learning curve

One of the purposes of this progressive learning module structure is for learners and their managers to be able to choose the training appropriate to their level of knowledge, experience and skill. Another is to take into account the progression of the typical project team member up the 'cultural learning curve' (see Fig. 6.1).

Learners come into the programme bringing different levels of experience, education and personal aptitude with them. One of the more subtle workshop design issues is to build in enough variety and open space for people at different learning stages to glean what is meaningful to them.

Interaction training

In the remainder of this chapter we will look in detail at some content and design issues for level 4 training measures (interaction training) which are well-suited to a fairly heterogeneous group of learners in terms of the cultural learning curve. However, participants in these interaction training workshops should have had at least 6 months' prior experience of living and working in the 'foreign' culture. This ensures that patterns highlighted in the workshop may be compared with and validated against on-site experiences and also that useful learning material from daily life is brought into the workshop by the participants.

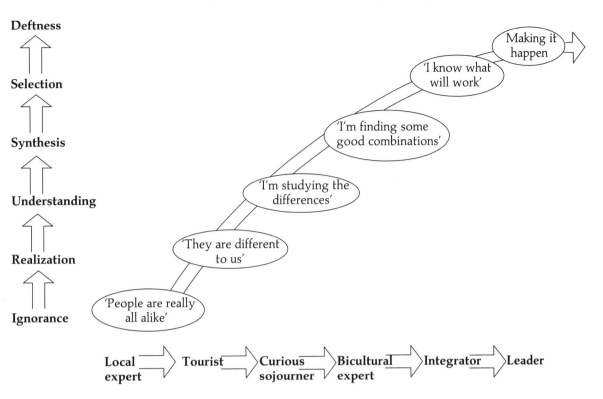

Figure 6.1 *The cultural learning curve*

Interaction training architecture

As a rule, six Americans and six Germans learn together in a 3-day workshop. On the first day they observe how people from the other culture interact with each other. On the second day they observe, and analyse what happens when the two different ways of interaction meet and mesh or fail to mesh. On the third day they seek solutions to recurrent misunderstandings and interaction breakdowns.

Ideally, three interactive workshops should be run at intervals of 6 to 12 months, dealing with progressively more challenging situations. In the first, the focus is on learning to understand each other, to understand that there are culturally determined differences in perceiving and handling tasks, problems and team processes, and how to handle these differences. In the second, the focus is on conflict resolution processes. In a third workshop, which will not be described here, participants learn about innovation and creative team processes.

Methods

The main methods used are:

- Simulated business meetings (e.g. planning a presentation)
- Analysis of video recordings made of the work done in monocultural and bicultural groups

- Development of constructs (i.e. attitudes, behaviours and assumptions) which differentiate cultural difference
- Open discussion of assumptions, expectations, behaviour and reaction patterns and of the underlying value systems

Training in understanding

In the first workshop, entitled 'Effective Interaction at the German–American Interface', people learn that cultural differences exist and learn how to learn about them. Care is taken to keep these discussions on the level of objective description, of trying to understand why people from another culture do things the way they do and make the assumptions that they do. Learners are encouraged to suspend all judgements, evaluations and moral or other verdicts during this phase. Learners go back to their workplaces knowing that differences can and must be accepted, lived with, described and understood before they are weighed up or labelled as good or bad. Learners then appreciate that only after understanding the differences in depth can the next challenge be tackled: to find effective combinations of the strengths of each culture.

Conflict resolution training

The second workshop, entitled 'Effective Interaction in Difficult Situations at the German–American Interface', deals with conflict resolution patterns in each culture, and the particular chemistry taking place when they collide. The same basic methods are used as in the first workshop. However, it presents several additional *methodological* as well as *content* challenges.

Approach to conflict

We found that Americans, for instance, handle the subject of conflict much less directly than Germans. This was a methodological challenge that became evident when we advertised early pilot workshops under the title 'Effective Conflict Resolution at the German–American Interface'. Experienced US trainers recommended that the title be changed, as it sounded 'too confrontative'. We hypothesize that Germans think much more comfortably in terms of problems and conflict resolution than Americans, and are much more inclined to work explicitly with them. So we decided to talk initially about 'difficult situations', and only gradually increase the level of explicitness during the course of the workshop.

The second methodological problem was that of generating emotional conflict in a workshop in which the learners had had no previous opportunities to get to know each other at work and develop normal levels of interpersonal tension and friction. These had to be contrived in an accelerated fashion during the workshop in order to generate learning material that approximated real-life situations.

A third problem was how to handle destructive conflict resolution or 'win–lose' strategies. This was met by stating quite clearly from the outset that we would be studying constructive conflict resolution patterns and concentrating on how people in each culture go about handling tension creatively. One exception was made to this general rule: a section in the workshop makes use of a variation of the 'prisoner's dilemma' game, in order to experience and reflect on the effects of using skulduggery in a conflict situation. This section also generates the highest level of emotional energy, and for this reason the game is played late on the second last day, with ample time informally to work through any animosities arising during the last evening, which had to be designed accordingly.

German– American patterns

On the content side, pre-workshop research showed up several major differences in the way Germans and American manage conflict. Two of them—conflict cycles and 'crossed purposes' must suffice as examples with which to trace the learning track for getting important insights across and transferring them to the workplace.

The conflict cycle

Conflict resolution can be represented as a cycle (see Fig. 6.2). This cycle is probably a universal pattern, with cultural variations playing a major role. It was given to participants as part of a pre-workshop reading assignment.

Time horizons

We found out that there is a great difference in the time used to 'go through' the conflict cycle. Conflicts will be recognized, addressed, dealt with and 'resolved' in a much shorter time in America than in

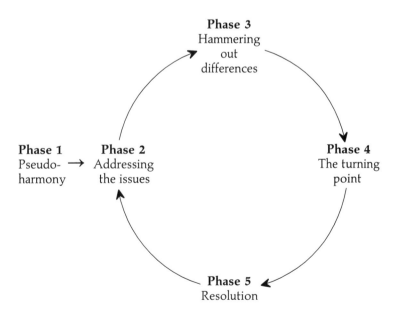

Figure 6.2 *The conflict cycle*

Germany—in fact, any cybernetic feedback loops are much shorter in the USA. Feedback is given more frequently, progress is evaluated more frequently, strategies are adapted with greater alacrity, alliances are formed and dissolved more quickly, and project goals are reviewed more often.

A German team will address issues more comprehensively and cerebrally, in comparison to the action-oriented treatment by an American team. Thus, the time taken to hammer out differences is longer. A team will discuss the inputs from more points of view, struggle to analyse the interrelationships of more elements in a system, argue more doggedly about detailed aspects of a problem and adjourn meetings more often to go over the homework again before making another attempt to find a consensus. Consequently, a German group will go into and through the 'turning point' in a conscious and concerted fashion. In contrast, the turning point for Americans is marked more by the feeling: 'let's split the difference and get on with the action'.

Transfer to working life   Once an insight like this is 'discovered', hopefully by means of participants themselves observing and naming the pattern and the facilitators limiting their inputs to pulling together and recording the observations, the group is then faced by the question: 'What do we do with these differences, now that we have recognized them?'

One American, who had been struggling against this German pattern for several years, realized in the workshop that this pattern was the real reason for what he had previously called 'heavy handedness', and assumed to be a tactic to dominate discussions. Back on the job, he was able to sit back, listen, and let a German 'unfold his concept' before interacting on single aspects.

Such gut-level learning is *serendipitous*. The learners determine when an insight lights up and translates into everyday behaviour, not the trainers.

His German colleagues were thereafter much better able to handle his American 'linear bullet-point' inputs, because he had given them the chance to 'spell things out'. The American learned when and how to interrupt a German speaker who had actually said what he had wanted to say and was hoping for someone to interrupt smoothly and fill out the picture from another point of view. The American also learned when and how to interrupt with a factual correction to an essential point in a speaker's line of argument.

He got to the point of 'making it happen' in Germany, and German colleagues came to appreciate his American 'businesslike' more.

'Crossed purposes'   This second example illustrates the value of 'construct development'. Monocultural groups prepare and then meet in a bicultural exploratory joint venture meeting. After a dozen or so workshops a pattern became clear. Germans would start by describing relevant facts and expect to get confirmation or correction from the other side. Americans would start by describing their vision for the joint venture and expect to feel a degree of commitment to this or another vision from the other side. Germans were irritated by the American 'superficiality'; Americans were irritated by the Germans 'getting stuck in details'. The construct that emerged is presented in Table 6.1.

Table 6.1

	Germans	Americans
Phase 1 of a simulated joint venture meeting	Concentrate on comparing perceptions of reality—what is	Concentrate on comparing visions of the future—what should be

This juxtaposition of expectations is usually overcome by Americans accepting the 'German toughness' and Germans accepting the 'American friendliness'. So in the second phase, the Americans, who usually get tougher as the negotiations proceed anyway, did so with even more emphasis than usual. And the Germans, who usually get more 'compromise-willing' as negotiations proceed, did so with even more emphasis. Most joint venture meetings were at breaking point after the second round. Only after viewing and discussing the video scenes did these patterns come onto the table. The construct was continued as in Table 6.2.

Table 6.2

	Germans	Americans
Phase 2 of a simulated joint venture meeting	Look for workable compromises	Go for a good deal, drive a hard bargain

In one workshop we gave the total construct, covering both phases, the title 'Crossed purposes'.

At this point, participants who had had several years of experience in German–American joint venture negotiations told stories of big projects which did not get underway due to this fundamental misunderstanding. Subsequent feedback from participants confirmed the validity of this construct, and its usefulness in keeping joint venture negotiations from becoming shipwrecked on imaginary shoals.

Style enhancement   The transfer of learning to the workplace is encouraged by inputs from the trainers on 'style enhancement'—learning to play the game according to the expectations of the negotiating partners, without relinquishing the inner strength of one's own approach. In the case above, Germans learned to think in terms of visions and goals, but based on thorough cognisance of a wide range of relevant facts. The Americans learned to work more with 'specifics', using their future orientation to work out operationally-feasible lines of action towards the goal.

Reports from past participants indicate that this type of cross-cultural conflict resolution training generates habits of perceiving, interpreting and coping with conflicts that are much more reality-based than the stereotyping approach normally used to a greater extent before coming to the workshop. One study carried out by the University of Munich showed substantial differences between competency levels of trained and untrained members of international project teams.

Eastern cultures

This method of interactive construct development has been shown to be effective with German–American teams, but now we are facing the challenge of modifying the methods for participants from Eastern cultures. It has become clear that Westerners are comfortable with words—digitalizing their learning in the form of pattern descriptions, constructs, abstract concepts and verbalized thoughts. But how should an interactive workshop be designed for Eastern participants, whose language and thinking structures do not include pattern descriptions, verbalized in these forms? How are trainers to structure the time in a workshop to enable everyone to see an event and formulate their observations in terms that make meaningful exchange possible?

As far as conflict resolution training is concerned, Westerners are emotionally comfortable with talking about conflict, with Germans (and possibly French) being much more so than Americans and Britons. But how should an interactive workshop be designed for Eastern participants, avoiding confrontative statements which cause the other side (or a senior member of one's own group) to lose face?

Need for professional exchange

Ongoing pilot projects are beginning to provide answers to such questions and should one day be the subject of further reports. Training architects should be open to opportunities for exchanging experience and know-how, in the interests of furthering the art of helping people who work at cultural interfaces to move faster and more surefootedly up the cultural learning curve.

Introduction to Chapter 7

'Team Building at the United Nations Industrial Development Organization', by Bing and Gardelliano, describes a major organizational change initiative in the extremely multicultural setting of the United Nations Industrial Development Organization (UNIDO).

The training was a key element of an overall strategy, implemented to increase participation in decision making and to improve overall efficiency. The first element of the strategy was to flatten the structure, convert it to a matrix form and enable the use of temporary project teams. It was recognized that the structural change would only work if the teams were empowered, if individuals in the team were able to work collaboratively and if senior managers were supportive of the change.

The second element of the strategy was a series of team-building workshops aimed at people learning skills of effective group work, developing cultural awareness and understanding how to accelerate group development.

The major themes of the training workshops were the key factors that influence team performance:

- Understanding individual differences, achieved to a large extent through the use of the Myers-Briggs Inventory, which can impact on their style of management.
- Recognizing cultural differences and their possible effects on team work. Culture was examined at the levels of country, ethnic group, generation (age) and profession.
- Development of key organizational skills needed for team effectiveness, including leadership, motivation, agreed purpose, and clear structure.

The training was aimed at increasing tolerance of people's behaviour and suggesting methods for constructive synergy. These themes were presented within the context of understanding the phases of team 'performance process' along with guidelines for accelerating the team's handling of the key issues of each phase. For example, early on in the group's life, purpose, trust and communication are important. If these issues are dealt with thoroughly, then they provide the foundation for such later phases as decision making and implementation planning.

The chapter describes how to build cross-cultural teamwork in a large, very diverse organization. First, it details the context of a major organization change strategy which recognized the need to change the formal structure and to give people the team-building skills needed to operate the new structure.

The second important aspect of this chapter is the way in which the training blended cross-cultural learning with organizational 'project team' skills. A third aspect involves how to address the common dilemma that people from different cultures will have different expectations about the amount of participation and consensus that is appropriate. The resolution the authors found was in the introduction of a structured approach to building openness, participation and flexibility.

7 Team building at the United Nations Industrial Development Organization

John Bing and Sergio Gardelliano

This team-building programme was presented to the managers operating within the United Nations Industrial Development Organization (UNIDO) headquarters in Vienna. The programme, therefore, has complex and many-layered levels of cultures both as the context of the programme and as representative of participants in the programme. Of the 100 national cultures represented in UNIDO, there are typically more than 10 national cultures represented in each team-building programme. This presents special challenges, especially when many of the participants—often veterans of UN and other international service—have lived and worked in many countries and thus may claim more than one culture. It is for this reason, among others, that we have chosen a cultural assessment questionnaire to provide each participant with his or her own cultural profile (as distinct from using national cultural generalizations).

The two basic reasons that UNIDO has organized these team-building programmes are to empower employees to contribute fully to the improvement of their work and thus to increase organizational productivity. These two factors go hand-in-hand; it is not a matter of 'either/or'. The main value of teams is their ability to assemble and empower employees to make better use of their talents to improve the organization.

Organizational culture

An equal force in the workings of these teams is the organizational culture. UN organizations differ significantly, by history, structure and purpose, from the private sector. There is no profit motive and consensus building on such typical business concerns as the 'market' and the 'customer' is limited. Rather there is the ethos of UN organizations as providing international service of various kinds.

Moreover, UN staff are divided into top level (politically selected), senior managers, professional levels and support staff. As in the diplomatic corps, this division affects many aspects of operations including the perception of the function and importance of teams within the organization. Therefore, there are at least three cultural levels in the UNIDO context: national cultures, organizational cultures, and professional cultures. Each of these influences the composition, purpose and efficacy of the teams within UNIDO and each individual may represent more than team interest alone.

Teams within UNIDO

The concept of teams within UNIDO is relatively new. Before a recent reorganization, there were five divisions and, although three were occasionally cross-functional teams operating within the agency, they acted less in the sense of co-ordinating teams than as collections of representatives of the division—that is, as individuals representing more their divisional interest than team interests. Hierarchical structures and centrally-controlled organizations are being replaced by a flat matrix structure with multiple information networks and more participation by the employees in decision making. Team-building integrates these concepts.

In the reorganized, flatter agency, the concept of teams has assumed greater importance because the activities of the agency must now be co-ordinated more closely across a greater number of smaller divisions as well as with respect to field projects which the agency oversees. The new UNIDO will likely be characterized by emerging 'adhocracies' in which a temporary group is involved in a function with temporary lines of authority. Today, project teams are comprised of a variety of skilled specialists from diverse fields. At the same time, functional arrangements are being established among different organizational units, hence line and staff duties are overlapping and merging.

Effective team development programmes are required within the new divisions (and branches and units within these divisions), within cross-functional groups and within project teams within and outside the agency. Given all these considerations, it was decided within the Division of Personnel that team-building courses should be instituted. A team-building process cannot be started without an adequate management development process and supportive organizational climate. This management development programme must have the full support of senior managers; without their commitment, the teambuilding process would fail.

The model we present is itself an important component of the management development strategy. It integrates many management/organizational concepts and enhances cultural synergy, which is essential for effective management practices in the kind of multicultural environment found in UN agencies.

Programme design and development

The goal of developing and implementing a team-building programme at the United Nations Industrial Development Organization is to improve overall organizational performance at a time of restructuring. The programme has been designed to help participants visualize the interrelation of the main components of a team-performance improvement process, namely *the phases of team development* and *the four factors influencing team performance*—that is, *individual differences, cultural factors, organizational context* and *environmental factors* (see Fig. 7.1).

One of the main components to consider while creating and sustaining high performance teams is the *team development process*. The six basic phases we utilize were identified by Drexler, Sibbet and Forrester (1988) and are always present in a team; however, each of them comes

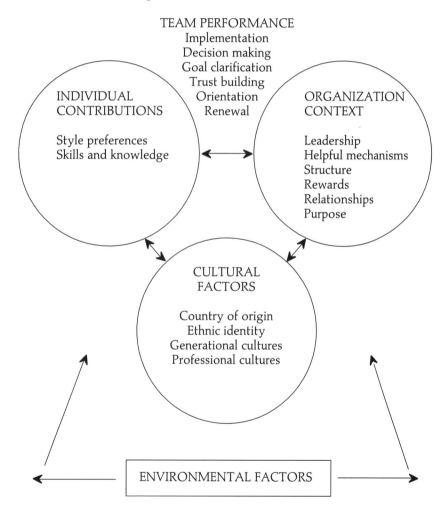

Figure 7.1 *Integrative model for cross-cultural team effectiveness* (© 1994 ITAP International)

into focus at a particular stage. A team that resolves the questions of each phase and builds the next phase over the last one is better prepared for a higher level of performance. Unresolved questions in each phase will diminish the level of team performance, making the team increasingly ineffective. A brief description of each phase follows.

- **Orientation**   In this phase a certain ambiguity exists in the minds of the team members as to the purpose of their coming together. They need a clear answer to *why* they are there. If this question is unresolved, team processes will lead to disorientation, uncertainty and fear which is not the appropriate condition from which to enter into the next phase.
- **Trust building**   During the second phase, members are engaged in sharing their expectations, competences and hopes with other participants, thus building the basic trust and rapport needed for effective communication.
- **Goal clarification**   Phase three emphasizes discussion of team and individual priorities among members. Additionally, members' roles are clarified and the task to be undertaken is identified.
- **Decision making**   At this phase decisions are taken by participants as to how the team will be managing resources, time, work processes, constraints, etc.
- **Implementation**   During phase five, the members actually begin to sequence their work according to a time schedule and a shared vision. If the team was able to resolve the key questions of the preceding stages, a higher level of performance can be expected.
- **Renewal**   This is the final stage, in which the team members look back and reflect on what they have achieved, work on their shortcomings and prepare themselves for the future.

Each of these phases of team development is an essential part of the integrative model of team performance and is influenced by the organizational context, cultural factors and individual differences. Now we will examine each of these main areas of influence separately.

Organizational context

What outside factors influence the capability of the team to achieve goals? This short question makes relevant the need to analyse how the *organizational context* affects team performance. The following factors are considered:

Leadership

The type of leadership and its effectiveness needs to be examined, which includes leadership within the team and within the organization and leadership styles which contribute to effective or ineffective management practices. Consideration was also given to situational and principle-centred leadership and its relationship with followership and strengths and weaknesses of the organization's leadership norms.

Purpose   Every team needs a clear mission. Determination of the purpose of the organization or division results from the negotiation process between 'What we want to do' and 'What we have to do'. Goals of the team and purpose of the organization or organizational units could also require some adjustment.

Structure   It is important to analyse the organizational structure and its impact on group work and team performance. Structure is supposed to solve division of labour problems, not create them. Three main ways to organize are by

- function;
- product, programme or project; or
- a mixture of both.

An assessment should be carried out to determine the fit of team members' roles within the organizational structure.

Rewards   Formal reward systems are no guarantee that staff will act in the way the system is attempting to prompt them. Formal or informal rewards should satisfy team members' needs, i.e. professional growth, esteem, acceptance, safety. Motivational or hygienic factors should also be considered, such as achievement, responsibility, team recognition and working climate. The strengths and weaknesses of the reward systems should be evaluated to determine if the system properly reinforces team goals and behaviours.

Helpful mechanisms   Mechanisms are needed to help people in working together more effectively. Mechanisms are helpful when they assist in the co-ordination or integration of work or assist people in keeping track of whether things are going well or badly. Examples include management informational systems, performance appraisals, weekly problem-solving meetings and *ad hoc* brainstorming sessions.

Relationships   This analysis is centred in the relationships:

(a) among people, peers or manager–subordinates;
(b) between organizational units and tasks performed; and
(c) between people, systems and technology.

It is important to explore how these relationships affect team performance. The quality of relationships and their interdependence are highlighted. (This area dovetails with the analysis in the section on cultural factors.) The relation with the external environment of the organization is also explored.

Cultural factors

Increased awareness about the nature and effects of cultural differences can overcome barriers to adjustment and peak performance within the team. The participants analyse their own cultural profile using the following dimensions from Fons Trompenaars's schema. This analysis focuses on cultural factors rather than professional or other issues.

- **Relationships with people**   Participants explore ways in which they relate to each other. For example, some may feel that friendship has special obligations and should come first in working relationships, while others may give more emphasis to following rules first and less importance to helping friends.
- **Attitudes towards time**   Individual team members may have differences relating to how strongly they are orientated to the influence of the past (for example, the importance of precedence and history), the present (for example, current organizational politics and concerns) and the future (for example, a vision for future development).
- **Attitudes towards nature**   Some people view the environment, fate and current circumstances as acting powerfully on individuals and will seek to live in harmony with these factors. Others may want to manipulate, control and even exploit the environment. These views may lead to very different ways of analysing the feasibility and importance of projects. These attitudes are also highly important in anticipating reactions to field projects.

The analysis of cultural differences using a cultural profile questionnaire first helps participants understand how they may be perceived by others and, second, helps them to modify and expand their understanding of the behaviours of others. Cultural differences can either inhibit or augment the effectiveness of teams, depending in part on the awareness that each member brings to the team regarding these differences. If members view such differences as annoyances or barriers, then the team's effectiveness will be inhibited. If, on the other hand, members sees these differences as representing alternative ways of both understanding and implementing the work of the team, the capacity of the team will be enhanced. Since there are within all cultures both effective and difficult (counterproductive) people, it is not the presence of individuals from multiple cultural backgrounds that causes problems but rather the presence of those who are either unwilling or unable to carry out the work of the group. This is an important distinction, since it is often assumed that the cultures themselves may inhibit the work of the team.

Recent research has suggested that although diverse teams take more time to complete tasks in the short run, in the long run they find more *creative solutions*.

Individual differences

In the analysis of individual differences, participants explore their personality type and reflect upon their working styles and management preferences. With the help of the Myers-Briggs type indicator, participants gain a perspective on how they are energized, acquire information, make decisions and relate to their fellow workers. Within the context of these four scales they are helped to understand themselves and their behaviours and appreciate others, so as to make constructive use of individual differences. By knowing their own preferences and learning about those of others, they come to know their special strengths and how people with different preferences can relate to each other and become valuable within teams.

Additionally, using the Myers-Briggs Type Indicator, the weighting of types within the team as a whole is analysed and discussed with participants, with regard to the impact on the team as a whole and on the larger organization. In the present format of this team-building workshop, the individual differences resulting from technical competences or knowledge and experience levels are not analysed. However, we believe that in the initial formation of teams, professional competences and complementary expertise should also be taken into consideration.

Prerequisites for development of the UNIDO cross-cultural team-building programme

Training in team-building is an important component of the UNIDO Management Development Programme and integrates skills developed in other management training modules, such as 'Interpersonal/Intercultural Skills Development' and 'Leadership Styles and Effective Management'.

Before team-building sessions are conducted it has been found to be advisable to create a positive atmosphere in which such sessions can be conducted effectively. The following activities can be useful in building receptiveness.

1 It is necessary for participants to have participated in a primary workshop on intercultural skills development prior to attending the team-building programme. This workshop provides participants with analytical tools to distinguish between different causes of management behaviour; assess how their own cultural management preferences may affect the workplace environment; develop skills and strategies for working effectively in a multicultural, gender neutral environment; and increase their awareness of research in the field of intercultural and gender management practices.

2 Prior to the team-building programme, team members should be selected or trained for the knowledge, information and expertise needed to help the overall group with its mission and should display competence in managing small- or large-scale projects. This involves skills in the areas of time management, negotiation, conflict management, presentation and intercultural communication.

3 Team members should attend the course: 'Leadership Styles and Effective Management', during which participants reflect on how job performance and managerial effectiveness are related to the way they think about themselves and others. This workshop provides middle-level professionals and senior managers with the opportunity to examine their working styles as leaders, as well as the processes of managerial change and self-improvement.

4 One of the facilitators may meet with a group before it begins the team-building process to do a thorough needs assessment and inform the group of the structure of the programme.

5 Team input sessions are arranged with an organizational development practitioner to provide education in group decision making, communication, problem solving and skills of interfacing with other teams.

6 Team sessions are held on forecasting, budget planning, member replacement and impact of technological or organizational changes on the team.

Ground rules during the programme

In order to create a positive attitude towards the training programme, the following guidelines are offered:

1 Group participation and consensus building should be encouraged. Group communication should have a specific content focus. Disagreements should be permitted, while effective listening should be considered a valuable asset.

2 Constructive criticism should be encouraged. The members should also be assisted in expressing their feelings, clarifying their roles, and discussing relationships, assignments and responsibilities.

3 There should be sharing of leadership functions and utilization of total member resources. From time to time there should be a re-evaluation of team progress and communication. Team members should be sensitive to the team's linking function with other work units. The whole approach of the team should be goal directed, fair in dividing the work and aimed at synchronization of efforts.

4 In order to implement the integrative model for cross-cultural effectiveness, there are short lectures, assessment tools, group discussions and group work. The target group for the cross-cultural workshops can be professional staff, general service staff (administrative support staff) or a mixture of both.

The role of the facilitator

The facilitators (also the authors of this chapter) are the chief, staff development and training section of UNIDO and the head of an outside training organization (ITAP International). The principle that has been used here is that an inside facilitator brings to programme development and implementation an understanding of the organization. An outside facilitator brings new ideas, approaches and the insight of someone freed from local politics. Of course, both of these virtues are shaded by their opposites: the inside facilitator may have his or her own limitations within the training programme itself; and the outside facilitator may not be interested in risk taking, in order to perpetuate his or her position as a consultant. These are the risks that any such 'inside–outside' endeavour brings. However, one has only to consider the limitations of two inside facilitators, or two outside ones, to understand the advantages of mixed roles.

Equally advantageous in a course on cross-cultural areas is to use facilitators with different cultural backgrounds. One of the facilitators is of Argentinean–Italian background; the other is German–American. Given this mixture, the facilitators have the opportunity, in miniature, to demonstrate an effective multicultural team. Facilitators from only one cultural background will prima facie be unable to model a multicultural team.

In these ways a sense of rapport and trust can be built with the participants. There are many other factors, of course, which contribute to rapport and trust but, in the case of cross-cultural team-building, these stand out.

Opportunities and obstacles

Courses in the UN system are generally taught in English, and this was the language of the course. Because English is native only to a minority of participants, it is necessary to rethink exercises and presentations to allow for alternative ways of presenting ideas and facilitating communications within the groups. Methods include presenting materials in written as well as in spoken form and the use of overhead projections to convey ideas more through graphics than by words. Experienced facilitators also often use alternative words and phrases to describe the same phenomenon, making use of repetition.

The problems and obstacles that have arisen in the programme are both internal and external in nature. Over the course of the development of this programme, from its pilot state to its present form, the interrelationship between internal and external problems has been complex. Early in the pilot process, one of the programmes was in the final 10 minutes when one of the participants re-entered the training room after a lengthy absence complaining that he had just heard that some staff would lose their jobs due to financial constraints. The reader can only imagine the effect of this emotional pronouncement on the rest of the group. (At that time there were three trainers, one of whom observed: 'This is a learning opportunity!')

Problems can arise because of stresses within the organization itself, which cannot be banished from the classroom. On the contrary, in later courses, the facilitators have used the issues which cause their stresses as examples and discussion points within the programme itself. Thus, the real institutional issues become the stuff of the course itself, strengthening both the course and the participants as well.

The results of the team-building courses to date indicate the programmes are exciting more interest than before as participants leave with both theoretical and practical approaches to strengthening teams of which they are a part. A recent exercise which required the participants to negotiate their team cultures, based on the Trompenaars's model, is an example. One team member noted that the teams started their negotiations from significantly different cultural positions, and they had had to learn each others' preferred style before they could go on to resolve these. What were once perceived as academic issues suddenly become real ones as the participants debated what type of decision-making style to use and what qualities were associated with successful team members. Let us take one example from a team culture questionnaire:

'Should team members

(a) Make decisions together with reference to UNIDO's processes?
(b) Leave some decisions to individuals, the rest to the team?
(c) Leave decisions to each member to decide?

This question brought individualistic team members up against group-oriented members. To develop their team culture, they had to learn both what their teammates preferred and how the context helped to define the appropriate course.

The principal challenge for the authors is to understand how team issues are embedded in a forcefield that includes organizational culture and issues, individual (as opposed to cultural) preferences and larger environmental forces, such as changes in the UN system itself. Teams are composed of individuals with different preferences, based on their different cultures, and who are also strongly influenced by current organizational and environmental characteristics. For training to be effective, analytical tools must be provided to team members to utilize in their daily work, and practice given in how to forge a team in the face of differences and difficulties.

Conclusion and general recommendations

Since effective working arrangements across departmental functional lines are difficult to introduce in multicultural and intergovernmental organizations, management and human resources development specialists have a responsibility to lay the ground work for cross-boundary collaboration.

Top management must provide the institution with an effective team model and a rationale for team work. Top-level commitment is essential. Without such commitment, teams which could be established at middle levels within the organization may fall apart because of lack of effective, supportive teamwork in other parts of the organization.

The training and development group must help to develop this model and convey its rationale to the staff of the organization by providing skill-building opportunities. Equally important, reward systems must be revised to acknowledge the contributions of individuals to overall team efforts. In order to develop specific skill sets in the organization's managers, we strongly recommend that professionals and administrative staff attend an initial workshop on 'intercultural and interpersonal skills development'.

Team-building workshops should be conducted with staff at all levels. The aim of these team-building workshops should be to help participants define their performance and effectiveness and to establish norms of team development and support within groups within the organization.

Follow-up workshops should be conducted to review what the participants have learned and how much they have incorporated their new skills into their daily working lives. It is also advisable to follow up *in situ* the performance of specific teams by analysing the change in quality and quantity of their outputs.

In a recent keynote address to the Society for International Education, Training Research, Nancy J. Adler, Professor of Management at McGill University noted that transnational organizations develop through negotiated cultures: 'The United Nations ... is definitely not transnational, but rather quintessentially a multidomestic organization'. In other words, the United Nations, and by inference its specialized agencies, has not yet developed its own culture from within, from negotiations and reconciliation of cultural values among those that work within its structures.

We realize that the UN system is in the process of creating a new organizational culture, one which reflects the enormous changes that have occurred in the recent past in relationships between states throughout the world. Therefore, we believe that programmes such as this one, which teach the skills of team development in a multicultural context, can reinforce a positive process to lead UN managers toward transnational operations in which each specialized agency can develop its own unique approach towards solutions of their related issues. We are also aware that in order to take root, such approaches must be supported by upper management and—ultimately—by the countries' representatives which comprise the boards of these organizations.

The views expressed in this chapter are those of the authors and do not necessarily reflect the views of the United Nations Industrial Development Organization.

Notes

1 Myers-Briggs, I. (1996) *Introduction to Type. A Guide to Understanding Your Results on the Myers-Briggs Type Indicator*, 5th edn, Consulting Psychologists' Press, Palo Alto, CA.
2 The authors are indebted to the pioneering work of Marvin R. Weisbord. For more information on this analysis of organizational context, see Weisbord, *Organizational Diagnosis: A Workbook of Theory and Practice*. Addison-Wesley, Reading, MA: 1978, repr. 1992.
3 Fons Trompenaars (1993). The cultural profile questionnaire utilized in this programme was developed by Trompenaars through his Centre for International Business Studies (CIBS) in Amsterdam. Chapter 2 describes Trompenaars's seven elements of culture in detail.

References and further reading

Drexler, Allan B., David Sibbet and H. Forrester (1988) *The Team Performance Model*, NTL Institute for Applied Behavioral Science.

Trompenaars, Fons (1993) *Riding the Waves of Culture: Understanding Cultural Diversity in Business*, The Economist Books, London.

Weisbord, Marvin R. (1978, repr. 1992) *Organizational Diagnosis: A Workbook of Theory and Practice*, Addison-Wesley, Reading, MA.

Introduction to Chapter 8

'Team building in Asia', by Helen Price, focuses on the uniqueness of Asia and on managing the interface between Asian and Western cultures. While recognizing that considerable differences exist between Asian countries, there are, nevertheless, some common values that will reflect most of them. The Asian cultures tend to be more collectivist than individualistic, therefore the group is of primary importance; hence team building is valued. However, the Asian emphasis is on harmony and loyalty rather than on openness and independent thought. Additionally, high status members are accorded great respect and obedience, much more so than in Western cultures where status must be 'earned'.

The chapter gives in-depth attention to how the unaccustomed Western trainer must adapt. First, greater formality of style and instruction will be expected. Second, the intensity of personal feedback will need to be moderated, particularly with regard to high status participants. Third, participation will need to be regulated to prevent 'eager' Westerners from excessive talking at the expense of the naturally polite Asians. And, of course, it is essential to remember the great importance given to 'face' by the Asians. Throughout the chapter, practical advice is offered.

The author concludes by suggesting that cross-cultural team building can often be accomplished indirectly through the course design, composition of syndicate groups and tasks, and even social events.

8 Team building in Asia

Helen Price

This chapter was conceptualized during a conversation with a colleague while we were waiting at Manila airport, in 28°C heat and 90 per cent humidity, for a bus to take us to a team-building workshop. The young lady from the local office whose job it was to organize the trip had taken half an hour to contact us—she was not allowed up into the arrivals hall and we did not know to go downstairs to meet her. The bus she had ordered did not turn up and there was no apparent explanation.

Nevertheless the group of 16 of us—British, New Zealanders, Australians, Indonesians and Chinese—were conversing merrily about the weather, the latest cricket results, the share prices in Hong Kong and constantly reassuring the young lady concerned that 'these things do happen'. All of us knew the potential loss of face, not only for her but also for the local office who were responsible for the arrangements. We were also aware of the potential difficulties which can often arise with arrangements in the Philippines.

One hour later the bus eventually arrived and, after a 6-hour journey across volcanic dust and over roads splattered with mud slides, we finally reached the hotel where the team workshop was to be held. It was a haven of tranquillity—a world away from the sultry heat of downtown Manila. I realized, once again, that Asia is not a single place but a myriad of environments.

Despite this vast diversity there are common challenges for the team builder. This chapter examines the preconditions for successfully building teams in Asia with members of different cultures. My aim is to give practical guidelines for trainers and facilitators who are new to or inexperienced in Asia.

Based on 15 years of living in Hong Kong and working in the multicultural environment of the large Asian trading companies, known in Hong Kong as the 'Hongs', I have taken a practitioner's view and describe how the insights into the broad differences between Asian and Western cultures, which we have gained from academic studies, can be used to improve the effectiveness of team-learning events. The 'hints and tips' may seen obvious to many of you, particularly to those of you who are more experienced in Asia and Asian culture, but I must confess that too many of them I learned the hard way.

Before we look at team building in Asia it is worth asking what to some may appear a fatuous question: 'Does Asia exist?' 'Of course', people say, 'look at any atlas or encyclopedia—it stretches from Turkey to Japan and covers 17 million square miles'. However, as team builders we are interested not in geography but sociology. Asia does not have a unitary culture: the largest continent embraces a multitude of different countries, races, religions, languages and peoples—each with their own very ancient histories, traditions, norms and values. Team building in the Philippines has subtle differences from team building in Thailand which will be as different again as running similar events in Japan and Korea.

I will not attempt to encapsulate all significant differences of national character which may affect Asian teams as this would require a book of encyclopedic dimensions. Rather the emphasis is on practical theories and key points from experience, focusing on the broad differences between East and West.

The trainer new to Asia has to answer four questions:

● How do Asians view teamwork?
● What is the appropriate stance for the trainer?
● What techniques of team building are likely to be effective?
● Are there any special multicultural dimensions that need to be managed?

How do Asians view teamwork?

In many Asian countries the group is seen as the primary unit—and is more important than the individual. The preoccupation that many Westerners have with autonomy is not shared by their Eastern counterparts. The success of quality circles in Japanese companies is just one example of the importance of groups in Oriental countries. The group provides identity and so Asians are disposed to see their lives in terms of membership of an interconnected network of groups.

The most important group, particularly for the Chinese, is the family which is enmeshed in a web of rights and obligations. Society is structured around the strength of the family which provides many of the functions (such as caring for the elderly) that have been taken over by the state in the West.

Collectivism versus individualism lies at the heart of many of the differences which the Westerner experiences in an Asian environment or vice versa and it is often at the heart of the differences in behaviour from Western and Asian participants on a team-building event. This is a dynamic which needs to be most carefully managed in order to maximize learning.

Although Asian people are committed to functioning in groups, many of the concepts that we take for granted in the West as being essential for effective teamwork are no longer self-evident when working in the East. There are four differences which require special explanation:

1 The value of 'openness' is accepted by behavioural-science-based trainers as generally, a 'good thing'—almost without question. Most Chinese (and there are 1.2 billion of them) place harmony far above openness. If there is a risk that saying what you really think will embarrass or offend another or cause disharmony in the group, many Asian people will choose to avoid expressing their opinion.

2 Strong external control by the leader is under threat in the West as it is increasingly seen as a relic of a class-structured society that has no place in today's world. This is not true in the East, where direction is generally expected and accepted. In the East the team manager may act paternally without a hint of criticism. Indeed some of the most successful firms are highly centralized and figures in authority are highly respected.

3 Attitudes towards authority are different in many Asian cultures (described by the academics as 'high power distance'). For those working in multicultural teams this means that within the same group you often get participants from very high and very low power distance cultures plus those in the middle. The former could be Asian born, brought up and working within an Asian culture; the latter could be Australian or American and your programme is his first time in Asia. The middle ground may be occupied by Western expatriates who have lived and worked for many years in Asia and have made the necessary adaptations or Asians who have lived and worked in Western countries or for Western companies.

4 Discipline is a virtue in the East where school children spend years memorizing such complex matters as Chinese characters. The West prizes questioning highly and praises independent thinking. Few Westerners, but many Asians, would view obedience as a great virtue.

This complexity of racial and national differences does affect the structure of thinking of the individual. However, the fundamental orientation in Asia towards supporting the group means that even multicultural teams and firms can work together with a high degree of effectiveness—if they learn to manage the diversity points outlined above.

What is the appropriate stance for the trainer?

There are three major issues which affect you as a practitioner: first, your role as the teacher or expert; second, handling mixed status within the group and, third, stimulating critique and feedback.

The role of the teacher or expert

In Asia the teacher is a respected person, regarded as a source of expertise and knowledge from which the student is expected to learn. This status will often be acknowledged by the group with courtesies, deferring to your expert status and you may receive expressions and tokens of appreciation. The expectations of your role and the type of educational experience which many Asian participants will have been subjected to may make it difficult for them to adjust to some of your methods—especially the participative approaches so beloved by Western trainers.

It is possible to adjust to such different expectations. One of our external contributors on the 'cross-cultural management' event always begins his seminar with two introductions. First the European introduction, which is to tell a joke about himself, underplaying his knowledge and importance; he will even single out a participant and start some competitive repartee. The other introduction is the Asian one where he stresses his qualifications and experience, the important people he has dealt with before and he is similarly flattering about the audience—their importance and expertise, how honoured he is to be with them and how unworthy he feels for the task.

This stereotype, which immediately brings smiles of recognition from his multicultural audience, is a caricature of an underlying truth *vis-à-vis* the tutor and the group. You will ultimately have to judge how far to adapt your usual style. However, if you move too far away from expectations that you are not an expert, then in many participants it will create confusion—a cognitive dissonance. Or in some of the more pragmatic souls which one finds, particularly in Hong Kong, they will feel they are not getting value for money—i.e. you are not sharing your knowledge so why are they there? They have come to learn from you, not fellow participants with whom they can interact at any time!

How do we accommodate this? First the trainer needs to accept that the facilitating/coaching style will have to be moderated. At the beginning of a training event it is important to reassure participants regarding the academic credibility of the theories used, and assure them that the trainers have previous experiences and success with suitably prestigious companies. It is necessary to point out that the trainers are the experts in the process of analysing the team and developing them. In addition, trainers should be prepared to offer more comment and critique than would perhaps be necessary, or acceptable, with a Western audience.

Respect and appreciation will probably be shown to the trainer in a myriad of obvious and less obvious ways. For example, you will be called by your surname and any academic title will always be mentioned. It is important for you to clarify what the norms are regarding what you call participants and particularly the boss. When in doubt refer to the latter by his title and you will not be wrong. Similarly, with Chinese participants it is more polite to call them by their family name—Chan or Mr Chan—than to presume to use their given names. In any case the latter will often only be indicated by initials and one of the early traps for the unsuspecting trainer is differentiating K.C., K.Y., or T.S. from T.Y.

You will often be accorded privileges, the best seat at the dinner table, the best room in the hotel or have your lunch paid for when everyone else is paying for themselves. Mementoes are often presented to trainers at the end of programmes. In most cases it is best to accept *modest* gifts gracefully, otherwise you risk offending the givers. If a present has been given on your first visit you might consider bringing an appropriate memento from your country on your return visit. If there have been many treats or outings then it is courteous to arrange something special in return.

As with most situations, balance is the aim and achieving a 'both/and' approach rather than 'either/or' is the key. If a trainer is wedded to facilitating and experiential learning, he or she may have to moderate this at first and introduce it gradually to participants. I have already recommended that you must be prepared to comment and criticize from an expert standpoint. But be aware that your pronouncements will have a profound influence and will be taken more seriously than by many of your Western audiences. I have found, to my cost, that casual remarks and informal comments are often quoted and relayed back to surprising levels in the organization.

Handling mixed status within the group

Authority is respected and deferred to more within Asian society and the boss—subordinates dynamics will probably be quite different from those operating in the West. The dynamics between Asian bosses and their subordinates also have to be managed carefully by the trainer to preserve face on all sides.

Contracting is always an important issue for team builders and one that is sometimes skimped as we get more experienced. However, in Asia this is particularly important. It will alert the boss (or bosses) to the potential for public critique; it will help you to establish boundaries and to identify the discussable and undiscussable issues. Focusing the senior people on the potential of the event for learning can also encourage them to adapt their role within the group and facilitate more even participation during the event (i.e. by giving senior people a legitimate reason to play less prominent roles).

There are various techniques that can help. Early videoing of group exercises helps the boss to see how he or she is dominating discussions; moving high status individuals around groups and ongoing coaching from consultants are all beneficial at times.

In general you must accept that the plenary sessions will tend to be formal and that the usual status roles will tend to predominate, with the most senior people contributing significantly more than others—or sometimes exclusively. A carefully balanced small group is the best forum to solicit opinions from everyone in the group, and creating informal opportunities for bosses and team members to mix after sessions is a constructive step.

Stimulating critique and feedback

Diversity brings strength if it can be managed properly. The challenge for us as trainers and consultants is to create this strength by managing learning events so that all cultures can and will contribute and benefit. Some of the cultural difference points I made earlier need to be expanded to deepen our understanding of how to manage participation, critique and feedback within an Asian context.

In most cases Asian participants will have been trained since childhood for lifelong relationships to a group. The personal characteristics which are admired are those which promote harmony within the group— loyalty, moderation, self-discipline, modesty and self-sacrifice. Translated into the context of a team training event, an Asian participant will typically come dedicated to learning from the experience and, in particular, from the teacher or expert. The Asian participant will want to create a cohesiveness and harmony within the group, not wanting it to be too tough or to be personally exposed to public failure or ridicule. The same fundamental team dynamics probably exist as within Western groups, however, feedback is much more threatening to the giver and the receiver in Asia.

On the other hand the typical Western participant will have been raised within an environment where children are trained for independence, freedom of self-expression and encouraged to relate to a wide range of new people. The characteristics which are valued are those that protect the expression of self-interest while protecting the interests of theirs— truthfulness, enterprise, fairness, sociability and openness. The Western participant approaches the programme often with a more sceptical perspective, wanting to have a say in the design of the learning event, wanting to participate and willing to debate with fellow participants and the facilitator who has to 'prove' him or herself worthy to facilitate. The Westerner may frequently see it as a vehicle for airing latent conflicts in the group or, in the case of the boss, as an opportunity to find out what subordinates really think—good and bad.

If we look at these polarities—which sometimes have to be managed— the Asian participant will be a keen and conscientious student, eager for structure and guidance from you as the 'teacher'. They are unlikely to be aggressive towards you or fellow students and will work towards harmony in the group, suppressing personal needs and fostering those of the overall group and fellow students. On the other hand, the Asian participant may have a web of obligations and involvements which may intrude upon 'efficient' management of the seminar and lead to a fairly flexible attitude regarding time-keeping and attendance (if something judged to be more important comes along). One problem that may crop up for the trainer new to Asia is that participants frequently engage in conversations with fellow participants or on mobile phones while you are expounding your most important point. Handling this is discussed later when I come to deal with 'face'.

Collectivist cultures are often described as 'phobic' about verbal disagreement and, indeed, my experience has been that with Asian teams and groups it is often difficult to get good quality critique going. Members with problems find it difficult to surface these with the rest of the group and Asian participants on team building events are less likely to provide strong critique or engage in public debate. Similarly, for you as a trainer seeking feedback on your own performance, it is often difficult to find out if you are meeting their expectations or delivering anything that is useful to them.

On the other hand Western team members have fewer problems expressing emotions in public and frequently want to have humour used as a vehicle for learning. They will try to achieve their own learning goals and satisfy their own needs—often at the expense of other participants because they are not aware of the latters' needs. Westerners are more likely to profess to speak 'on behalf of the group' when they are, in essence, expressing their own opinions or those of their compatriots. Upbringing and language will often give them the ability to dominate and influence the group unduly and they may often be pressing for a pace of learning inappropriate for the Asian participants and second language speakers.

Some practical points will be useful:

- Use an ice breaker early on which allows everyone to mix informally.
- Remember that jokes and humour vary widely from culture to culture and can be exclusive rather than inclusive. Sarcasm and cynicism are rarely appropriate in Asia.
- Compose groups carefully to manage, as far as possible, the status issue. Balance senior Asians by allocating them to a group where they are not in their expert field. Those less skilled in language or lower in status thrive best within their expert groups. Split the foreigners (or isolate them in one group). Balance the boss or the foreigner with a Westernized Asian, someone senior, someone from another department or a fluent linguist.
- Do not insist that older and respected Asian managers participate fully if they show some reluctance (particularly in exercises which involve identifying personal strengths and weaknesses). This will be most embarrassing for everyone and is likely to fail—I learned this lesson after a president skipped the second seminar in a series after he found the first 'uncomfortable'!
- Establish an environment which is non-threatening so that participants feel at ease. Accept that some messages may be put much more subtly and diplomatically but will just be as effective

within the Asian context. If you want feedback about your own performance ask specific questions: 'I felt the finance was a little too long—what do you think.' 'I would like to improve the team reviews, have you got a suggestion?'

- Allow the volunteers to make the early contributions before insisting that everyone contributes. Make positive critique of early contributions.
- Avoid public criticism of individuals or leadership. As the 'teacher' your words and pronouncements have potentially more impact—bear this in mind and ensure that you give feedback only when it is sought and in private.
- Allow informal opportunities for interaction, e.g. a nationality group may wish to disappear one evening to Karaoke and one can predict that some useful opinions will be exchanged.
- Do not labour publicly over 'problems'—allow teams and individuals to diagnose their own situation and identify their 'weaknesses' in their own terms. For example, be sensitive when feeding back results of climate surveys publicly where distinct differences in departments may cause some embarrassment and lead to defensive behaviour which would not be helpful in tackling the problem.
- Provide a clear structure for feedback and insist on both positive and negative points.
- Defer feedback until the later parts of the team-building event, when you are sure it will be appropriate.
- Restrain the Europeans from excessive speaking and encourage the Asians to offer ideas and suggestions.

What techniques of team building are likely to be effective?

In my experience, taking into account 10 factors additional to those mentioned above in subtle and often simple ways will help to improve the effectiveness of team-building initiatives within the Asian context.

1 Norm setting

Early in the team-building event establish the norms. To increase the credibility of the event invite the boss to introduce and set the scene. Try to develop a team charter where team members are explicit about the norms they will use in the workshop sessions.

2 Standard setting

Teams are often too complacent about their performance. Gently encourage self-critique. Get the team members to set both personal and group improvement goals.

3 Create fun

Team exercises create a high energy psychological environment which Asian people enjoy. This provides a structure for the team to mix, have fun and improve confidence.

4 Provide structure   The necessary degree of structure and an academic approach adds credibility and allays fears. This means providing notes, outline timetables, review and summarizing of learning objectives, etc.

5 Respect the individual   The well-known and much discussed issue of 'loss of face' is quite a *bête noire* for the uninitiated. After 15 years in Asia I am still surprised that particular debates are complicated by issues of 'face'. However, I have also come to realize that 'face' is important for all races—it is the subtleties and emphasis that are different. Organizing a team-building event in Asia that has concern for 'face' benefits all participants, in my experience.

Public critique, ridicule and sarcasm (however mild) are to be avoided, as is critique of any decision associated with the person—the choice of venue, dinner menu, etc. Public display of emotion, loss of temper or annoyance can also 'lose face' for the individual. Public questions can, therefore, be fraught with problems for the unsuspecting and it is usually safest, at least in the preliminary stages, to ask questions where you are confident the responder will be able to answer. Finding creative ways of saying 'no' is also problematical. Shortly after my arrival in Hong Kong when I consulted a very experienced Chinese colleague on this issue she recommended saying, 'you are partly right', 'interesting approach' or 'maybe so'.

The complexities of 'losing face' are perhaps best illustrated by referring to an issue mentioned earlier—participants talking on mobile telephones or to each other. The response of many trainers, unfamiliar with Asia, is to indicate their annoyance by pausing and waiting pointedly or asking the offenders to stop. However, this course of action in public is embarrassing for all concerned and everyone has lost 'face'—you for showing your annoyance and embarrassing the offenders and the group; the group for having participants who have annoyed the teacher; etc. The more appropriate responses would be to ignore it and talk louder or to approach one of the senior Asian members and ask them to deal with it for you as they see fit. You can be sure that they will find a much more effective and tactful means of handling it than you ever could.

6 Handling team conflict   Diplomatic, indirect and gentle are the key words when it comes to handling conflict in teams. Many of the techniques and approaches used with teams in the West are designed to surface grievances and conflict on the basis that they can be confronted and mutual agreement reached or solutions found. A different perspective would be that there are irreconcilable differences that have to be understood, accepted and tolerated. A note of caution here: the process of airing and confronting team problems may create such disharmony that irreparable damage may be done to relationships.

The traditional Chinese way of expressing dissent was by finding historical analogies. The choice of a good case study or exercise where people can draw parallels is the modern equivalent for the team trainer. Similarly, be alert to any feedback which is being given to you by use of a question about a hypothetical situation or involving a third party, e.g. another course, another participant.

Many of the Western methodologies which are designed to promote openness and the surfacing of issues are quite inappropriate in Asia. Anything which involves a public loss of face—in particular for older or more senior team members—would make everyone feel most uncomfortable and would rally support for the individual concerned. Allowing opportunities for informal mixing after potentially controversial issues have been debated helps ease the situation; it also provides a vehicle for giving feedback in circumstances where both the givers and receivers feel more comfortable, less threatened and in control of how much or how little is said.

7 Team role questionnaires and team exercises

Most of the well-known team role questionnaires can be used effectively in Asia. However, the patterns can sometimes be different and need careful interpretation within the Asian context. Credibility and applicability to Asia also need to be established and this is, of course, much easier for those of us who have had many years' experience with similar audiences. There is also a tendency to look for the 'right' profile and so the trainer must be extra careful with explanations and alert to negative responses.

Most team exercises can also work well but it is worth thinking carefully about two aspects. First, if the exercise is designed to create conflict based on status roles this will not necessarily emerge, because of the acceptance of authority which has already been described. Similarly an Asian group may be more collaborative than a Western group and competitive dynamics may not emerge quite as strongly. Second, think carefully about any aspects of the exercise scenario which are culturally specific, e.g. does it present a type of person instantly recognizable to a Western audience but less so to an Asian one? Is the underlying issue an issue in Asia? Is the prize or target a desirable one in Asia? It is always worth checking out proposed exercises beforehand with local contacts.

8 Watch your language!

Never underestimate the problems created by language. Over the years we have had to make significant alterations to documentation—simplifying it, eradicating slang, jargon and colloquialisms. Allow more time for people to read and assimilate material—this applies to team exercises, questionnaires and instruments. Allow more time if participants are having to present to the group. Not only is it difficult to be succinct and to summarize in a foreign language, but also the formality of the plenary session and the presence of seniors will make many participants approach this in a more formal and time-consuming way.

Use specific examples and take care with your presentations. Alter your own language to meet the needs of the team and allow more time for assimilating and responding to your questions.

Monitor the team to ensure understanding and use the 'buddy' system for poor language speakers. In the main Asians are pragmatic and concrete thinkers, more comfortable with the specific rather than the abstract where one has to generalize to one's own situations. As the trainer you must bridge the gap from theory to practice; do not leave specific application up to individuals.

Finally, never forget just how tiring it is to be working in a second language—so do not insist that all social time is spent together. There are times when one wants to relax in one's own language.

9 Socializing and sharing

Problems in this area depend on how the 'in-group' is defined by the collectivist cultures. As referred to earlier, collectivist cultures such as those found in Asia, see the group as central, harmony in the group being more important than individual needs. The 'in-group' is often the family but is also sometimes defined geographically by village, province or country. If the event which you are running is seen by the Asian participants as a training course and the group includes all the participants, this group orientation may have a positive influence— lunches, events, reunions, alumni will be organized. However, where there are existing differences and the 'in-group' is defined as the nationality or business grouping, schisms across cultural lines can develop.

In the working team context there is a 'win–win' goal in co-operating; there are often formal and informal ways of working which facilitate groups co-operating effectively. However in the social context we often return to our core culture and values and there is no structure to facilitate interaction.

It may be as simple as different interests and inclination. It may relate to language—the desire to relax and share a joke in one's own language— it may relate to perceptions of how one wants to fill the time. Ways of enjoying oneself differ from culture to culture and sometimes it is nice not to have to compromise. For example, Europeans often like to get to know each other in the bar or on the sports field, whereas an Asian group will prefer karaoke, shopping, games of mahjongg, eating a local delicacy or preparing for the next day.

Are there any special multicultural dimensions that need to be managed?

In Asia, more so than in the West, one is highly likely to find a very multicultural environment. In fact this is the type of environment in which I have spent most of my career. For the last 15 years I have been working mostly with organizations whose *raison d'être* is bridging cultures and which would not exist if they were not effective cross-culturally. Cross-cultural issues have to be built into the very fibre of the organization—a part of everyday operational thinking in the same way that profit and loss is for accountants and sales turnover is for a sales director. In this respect all aspects of the organization need to be potentially cross-cultural.

The history of my present company, Jardines, is described in a book *The Thistle and the Jade*. The 'Jade' is China itself, ancient and splendid, and the forceful independent 'Thistle' is the Scots firm of Jardine Matheson. The material contained in the archives that chart the company history also charts the day-to-day history of East–West relations in the nineteenth century.

There has always been great interest in Jardines. It is not only a firm founded before Hong Kong itself, in the days of true merchant adventure, but it is the only business from that time which is still flourishing. This connection with the days of the merchant adventurer and the association with the opium trade have already been used as the basis of fiction. The real story—of the opening of Japan, of railway building, of steamship competition and of surviving the upheavals of two world wars—is the foundation on which the current company is built and why, for many, Jardines is the quintessential multicultural company. This is symbolized in the logo: the Thistle with the Chinese characters for Jardines—EWO. The translation of EWO is 'happy harmony'. Achieving the latter (most of the time!) by a unique blend of Western and Oriental approaches to running a business may be why the company has survived and prospered for 150 years.

In such an environment every event for the trainer is, potentially, a cross-cultural event. It may be that the audience is multicultural, in which case the dimension will have to be carefully managed to ensure that the learning is maximized and *everyone* benefits. It may be that the audience is mono-cultural but that the trainer is of a different nationality. The guest speaker or visiting expert may be from outside Asia and the trainer has to work diplomatically with him or her to ensure that the material and the style will be appropriate to the audience.

The essence of our approach is to concentrate on improving the overall effectiveness of individuals and the business at the same time—thus creating 'win–win' goals while recognizing that team-building events are providing the opportunity for intercultural learning.

In keeping with this philosophy, one of the most extensive and successful initiatives was to run strategy and team-building workshops with 25 of our larger businesses. Since 1988 we have been conducting these workshops for the top teams of our business units. These initiatives were taken in response to requests from the businesses concerned and our decentralized costing philosophy also meant that units paid us for the workshops.

In many cases the reason for undertaking the workshop is in response to the need to regionalize it. The presenting problem can take many forms but, typically, the business may be particularly strong in one country and have a much smaller operation in another, and it may then wish to expand or to explore new countries altogether. Alternatively, there may be several successful but small businesses dotted around the region and the task may be to weld them into a regional business—to create the culture and the commitment for synergy and internal staff transfer.

The strategy workshop process consists of two 3.5-day workshops separated by approximately 3–4 months. At the first workshop, participants are given frameworks to analyse the existing situation of their strategic business unit. The format works by giving input of 20–30 minutes on subjects such as industry and competitor analysis, market segmentation and customer analysis. Participants then work in strategic business groups to analyse their particular part of the business and they report back to the group as a whole, using pre-set formats on overhead slides.

The advantage of this methodology is it gives everyone a chance to learn more about other segments of the business and a chance to advise on and criticise each others' assumptions and reasoning. We have also added a team-building component and use team role analysis and typical group exercises to enhance teamwork.

During the interval between the two workshops the participants undertake mini-workshops to research the strategic position of their business within a competitive environment and this research forms the basis for the next workshop. At the second workshop, new frameworks and methods are introduced to help the participants review strategic position, explore options and develop implementation plans. During this workshop a climate survey will have been conducted in the businesses and the results of this are analysed and reviewed.

The overwhelming logic of the strategy workshop programme is seen to be business-based. However, team relationships, even within a multicultural group, develop rapidly. In fact, team building happens obliquely, which is very suited to the Asian approach.

Over a period of 5 years we have run these programmes for over 25 businesses and the outcomes have been many and varied. In some cases, business decisions with measurable outcomes were taken—to diversify, acquire companies, close divisions, introduce new methods of cost control and service delivery, etc. Improved teamwork was reported in all cases, managers citing better relationships, more willingness to communicate and a better general understanding of the wider picture as the most detectable outcomes. A few initiatives were less successful but this could be attributed to inappropriate timing from the business point of view rather than the cross-cultural dynamics.

The process was successfully imported from the West. While no significant changes were made in the underlying philosophy the successful implementation relied upon awareness of many of the cultural issues outlined previously. The example of this programme leads me to the chapter's conclusion.

Conclusion

One of my key beliefs about cross-cultural team effectiveness is that the answer lies in the details—not in the generalities. A Western approach leads us to believe that by analysing team situations in detail we can identify laws and rules which can be applied, generically, to all situations. Maybe so, but for effective team action we would do well to adopt the Oriental perspective that everything is only true within its context and we must understand the whole.

As a team builder it is not enough to design an event on 'cross-cultural effectiveness' that will be universally applicable. You must understand why effective cross-cultural behaviour is going to benefit both the individuals and the company—the ways in which people need to be effective and how they will benefit from it.

Cross-cultural effectiveness in teams is only a means to an end *not* the end. It is only relevant if it facilitates the group in achieving better results.

Finally, of necessity I have concentrated on the broad dynamic of West versus East and ignored the inter-Asian dynamic. A cautionary tale will illustrate the importance of the latter, however. During a team-building event we were running in Malaysia many years ago, the local office had gone to trouble and expense to arrange a cultural evening of dinner and dance. One third of the delegation from another country were absent because their boss had decided to treat them all to an evening of gambling which was illegal in their country of origin. This created great offence and the workshop ended on a very sour note. Inter-Asian prejudices can sometimes be much stronger than the East–West dynamic and need just as careful management.

Asia has been a continent hungry for change and growth, welcoming help from the West to achieve this but wanting to do things in an Eastern way. Increasingly we are now seeing a growing awareness and sense of pride in the remarkable economic achievements of the past decade. This has created a desire to understand and develop theories and methodologies from within Asia, appropriate to Asia. Western trainers, consultants and team facilitators have much to contribute but it is worth remembering that the incredible vitality and success of the East is equally inspiring and we in the West have as much to learn as to teach.

Reference   Keswick, Maggie (ed.) (1985), *The Thistle and the Jade*, Mandarin Publishers Ltd, Hong Kong.

Introduction to Chapter 9

'Intercultural team building in the USA', by David Wigglesworth, describes the elements of effective team building and how cultural diversity adds a further critical dimension. Diversity is defined as relating to age, ethnicity, gender and many other aspects of people's backgrounds or personal preferences, not simply to international differences.

The USA culture contains much cultural diversity, more so than most other countries. These diversity issues can be similar to those between nations, but often with a greater imperative to find ways of working together. Within the same organization it is hard to avoid the implications of diversity. The author points out that the nature of diversity has changed in the USA, from the traditional 'melting pot' in which people adapt to the overall 'dominant' culture to that of the 'pizza' in which people retain their cultural background—they do not merge and, therefore, they need to learn how to work together while valuing the differences.

Diversity can be a strength in that by bringing together people with different perspectives the quality of problem solving can be improved. Therefore, the aim of team building is to increase openness and trust so that different perspectives will be raised, explored and built upon. Differences become strengths to utilize, rather than conflicts to by-pass.

An important element which diversity brings to team building is the need to work through the human tendency to stereotype. Stereotypes are particularly divisive because they offer a negative interpretation to the behaviour of others which reinforces the attitude that my group is 'superior' to your group, for example, 'Euro-Americans may see Latin Americans as lazy and not corporate goal oriented'. Latins, in contrast, may perceive Euro-Americans as being obsessed by work to the extent where corporate values are more important than family values. Team building can enable people to understand the customs and behaviours of others, to respect culturally-based differences and to work together creatively.

9 Intercultural team building in the USA

David C. Wigglesworth

Team building has gone through many iterations in the United States of America including, games and simulations, 'touchy-feely' sensitivity training, applied sports training techniques, task-orientated processes and the planned development of effective interpersonal communication skills. It has been accomplished by structured design and/or by indirect, informal processes that aim at creating strong interpersonal relationships and commitment to the goals of the team, project or organization. Traditionally, it has been focused on an *esprit de corps*, on direct interpersonal communications, on trust and on the integration of people from alternate disciplines into an effective unit.

The multicultural workforce adds new dimensions to the process of team building in the USA. The rich diversity of the labour force in the USA calls for new techniques and processes for intercultural communication and the creation of practical, functioning teams made up of members who, while having much in common, are definitely different from each other.

In discussing workforce diversity in the USA, Loden and Rosener (1991, pp. 18–21) separate the major dimensions of diversity into two categories. Their primary category lists the dimensions of diversity as: age, ethnicity, gender, physical ability and sexual/affectionate orientation. The secondary category includes: geographical location, income, marital status, military experience, parental status, religious beliefs and work experience. To this list one might logically add the disparate considerations of professional disciplines.

The changing degree of diversity

The workforce, at almost all levels in the USA, is undergoing—and in many instances has undergone—major changes in its demographics. What was once seen as a workforce dominated by Euro-American males, has now become recognized as multicultural in its composition. It is clear to see that there is a major shift which shows the Euro-

American (i.e. white) male majority becoming numerically diminished as the workforce becomes enriched by Hispanics (those from Latin America), Asians (predominantly from South-east Asia and China), Afro-Americans (i.e. blacks) and women.

The Report of the Hudson Institute, *Workforce 2000* (Johnson and Packer, 1987, pp. 15–19), projected that by the turn of the century the workforce population in the USA would have changed demographically, comparing the 1986 profile with that anticipated in the year 2000 (see Table 9.1).

Table 9.1

	1986 %	2000 %
White	80.9	76.3
Black	10.0	10.7
Hispanic	6.4	9.2
Other	2.7	3.8

Historical perspective on diversity

With the exception of the Native Americans (Indians) who crossed the Bering Straits in prehistoric times and appeared to have claimed North America as their own territory, the population of the USA comprises immigrants and the descendants of immigrants. Initially, the influx of immigrants came primarily from Europe. These groups, which came in waves of people fleeing economic, religious or political hardships, by and large came voluntarily—seeking a better life. While there was some resentment from those settled first against each succeeding group, generally succeeding generations were able to blend into the general mainstream population because they were white and came with value systems that could either be adapted to the American model or kept from public view. This led to the creation of the idea of America as a melting pot where foreigners came and were absorbed into the national mould.

During the history of the USA, a significant number of workers came involuntarily as slaves. Called in succeeding generations: negroes, coloured, blacks, and Afro-Americans, they have never been fully assimilated into the fabric of mainstream American life. Their roots were different, the causes of their being in the country were different, their political status was different and, for most of their time in the USA, their human rights were often ignored. It has been difficult for them to gain parity in the workplace.

Another large influx of immigrants to the USA came from Asia and, throughout America, there are sizeable pockets of Filipinos, South-east Asians, Japanese and Chinese Americans. They too are people of colour who bring alternate systems of values and who have some difficulty in making the concept of the melting pot work in practice. They appear to have gained a greater degree of parity in the workforce than the African Americans.

In the twentieth century, there has been a steady stream of immigrants to the USA (both legal and illegal) from Mexico, Central America and South America. These people, who often look different from the Euro-Americans, have faced considerable difficulties in being accepted in the community, as well as in business organizations. They have been seen, for the most part, as inexpensive entry-level labourers. However, succeeding generations have attained a greater degree of parity than their parents in the workforce.

Looking at workforce diversity, the role of women also has significance. Women came into the workforce in large numbers during the Second World War where they replaced the men who were off in the military. When the veterans came home, women in the workforce did not disappear. It has taken some 50 years for women to gain a reasonable measure of acceptance in the workforce. According to *Workforce 2000* (Johnson and Packer, 1987, pp.15–19), women account for nearly 50 per cent of all professionals in the workforce though, as Morrison et al. (1987) discuss, women have difficulty in reaching the upper levels of management—that is, breaking through the glass ceiling.

Benefits of diversity

Diversity in the workforce of today has been viewed by some as a problem that impedes safety, productivity and profits. The proponents of this view seem to argue that there is a need to Americanize all workers so that they fit the melting pot mould. Others are of the point of view that diversity in the workforce is an asset that management can employ to increase safety, productivity and profits. The proponents of this view seem to believe that within the diverse cultures of the workforce there may be new approaches to problem solving and decision making, for example, that can enhance the efforts of the organization and increase the bottom line. Within organizations, there is a range of these views among managers and workers which can, and often does, impact upon team-building efforts.

In the diversity arena, the concept of the melting pot has, to a large degree, been replaced by the concept of a pizza with everything on it or a tossed salad. In each of these dishes there is a variety of flavours, separate and distinct, and yet enhancing the overall flavour of the pizza or salad. This diversity is reflective of ethnicity, colour, national origin and gender.

Team building and diversity

The object of team building, traditionally, is that of harnessing people who are basically independent in a working environment to perform their responsibilities in a systematic or unifying way. This has never been an easy task; the objective becomes more difficult when working with individuals of different backgrounds who have different norms, values, expectations, traditions and priorities.

Essential elements of team building focus on openness, consensus building, mutual support, trust and task performance. Building teams in a multidisciplinary work environment has required an alignment of values that enable a team to develop the requisite trust for a functioning, open, consensual, supportive, task performing team. Building teams in a multicultural work environment requires an understanding of intercultural communication and a belief that people with differing values and behaviours can form a cohesive group.

Performance of diverse teams

Recent research has demonstrated (Watson et al. 1993) that, in the long term, heterogeneous (i.e. multicultural) groups perform equally as well as homogeneous (i.e. single culture) groups, in both their process and overall performance. This research has also demonstrated that heterogeneous groups performed better in identifying problem perspectives and in generating solution alternatives.

This same study indicated that newly-formed or short-term heterogeneous groups did not perform as well as homogeneous groups. This suggests that some basic considerations must be built in to the process of developing effective multicultural teams at the very beginning of a heterogeneous group's formation in order to enhance their effectiveness.

Diversity adds new dimensions to the team-building process because people with different value systems are often locked into varying and even conflicting perceptions and communication values that need to be addressed. It is potentially dangerous to ascribe certain tenets or behaviours to a group. Generalizations are noted for their exceptions and one thinks of the quote attributed to Voltaire that 'All generalizations, including the one that I am now making, are not necessarily true.' However, we must deal with perceptions and individuals' reactions, recognizing that they probably do not hold true in all cases.

Teams comprised exclusively of Euro-Americans are expected to pose few difficulties within the team-building process. Yet, members of different professions often have different problem-solving techniques, their own vocabularies and distinct perceptions of the other professions which can hinder the team-building process.

Stereotyping

Multicultural or multi-ethnic teams face similar problems to multi-professional teams, problems exacerbated by negative stereotypes that may exist within the group. Thus, Euro-Americans may see Latin Americans as lazy and not corporate goal oriented. Latin Americans may see these Euro-Americans as less than human because they are perceived as putting corporate values above family. Asians may be perceived as devious, while their perception may be that Euro-Americans are so direct that they are rude. Misperceptions can impede the development of effective teams—and cultural misperceptions are no exception.

Elements of multicultural team building

The factors that need to be addressed in multicultural team-building sessions, according to Casse (1982, pp. 123–7), include: self-understanding, understanding others, interacting with others, as well as two general skills: tolerance of ambiguity and persistent patience.

Casse indicates that before members of a team can appreciate and interact with co-workers representing the diversity of the workforce, they need to have an awareness of their own culture. That is, they need to recognize that their every behaviour is influenced by some basic cultural assumption, value or belief and this awareness needs to be personalized to the extent that their construction of reality is personal and different from the constructs of others.

Skills relevant to diverse teams

Some of the skills that may be employed in the understanding of other team members, according to Casse, are the practice of empathy; demonstrating a respect for cultural differences; learning from interpersonal interactions; avoiding the explanation of other people's behaviour from one's own frame of reference; trying not to pass value judgements; and avoiding stereotypes in as much as such generalizations tend to lead to misinterpretations and, often, ill feelings.

The development of interactive communication skills may require learning how to ask open-ended questions, the use of silence, paraphrasing and the reflection of feelings. There is a need to pay keen attention to the maintenance or supportive roles of a team, in addition to the task roles. Listening and observing can be highly useful and team members need to have the flexibility to cultivate and expand their range of options and to be able to adjust according to people's reactions by using all of the resources available. This brings us back to Casse's two specific general skills; the tolerance of ambiguity and the need to be patiently persistent.

Gardenswartz and Rowe (1993, pp. 99–150) list eight considerations for building effective multicultural teams. These are:

- To identify and build on shared values
- Gain commitment to the group's goals and objectives
- Reward excellence in ways that are culturally appropriate
- Demonstrate an appreciation for each person's cultural uniqueness
- Acknowledge cultural conflicts when they arise (but do not view all conflicts as caused by cultural differences)
- Learn to be a better team member by being more aware and sensitive to the cultures of others
- Utilize alternative activities to foster team building
- Acknowledge cultural differences by learning about one another's values and culture-based behaviours.

In some respects, the key ingredients of building an effective multicultural team are the same or similar to any team-building process, i.e. the need to:

- Acknowledge differences
- Find common ground
- Identify individual interest, strengths and preferences
- Clarify expectations
- Collectively develop a common group culture
- Create communication feedback processes

Communication and trust

Team building, whether task or process oriented, requires major communication breakthroughs and the development of trust and reliance on others who may have a high degree of independence and self-worth. Intercultural team building in the USA adds new complexities that require new perspectives and the application of new skills. As Watson et al. (1993) have shown, long-term multicultural teams are more adept than culturally homogeneous teams in the identification of problem perspectives and the generation of solution alternatives. In addition to the usual rationale of enhancing the effectiveness of a diverse workforce, these are eminent reasons for the development of multicultural teams in the workplace.

Multicultural team situations

While it is easy to reach agreement on the general principles of diversity training, in practice one is faced with difficult choices of how to work with a given group.

As a training professional, imagine that you are called in to facilitate the development of a team. The task of the team is to create substantive guidelines for the introduction of a new quality control programmes. The team comprises three engineers, two human resource professionals, one accountant and one senior level manager. The group is representative of the workforce and includes three Euro-Americans, two Mexican Americans, one Chinese American and one Afro-American.

The gender make-up is five men and two women.

In your interviews with the prospective team members you note that some of the males have expressed displeasure that women are members of the team. One of the engineers speaks disparagingly about human resource 'types' and one of the human resource professionals wonders what the 'bean counter', i.e. the accountant, can contribute to the group. The Afro-American expresses concern that the whites (Euro-Americans) will dominate, while the Chinese American is concerned as to how to avoid the direct confrontation that sometimes occurs in teams.

Your role is to help this group blend itself into a functioning team that can and will achieve the goals set for it. Consider the following options:

- Do you confront each of the individuals in your interviews with their prejudicial thoughts?
- Do you ignore these differences and hope that the task and its goals will overcome the individual biases?
- Do you present the full review of your interviews at the first team session?
- Do you do individual, one-on-one coaching with each of the team members?
- Do you start the first session with a review of intercultural communication factors and their applications in effective team building?

What other approaches might you employ, such as: enabling techniques, empowerment, process monitoring and role responsibility? The purpose of this case scenario is to remind practitioners that there is no easy guaranteed solution that will provide all of the answers and lead to a positive outcome of this team-building assignment. Reference to the ideas of Casse (discussed earlier in the chapter) may provide some insights. Also reference to the concepts of Hofstede and the dimensions of Trompennars (both discussed in various chapters in this book) should be considered. In conclusion, this assignment demonstrates the multilayered, intercultural, interdisciplinary factors that can have either negative or positive impacts on the team building process, and illustrate the complexity of dealing with cross-cultural issues.

References

Casse, Pierre (1982) *Training for the Multicultural Manager*, The Society for Intercultural Education, Training and Research, Washington, DC.

Gardenswartz, Lee and Anita Rowe (1993) *Managing Diversity, A Complete Desk Reference and Planning Guide*, Business One Irwin, Homewood, IL.

Johnston, William B. and Arnold E. Packer (1987) *Workforce 2000: Work and Workers for the 21st Century*, Hudson Institute, Indianapolis, IN.

Loden, Marilyn and Judy B. Rosener (1991) *Workforce American, Managing Employee Diversity as a Vital Resource*, Irwin, Homewood, IL.

Morrison, Ann M., Randall P. White and Ellen van Velson (1987) *Breaking the Glass Ceiling*, Addison-Wesley, Reading, MA.

Watson, Warren E., Kamalesh Kumar and Larry K. Michaelsen (1993) 'Cultural Diversity's Impact on Interaction Process and Performance: Comparing Homogeneous and Diverse Task Groups', *Academy of Management Journal*, vol. 36, no. 3, pp. 590–602.

Introduction to Chapter 10

'Reducing prejudice between workers and management', by Raymond Cadwell, examines cultural differences between different levels and departments of the same organization. Workers and managers can be viewed as having different cultures to the extent that each has their own way of being and of perceiving events. Indeed, there can be more intolerance between people who work closely together than between those from distant lands.

The chapter begins with a description of the dynamics of prejudice and oppression. It suggests that the dominant group sends messages to the subordinate group that is 'inferior', replaceable and subculture powerless. Often the subordinate group comes to accept this perception as reality, thus, the stereotype is reinforced and the distrust between the two groups is reinforced.

An understanding of prejudice is important for recognizing where cultural differences become devisive and manipulative, and used as a justification for control and exploitation. This chapter describes a strategy for breaking down these barriers. It is a three-pronged strategy which educates people about the nature of prejudice, establishes cross-group working parties to tackle real organization improvement issues, and encourages leadership and initiative at all levels of the organization.

10 Reducing prejudice between workers and management

Raymond Cadwell

Over the last number of years the author and his team have succeeded in achieving a significant reduction in the amount of prejudice between workers and managers in a number of Irish, UK and European companies. In some cases this reduction in prejudice has led to good relationships which have stood the test of time and quite serious upheaval in the business. In other cases there has been an extraordinary level of achievement in working together as a team and making their organizations highly successful. We have also had one or two failures from which we have learned.

This chapter describes:

- A short case study and the results achieved.
- What we actually did.

The case study is an Irish one which has applicability on a European basis. Although the industrial relations environments are completely different in some European countries to those of Ireland and the UK, we have found that the perceptions which shopfloor workers have of management and vice versa are almost identical across different countries. This would also include a project implemented in the USA, namely in North Carolina and California.

A case study

Background   We first started this work over 10 years ago when a plant manager asked us if we could apply some of the work we were doing on changing attitudes to the problems in his plant.

He described the state of employee relations as being very poor, full of conflict and misunderstanding and, on most occasions, reminiscent of a battleground. There had been many incidents of unofficial disputes which left both sides feeling angry. People on the shopfloor were highly suspicious and very reluctant to talk to us.

How the shopfloor perceived management

Our initial discussions showed the following in perceptions of management by the workers:

- Management are not to be trusted.
- They have double standards, do not tell the truth and lie about the facts.
- They are petty and small-minded, and tend to apply procedures and rules in a pedantic and bureaucratic way.
- They allow things to fester for a long time before taking action.
- They have superior attitudes, they lack respect and generally treat us as if 'we don't count'.
- They are anti-union.
- They are aloof and distant.
- They tend to take advantage whenever possible.
- They lack an appreciation of workers and their efforts and dedication.

How management perceived the unions/shopfloor

Generally speaking management perceived the shopfloor people in the following ways:

- They are irresponsible and have a tendency to want to drive us out of business in order to obtain their selfish ends.
- They do not stick to their agreements.
- They have a closed viewpoint which is difficult to change.
- They do not really care for the success of the company.
- A small group controls the shop stewards' committee and there is a small group of trouble-makers who contaminate the majority.
- They see militancy as a successful way of doing business.

We got the agreement of workers and management to try our prejudice approach over a period of two years.

Case study: the results

After two years the transformation—of the attitudes, physical environment and relationships between everybody in that plant—was remarkable. There were a number of outward signs of this. Beforehand the plant looked very dull, very drab with very poor working conditions and people looked glum and demotivated. A visit to the plant two years later showed a dramatic change in the plant environment. It was painted all kinds of different colours, people had new working apparel and the atmosphere was bright, friendly and clean.

Over the two years of the project we did an estimate of progress each year by asking each group in the plant to give their estimate of the progress that had been made. Some sample statements of the estimate of progress for both senior managers and shopfloor workers are given below.

Estimate of progress—senior managers

- An increase in the number of managers who think of both shopfloor and management interests when making decisions.
- Five senior managers are perceived to have made significant changes in their leadership styles while the other two have made intermittent changes.
- There has been a significant increase in senior managers' willingness to listen.
- The capacity of the senior management to work as a team is visible and apparent.
- There is an increased acceptance by senior management of the individual differences in philosophy and style of members of senior management.
- The managing director has become part of the senior management team.
- A great improvement in senior managers' ability to support each other as leaders.
- A big reduction in the use of force as a means of solving problems.
- The gap between senior managers and supervisors has been reduced significantly.
- The level of appreciation of shopfloor contribution has changed completely, for the better.
- There is a better understanding of shopfloor interests.
- Employee relations are seen as an asset.

Estimate of progress—shopfloor workers

- Professionalism of negotiations between shopfloor and management has increased significantly.
- The annual negotiations have now turned into two- and three-year agreements. These are conducted in a problem-solving way. Both sides have now worked out a formula which gives them an objective measure of the plant performance and allows them to settle the percentage increase in an objective way.
- Conditions of employment have become equivalent between management and shopfloor.
- Shopfloor earnings have increased.
- Work teams now take responsibility for quality and production.
- Morale and job satisfaction are high.
- Shopfloor workers' sense of control over their own destiny is high.
- All plant issues and difficulties are discussed with the workforce in an open forum with senior management in the canteen on a regular basis.
- There is an increased level of satisfaction with the quality of communications within the plant.

This particular plant suffered a major loss of market share about one year after the completion of this programme and they came through the trauma successfully by finding themselves some new products. People remarked on how well they worked together during this crisis and how open the management were with shopfloor people at every step during the recovery stage.

What we did

The components of our strategy can be divided into three sections:

1 An information strategy.
2 The use of temporary social systems to elicit change.
3 A new leadership perspective.

An information strategy

The purpose of our information strategy is to give people a set of concepts through which to view reality. Our hope is that these new concepts will change the way in which they experience reality and thus enable them to be more effective in conducting their relationships.

During this phase, we give people information on the content of the prejudice towards themselves and towards other groups, also giving them an appreciation of how they are carriers and agents for the prejudice towards other groups. This enables them to respond differently and more productively because they are no longer influenced by these prejudices to the same degree.

We look at three aspects of prejudice:

1 The content of prejudice towards workers.
2 The content of prejudice towards management.
3 The content of prejudice which people hold towards themselves.

The content of prejudice which people hold towards themselves—internalized prejudice—affects both workers and management and is discussed in relation to both groups.

Prejudice towards workers

In our workshops we asked all workers to brainstorm a list of all the ways they think people are prejudiced towards workers and trade unions. We asked the question 'What does the prejudice say about works?' This formulation of the question distances the issue from people initially, which is a useful way of getting some objectivity into the situation. This initial brainstorming session usually gets out into the open the content of prejudice which workers think is held about them.

We then gave people our analysis of the content of prejudice towards workers which breaks down into five different components:

1 **Your intelligence/thinking is inferior.**   It is almost universal that workers feel their thinking and ideas are not used for improving organizations. They make statements like 'We are only paid from the neck down'. Also there is an undervaluing of workers' education. Formal education is taken to mean that one is intelligent, whereas

education gained through life's experience has low value for workers. The basic message is that people in the position of being workers 'cannot really think'.

Furthermore, working class people are led to believe that their thinking is inferior and that they should look to superiors to provide the thinking. They should simply do the work and let others do the thinking.

2 **Your role is to toil or you exist only in relation to your job.**   This piece of conditioning says, in effect, you are 'nothing without a job'. Your value is determined by the fact of having a job; furthermore, it is also determined by the status of the job which you occupy. This is illustrated by the fact that managers cannot stand to see workers 'not working'— a worker's job is to be occupied all the time. Managers tend to feel guilty and ineffective if they find their workers 'not working'. The message here is: 'your lot in life is to work and nothing else'.

3 **Your wants/needs are in a danger to our survival.**   It is constantly communicated to working people, mostly by management, that their 'wants' threaten the survival of the company. If only workers would stop 'wanting', the future of the company would be safe. This is also constantly communicated when people demand benefits which are given as a matter of course to other groups within a factory. They are often labelled as trouble-makers and accused of threatening the survival of the whole firm. Managers often say that workers are prepared to go to 'any lengths' to satisfy their needs. This statement has to be seen as a piece of prejudice and a generalization and probably plays a part in justifying the way workers are treated.

4 **Your work is not as economically valuable as other groups.**   Generally speaking working peoples' effort, dedication and loyalty are not as economically valued as those of other groups in terms of rewards. The relationship of factory workers to an organization is on the basis of an hourly rate and hinges on the fact that if you do not work, you do not get paid.

5 **You are not central.**   Workers, generally speaking are not seen as being central to the operation of the business even though they obviously are. They tend to be treated as somewhat invisible.

Institutionalized prejudice   It is important to point out that the content of the prejudice towards workers has been institutionalized into organizations. This means that it has been built into the structures of responsibilities, role definitions, forms of organization, etc. It is mainly maintained through a system of control in which people called managers are put in place to ensure that people who are workers are made to work. It is set up in such a way that supervisors and middle management are 'paid to take responsibility', workers are 'paid to work'. This in fact leads to the institutionalization of irresponsibility patterns among workers. These patterns are internalized by workers, which again reinforces the cycle of oppression.

Internalized prejudice

To discover what prejudices workers hold about themselves, we asked them the question: 'How do you tend to feel as a result of this conditioning?' They generally listed the following:

- Stupid/inferior
- Do not feel valued
- Do not feel responsible
- Unimportant
- Like we do not matter
- Powerless
- Angry
- Despondent and hopeless about ever changing anything

In exploring the content of the internalized prejudice with workers, we pointed out that workers have done their very best to resist this conditioning and have always tried to operate as best they could, even in situations where they have been highly discouraged.

Working on workers' internalized prejudice

We have had varying degrees of success in assisting workers to deal with internalized prejudice. It mostly depends on the extent to which they are able to feel free enough to express some of the embarrassment that gets in the way of connecting to how valuable they really are. The following gives a brief summary of what we did.

We say that there are two processes in every organization: the appreciation process and a depreciating process. The objective of the appreciating process is to add value to people and materials. The main thrust of the depreciating process is to wear out and use up the value of people and resources. Prejudice tends to emphasize the devaluing/ depreciation process. We asked the workers to go against the conditioning by valuing themselves and others.

We pointed out to workers that, because we internalize the low value about ourselves, we also tend to internalize it about other workers and, therefore, have difficulty respecting, appreciating and valuing each other as workers. This is particularly true of workers' representatives such as shop stewards and union officials. The constant criticizing and knocking of each other, as workers, is part of the way which workers have been conditioned to undermine each other. We challenged the workers to stop this process of depreciating and start appreciating each other.

We stressed that we fully understand how much this process has been institutionalized and how counter the culture it is to appreciate each other as workers. However, in order to reach the level of empowerment we need, it is necessary and useful for workers to learn to appreciate themselves as well as each other. We, therefore, asked a series of questions:

1 What do you most appreciate and value about the people you grew up with in your neighbourhood?
2 What do you most value about working class culture?
3 What skills do you have or have developed and what do you most appreciate about these?
4 Tell us something you have accomplished with your level of skill in a particular area, e.g. woodwork, metalwork.
5 What do you most like/appreciate about the kind of person you have become?
6 What do you most appreciate about other workers here?

The workers enjoyed answering these questions and were pleased by the extent to which they were able to listen to each other without too much 'slagging'. After a number of responses to these questions it became clear that workers are very proud of each other, their background and the kind of people they are. Giving them a chance to share and explore this was beneficial.

However, the main purpose of the coaching process was to enable each worker to see which particular part of the prejudice they had personally bought into. This was very hard to ask directly as few workers are willing to admit 'that they have been got' by the prejudice.

The coaching process followed along the lines of a series of questions and answers:

Trainer   'What do you most appreciate about the kind of person you have become?'
Worker   'I like that I can solve problems.'
Trainer   'What quality is there in you that enables you to solve problems so well?'
Worker   'I never give up thinking until I have figured it out.'
Trainer   'What kind of person never gives up thinking until they have figured it out?'
Worker   'A committed person.'
Trainer   'Would you like to spend just a few minutes thinking about ways in which you are a committed person?'

As workers became involved in this coaching, they became aware of the internalized prejudice and gave examples of where they had given up on their thinking. In other words, the appreciation process acted as a contradiction to the content of the internalized oppression and brought it into the mind of the person.

Statements like 'I am afraid to say what I think' or 'I am not as articulate as managers' tended to be voiced. At this point the workers began to own the content of the prejudice as it is internalized and became motivated to work on it from the point of view of ridding themselves of it. This coaching process broke through the denial process and enabled people to see how they were personally affected.

Each participant was given a chance to explore how the conditioning affected them personally and, after one or two people led the way, others were keen to find out for themselves about the ways they might be personally affected by the conditioning.

The cycle of prejudice towards workers

The following is an example of the way we highlighted how the cycle of prejudice operates in relation to prejudice towards workers:

1 **Perception**   Workers are not intelligent.
2 **Treatment (mistreatment)**   Workers are not involved in important decisions because they are not regarded as having the ability to think.
3 **Resulting behaviour**   Workers stop thinking, give up, tend to withdraw and feel that there is no point in them taking responsibility.
4 **Internalized prejudice**   I am stupid, I am uneducated, I cannot think.
5 **How the prejudice is institutionalized**   Workers' access to training is close to zero within factories and it is only in recent years that worker education has become somewhat available. Through the operation of the hierarchy, they are often the last people to be consulted.
6 **Conditioning**   Our workers are conditioned not to show intelligence or ability to think.
7 **Reinforcement of conditioning**   Since workers do not show intelligence and thinking, this confirms the idea that they are not intelligent and, therefore, should not be consulted or treated as thinking people.
8 **Denial**   Examples of denial are empty statements such as: 'workers are our most important asset' and 'workers in this plant are treated well'.

Prejudice towards management

In order to achieve a breakthrough with management, it was necessary for them to understand at least two things:

1 They are an oppressed group themselves and are affected by the expression of this cultural prejudice towards management, just as workers are affected by cultural conditioning towards workers.
2 They are the agents and carriers of prejudice towards workers in 'role' terms. This is by far the most difficult thing to get managers to see as most managers would tend to perceive themselves in terms of being very liberal and treating people equally and in a fair minded way.

The difficulties experienced in getting managers to see the extent to which they are agents of prejudice are similar to the problems faced in getting men to see that they are the carriers and agents of prejudice towards women. The concept of role conditioning is important here.

Exploring the conditioning of middle managers

First of all we found it useful not to distinguish between what we traditionally call middle management and senior management. All managers in charge of organizations who are on a salary can be regarded as 'middle people'. That is, they are agents for the shareholders and are employed to represent the interests of the shareholders in the business. It is important for managers to understand that they are in an intermediary/representative role and, therefore, they tend to carry much of the programming and conditioning that the people they represent generally carry.

In order to get managers to identify the content of the conditioning, we asked them questions:

1 What does prejudice say about management?
2 What do you have to do to be 'a good manager' within this system?
3 What is good about how managers are treated by the system? What is bad about it?
4 What do you dislike about other managers?

We helped them to brainstorm on these questions. There were a number of themes which ran through their answers:

- 'Don't rock the boat'
- 'Conform, do not appear to stand out'
- 'Do not call any attention to yourself as being in any way different'
- 'Represent the company view whether you agree with it or not'
- 'You have to say you don't know even when you do'
- 'Be loyal to management'
- 'Invisibility and secrecy, have to keep a lot of secrets'
- 'You feel like an individual, you're never a member of a group'
- 'You stand and fall on your own merits'
- 'You feel expendable and disposable, if you don't do the job like "they" want you to then "they" will get somebody else who will'
- 'You are not to trust your colleagues'
- 'You have to ensure that you get all the credit for things you do'
- 'You're only as good as your last job'
- 'You have to keep proving yourself over and over again each day'
- 'Suppress any fundamental disagreements you have with policy or approach of the company'
- 'Don't get too close to people who work for you or else they will take advantage of you'
- 'It's OK to have values, as long as you keep them to yourself'

This is just a sample of some of the things people said in relation to identifying middle management conditioning. There seem to be four basic themes which emerge from this:

1 **'You are expendable'.**   This seems to be a message that managers receive from the organization culture and it is very similar to that part of mens' conditioning which says kill or be killed. In other words, if you do not kill off another person's idea or project, perhaps they will get you. Though this is it in its extreme, most managers recognize and identify with a constant battle for survival.

2 **Caring is cut off.**   Managers who care or exhibit symptoms of care are usually regarded as inferior, in terms of promotion, to those who

are tough minded and uncaring. Some organizations devalue managers who place their family first and their job second. Also, supervisors who show any tendency to care for their workers' interests are usually considered suspect. This again runs parallel to men's conditioning, as most managers are being cut off from being allowed to care for each other in any fundamental way.

3 **Responsibility overload.**   Managers are overloaded with responsibilities for the well-being of the total organization. This brings about workaholic patterns, separation from family members and children, and long working hours. This often results in the burnout of managers and addiction to alcohol.

4 **Isolation/separation.**   Most managers are conditioned to feel they 'have to go it alone'. They are also conditioned not to get too close to their peers because of career competition and certainly not to forge links with people who work for them, as this may lead them to become too easily influenced in relation to the interests of workers. Some managers internalize that unless they 'take charge of it, it will not get done' or unless it is done 'their way' and 'on their own', things will go wrong and the situation will turn out to be unsatisfactory.

We pointed out that many managers resist this kind of conditioning and operate very successfully outside of it. However, it is still there and does influence to a great extent how managers are perceived by other groups. We wanted them to try to visualize how the prejudice becomes internalized. We asked managers to list the ways that these kinds of things made them feel. They said it made them feel:

- 'like we do not really matter or were not really valued'
- 'cautious and careful'
- 'managers are not important as people'
- 'isolated and have to go it alone'
- 'our own well-being does not really matter as long as the job gets done'
- 'invisible'

Our experience of working with middle managers on their internalized prejudice shows that the heart of the matter is that 'they do not really feel all that important'. Since the role is a representative role and, as a manager they are required to conform to the thinking of the company, then people internalize on a deep level that they are not important as people in their own right.

The notion that they are replaceable is generally acceptable by managers as 'being normal'.

The coaching process   The main issues in working with managers on this material was to get them to see the extent to which they internalize this information about themselves as people as a result of the conditioning. The steps we used to forward this process were:

1 Appreciation of your own background: what you liked about the people you grew up with, what you learned from them and what you gained from them. As many managers have had working class backgrounds this is a useful area of discussion and they can be encouraged to reclaim their connection to their working class roots.

2 What part of your humanity have you had to give up in order to be 'a manager'? Which values have you had to leave behind; have you had to compromise yourself and your best thinking?

3 How important, significant and essential are you? This is an important question as, generally speaking, the conditioning of management is to make them feel that they are not very important and significant. As soon as we ask this question, the person usually will tell us the way in which they feel unimportant and insignificant—in fact, the content of the middle management conditioning.

4 We usually ask each manager to see if they can identify, on a personal basis, the ways in which they have been affected by conditioning of middle management.

Trust and middle management conditioning

It was useful to explain to both workers and managers the effects which the content of middle management conditioning can have on the issue of trust. Middle managers are supposed to conform, be invisible, keep things secret, etc. When they speak and communicate, they tend to do so in terms of generalities and bland language. Their tones tend to be careful and cautious and they are often speaking in ways that seem vague. This generalized vague way of communicating, which is primarily as a result of the role, comes across as being untrustworthy to the ears of workers, particularly when relationships between management and workers are not good.

The example we often give is of the trade union activist who was promoted to be on the national executive of the union. What was noticeable was that, after a month or so of being on the executive, the language used by the previous activist tended to become general, vague and somewhat bland. What had happened was in effect, that he had taken on the conditioning of the middle role. This role is not just confined to people in management.

Generally speaking, our experience is that the more managers work on the internalized prejudice in respect of their own role, the more credible they will be and sound—both to workers and to themselves, as they see how they have internalized the conditioning of their management roles.

Management as the agents for prejudice

After managers had done a reasonable amount of work on the content of their own prejudice, it was useful to work with them on how they are agents or carriers for the prejudice towards workers. We found it useful to go through the following steps:

1 What is great about being the kind of manager that you currently are?
2 List the groups in society towards which you think cultural prejudice is held.
3 List the groups in society you think are the agents or carriers of prejudice towards other groups, e.g. parents, men, gentiles, able-bodied people etc.
4 Taking young people as a group, what do you remember about how you were treated well and how you were treated badly as a young person?

It is important when working with a group who are the agents for a particular piece of prejudice, to give them time to look at how they have been hurt by prejudice first and foremost before moving on. Sometimes working on how they have been hurt as managers is sufficient but, mostly, it is not because the acceptance of mistreatment as being part of the job is so pervasive and ingrained in some managers.

5 List all the ways you think you have stood out against prejudice towards workers. This is particularly useful in breaking down barriers between senior management and middle management. These team-building events can take place over a 2 to 3-hour period in which each team works on building a vision of how it would like to function if it were free of prejudice, followed by some coaching for each team member on how to make the changes in their own behaviour to be consistent with this. This has been a particularly useful approach for breaking down the barriers between formal supervisors and middle/departmental managers.

It is useful to include here some work on how managers currently treat the people who work with them.

6 What are some examples of ways in which you have unconsciously gone along with prejudice towards workers?
7 Are there some ways that you have perhaps unconsciously related to workers or treated them which you now think might be prejudicial and discriminatory?
8 Can you think of individual workers with whom you would like to improve your relationship or who you think you may have discriminated against or been prejudiced towards in the past?
9 What needs to be communicated from you to them in order to be able to repair the damage and raise the level of trust and credibility in the relationship?

Attitude of the coach   We cannot stress enough how important it was that managers understood the notions of prejudice and internalized prejudices as a prerequisite for being able to work on the ways in which they were agents and carriers of prejudice.

The attitude of the coach throughout this process was relaxed and accepting of everything that was said. It was not useful for the coach to get into arguments and persuasive discussions with managers on how they are prejudiced towards workers.

Generally, it is important to be welcoming and interested, particularly when managers mention things they have done or do not feel very proud about in relation to workers. In our work on this question, managers have admitted to doing some nasty things to workers and it is important to be non-judgemental when listening to this material.

This work brought up a lot of guilt and heaviness in the situation and it was important to maintain a balanced view of the reality of the work situation; managers were all doing their best and had been very strongly influenced by prejudice towards workers and trade unions.

The information strategy   The concepts of prejudice and internalized prejudice act as information processors, which people use to deal with the information they have about each other. For example, using the idea of internalized prejudice as a way of processing information about internal feelings proves to be a very powerful mechanism for transforming peoples' experience of prejudice. This results in a paradigm shift such that it can transform the quality of relationships within an organization.

Temporary social systems to elicit change

A temporary system consists of a workshop or a project group which lasts a finite amount of time. It is constructed and composed in such a way as to elicit and encourage new kinds of behaviour and attitudes in the participants.

Such social systems are usually composed in such a way as to bring together people from different levels within the organization and are non-hierarchical in the sense that participants 'get out of their current position' for the purposes of completing the workshop. There are also recommended procedures for discussing and thinking within the workshop which ensures that there is a high level of equality of participation.

Project groups, also constructed in a non-hierarchical way, have wide representation and are facilitated in a way which emphasizes quality of contribution rather than status or position. Project groups are called *interim systems* because, in their design and structure, they are in between or at the medium point between a completely-changed culture and the existing organization. These projects are the engine room of any change strategy and are also a forum in which the benefits of the workshop on prejudice reduction can be realized.

We also use a steering group mechanism which has mixed representation. At least half the group change every 12 months and it is empowered to manage and promote change within the organization.

Inter-level and inter-group workshops with shop stewards and senior management, engineers and technicians, etc. are also used. Our most often used inter-level workshop is that between senior and middle management. Very often we find a gap here which hinders progress.

These workshops enable each group to build a common vision and identify the goals they have in common and the goals they have in conflict. Quite a lot of work goes on in these workshops on reducing prejudice between the groups in practical ways and also in reducing the fear that each group has of the other.

To give an example, a shop steward/senior management workshop goes through the following process:

1 Each group sharing its vision of how they would like to see the factory within five years.
2 Identifying and recognizing consensus between the shop stewards' group and the senior management group.

   During this phase they are asked to agree which goals they have in common and which goals they believe are in conflict. They then agree a strategy for pursuing the goal they have in common and for figuring out ways of best managing the areas of conflict.
3 Each group gets to work separately in the workshop on what they would like the other group to know and understand about what it is like to be a worker/manager. This information is then shared in a general session in which no argument or disagreements are allowed; each group is invited to listen and understand as deeply as they can what it is like to be in the shoes of the other group, Once the groups have shared their ideas with each other, they are encouraged to ask questions that would enhance their understanding of what it is like to be a member of the other group, i.e. what is good about it and what is hard about the role.
4 Having split into two mixed groups, combining workers and managers in the same group, they are invited to explore what attitudes and prejudices get in the way of their working better together. The trainer then coaches both managers and shop stewards how to work on these attitudes and prejudices.

   Each group is then given the opportunity to work out guidelines which are useful for conducting their business in the future. This leads to a fundamental change in the way both groups do business.

A new leadership perspective

The effect of having a new leadership perspective is that managers tend to define their jobs as:

1 Accomplishing the organizational tasks effectively.
2 The undoing of the cultural conditioning which inhibits the growth of effective leadership at all levels. This means, in particular, undoing

the dynamics which tend to reinforce prejudice towards workers and other leaders within the organization.

It is also clear that there is quite a great deal of prejudice towards leaders within organizations and that this has to be undone in order for people to perform effectively.

Prejudice reduction between nationalities

This work also has wide application when working in intercultural situations. We have used concepts of prejudice and internalized prejudice for working in such settings as:

1 A top management team of a multinational which consisted of French, German, American, Belgian and English managers.
2 Working with a project team including an Irish manufacturing facility and its European-wide sales and marketing.

These have been very successful.

The approach we use is similar to that of reducing prejudice between management and workers and consists of the following steps:

- Pointing out that national identity is not something which people choose, it is something which they find imposed upon them. National identify also contains quite a lot of conditioning which arises from a local identity, namely, a town or a district.
- Encouraging participants to choose again on a conscious level their national identity: 'I choose to be Irish', 'I choose to be Belgian', etc. It is useful to look at what kinds of feelings, ideas, faults and insights the claiming of national identity brings up for each person. You may also find that there can be a great deal of denial in relation to the impact of national identity on a person's behaviours, thoughts and feelings. It is useful to encourage people to reconsider the fact that national identity has a fairly big impact on how they behave in relation to other cultures and within their own culture.

The most important part of this work is encouraging each person to identify and appreciate what they like most about their cultural background, particularly in relation to what kind of benefits and contributions their cultures have made to them personally in terms of character, personality traits and competences.

The use of the concept of internalized prejudice is most important in reducing blockages between different cultures. We have found that working with multinational groups on undoing the internalized prejudice which arises from their particular national identity is very productive. It also has a very powerful effect on removing stereotyping (at least temporarily) so that each person sees the other as the person they are, rather than as an embodiment of the national identity.

General conclusions

All of the work in this area is far more extensive than we have space to go into here. Generally speaking we can say that at least three out of five cases of working on reducing prejudice between management and workers have been successful and have made a distinctive difference to the organization. Most of the unsuccessful cases have been due to one of two basic errors:

1 Our own lack of expertise, insight and understanding of the dynamics of the particular situation.
2 A lack of constancy of purpose, particularly during the period 6 to 9 months after getting started. This is usually the period when most of the big difficulties arise and it is quite important for the management to remain constant in their purpose during these difficult times. Management who have done this have reaped rich rewards.

In conclusion, the intercultural work has been quite successful at giving managers real insight into the dynamics of national identity and how it influences both them and their relationships with people from other countries. We have found that having an intercultural event, in itself, has been enough to make significant changes in the quality of the work being done by people from different nations.

Further reading

Technical Bulletin No. 15–*Leadership as a decision*, available from the author on request.

Introduction to Chapter 11

'Leading and facilitating international teams', by Sue Canney Davison, holds a magnifying glass up to the processes and elements of team building. It is filled with detailed guidelines and examples of 'how' team leaders and facilitators can build multicultural teams. It also highlights the crucial issues which practitioners need to investigate before embarking on team-building activities. Her guidelines are based on an extensive research project which analysed teams and task forces in large multinational organizations.

Effective cross-cultural teams need similar group skills as single culture groups, but they are more complex and will therefore require 'three times' longer to prepare and implement. The added complexity relates to eight cultural and organizational factors including:

- The degree of similarity that exists between the cultural norms of the individuals within the group.
- The level of fluency in the common language.
- Cultural differences in preferred leadership styles.
- The status of different cultures within the organization.

Procedures for handling these issues are illustrated within the context of the need to manage the phases of group development. These procedures rely on understanding team issues and concerns, potential conflict areas and cultural differences that are likely to emerge during a given phase. The failure to work through these issues is likely to result in a polite stand-off in which issues are avoided, with domination by one subgroup resulting in bad feelings by others or the exclusion of team members. Success should result in a high level of team work and synergy. The strong 'moral' of this story is to start slow and prepare thoroughly in order to finish fast, rather than starting quickly but not finishing at all.

11 Leading and facilitating international teams

Sue Canney Davison

Do international teams require different facilitation skills to national teams? Research and experience suggest they do. This chapter sets out to explain why and illustrate some of these skills. The research findings come from two large research projects. The first project featured video analysis of the cultural processes in 23 teams in European and East Asian multinationals. The second project consisted of in-depth interviews of 17 teams to elicit the strategic focus and human resource (HR) needs of transnational teams and a survey of staffing, processes, rewards and outcomes in 30 transnational teams in multinationals from all three trading blocs. This chapter will focus mainly on the role of the team leader with additional comments for external facilitators. Above all, the intention is to get across three main features of facilitating international teams successfully:

1 The need to manage eight cultural and organizational factors that differentiate international teams from national teams.
2 Recognition that the effect of these factors on the team's dynamics means that three times as much preparation is needed to lead international teams effectively than for national teams.
3 There are effective procedures that international teams can utilize at each stage of their life cycle to overcome any cross national and organizational difficulties and which increase the chance of benefiting from the diversity.

Throughout this chapter, 'team' is defined as a group of people working towards a common goal. Many employees work in loosely-coupled international networks or work groups and regard the word team as too strong. They would point out that often the membership is fluid, below the overall corporate mission the goals are numerous and being asked to do 'team building' is perceived as the training department being over-zealous. These networks do have specific difficulties such as, in achieving mutual accountability, communication flow matrices and local problem solving. Despite these specific reservations, the factors and procedures explored in this chapter are relevant even though a given group may not fit into a tidy life-cycle framework or organizational permanence.

The first question most people ask about international teams is: 'Are they only more complex versions of national teams, or are they something completely different?' The reason for asking is usually to find out if incorporating some cross-cultural awareness into regular team-building programmes will work for these teams as well as for the national ones. Over eight years' experience working with these teams does show that international teams need to practise the same generic 'team basics' as national teams and so far the difference seems to be in degrees of complexity rather than substance. Often the levels of complexity and the resulting logistics are much greater than most mangers and team members anticipate.

Many international project leaders are technicians or experts who 'don't have time for the soft stuff'. Before starting any facilitation or training programme, the organization needs to calculate and benchmark the cost benefits of improving the interaction of their teams. For instance, one company calculated that the daily standing cost of each of its product development teams was $150 000. If one department takes two days to send out a report that could have gone out the same day, that is a $300 000 delay. They also calculated that each of their best selling products make around $3 million a day profit for the company at peak sales periods. With the corporate aim of cutting development time from 12 to 5 or 7 years, project leaders are beginning to realize the enormous earning power of improving their teams' interaction and avoiding difficulties before they arise. Spending a few days agreeing the task and process ground rules falls into perspective.

The uniqueness of international teams

The dynamics of all teams will be affected by the personalities, levels of knowledge and experience, differing levels of status, motivation and attitudes of the individuals involved, as well as by the team and organizational characteristics, and the nature and structure of the task. Leaders need to know something about all of these in advance. As one experienced human resource director pointed out, the nature and structure of the task may strongly influence any one individual's role and their level of motivation. The resulting power plays within the team can lead to uncharacteristic behaviour that can disguise cultural differences or overemphasize them if the power struggle falls across national boundaries. Both these possibilities stress the need for the extra preparation in international teams due to the added cultural and organizational factors that influence the team dynamics.

The factors in the composition of international teams that affect the team dynamics and performance are divided into cultural and organizational factors and are listed below.

Cultural factors:

F1   The degree of difference or similarity that exists between the cultural norms of the individuals within the group
F2   The degree to which individuals might manifest their cultural norms
F3   The level of fluency in the common language
F4   The different expectations about what constitutes effective group behaviour with a team and different communication styles
F5   Culturally different leadership styles

Organizational factors:

F6   The status of different cultures within the organization
F7   The geographic spread of the team members
F8   The similarity or difference between functional and professional 'cultures'

Cultural factors   The boundaries between national culture, ethnicity and regional cultures are hard to define. Culture and ethnicity are expressed through language; cognitive preferences; values; beliefs; status; artefacts; behavioural, occupational and functional norms—that is, both internal and externally-visible criteria. This chapter supposes that cultural norms around these factors are internalized by individuals while growing up within a certain cultural group and are then manifested through their individual thinking, values and behaviour. There is little agreement about what can be ascribed to culture and what to personality. All of these factors will probably affect how an individual responds in a particular group setting. However, it is not yet possible to prioritize or predict which of the above factors will have the most effect in any one team. That said, it is useful to identify five factors that arise from cultural differences that will affect the team dynamics in international teams as opposed to national ones.

F1: degrees of similarity between cultural norms of individuals within groups   Large differences, such as between Japanese and Kazaks or French and mainland Chinese, enhance the potential for richer solutions, but they may also cause greater communication difficulties within the team—and not just through having to use a second language or interpreters. One common trap is to assume that compared to a Japanese/Italian team, the British and Americans, or Dutch and Belgians, will have no difficulty working together. Experience in companies such as Wellcome on US/UK teams and BP Oil Europe on Dutch/Belgian teams have historically proved otherwise.

Hofstede (1980) and Torbiorn (1982) have both attempted to quantify degrees of difference between whole cultures, but such quantification is difficult to apply at the individual level. One reason is that individuals may express their supposed cultural norms to greater or lesser degrees.

F2: degree to which individuals may manifest their cultural norms

In some people, international exposure or different life experiences will mean that they only loosely identify with or manifest their original national cultural norms. In contrast, others may identify very strongly and be quite inflexible. Cultural norms have traditionally been established by taking some dimensions—such as how individually- or collectively-oriented an individual is—and collecting data from large numbers of people from one nationality and comparing them with other national groups. The national norm is expressed as the peak of a normal distribution. However, any one individual may be anywhere on that distribution, especially in nationalities which are not very 'cultural' homogeneous such as China, India and the USA, which can differ enormously coast to coast and north to south.

Individuals also adapt their behaviour to different situations and people in different ways, creating more variety or greater similarity. Global companies may select people who fit in with the corporate culture rather than represent their national norms, creating unrepresentative homogeneity across nationalities. Bicultural minorities may adapt their behaviours to the majority norms, but retain their own internal cultural preferences. So knowing what passport someone carries and a list of behavioural norms for those nationalities will not predict what could take place in any one international team. That said, legitimizing differences and discovering similarities is a key part of preparing a team to work together.

F3: levels of fluency in the common language

It is very difficult even for fluent common language speakers to interrupt mother tongue speakers using idioms at full speed. Experience shows that a team can adjust to one non-fluent speaker, but has difficulty including two or more. The language medium chosen will also imply norms for interrupting and gaining entry into the conversation (see Canney Davison, 1994). These can easily exclude second language speakers. For instance in their mother tongues, Japanese, Italians and Americans all like to talk a lot at the same time; the Japanese to build a synchronous and harmonious rhythm, the Italians to show involvement and feeling and the Americans usually to interrupt each other. However, Japanese and other nationalities working in English under US or UK norms in US/UK companies, usually wait for a pause, just as Finns do in any language.

People also respond differently in different languages, even if they are fluent. One young international team in Daimler Benz discovered that their boss seemed far more friendly and amenable when she spoke English rather than her native German. Despite all being fluent in German, whenever they wanted a favour they asked for the meeting to be run in English.

F4: different expectations of effective group behaviour

As well as language, cultural conditioning will also affect communication styles and expectations about how the team can best work together. In one team, a Nigerian kept asking if the whole team could work through the problem together. Rather than recognize a different approach, a nearby Norwegian rebuffed his suggestions with comments like, 'don't be ridiculous, there are six of us, we would all end up arguing' or 'that would waste four people's time'. Although the Nigerian contributed a lot during the course of the teamwork, his input was regarded as repetitive and disruptive.

National team members can more easily assume that they share similar expectations and norms about the most effective way to work together. International teams have to bring them to the surface, and rework and agree them so that everyone is involved.

F5: culturally different leadership styles

Despite what has been written in search of a universal leadership style, in some cultures, especially those where authority is often ascribed, e.g. Latin America, the Middle East, Asia, (see Trompenaars, 1993), team leaders are expected to direct the interaction and take final decisions. They may also be appointed because of their higher level of influence within the organization, rather than their higher level of technical or managerial expertise in the task. On the other hand in North America, Scandinavia and Northern European cultures, the most effective style is more participative and low key and the team leaders are more likely to have earned their positions because of their expertise. The leaders need to agree the appropriate style within the team and be flexible. The leadership style will also determine how much an external facilitator can intervene and guide the team.

These are the main factors that will be directly affected by the different cultural conditioning of the team members. There are also three organizational factors that will affect teams in companies working across geographic boundaries.

Organizational factors

F6: the status of different cultures within the organization

Different nationalities may have different levels of status within the company. If an Italian company has acquired a US company, the Italians are likely to assume higher status. Managers from the company headquarters—or in some companies, the 'international' managers—are often seen as having more status than managers from the regional offices. Preferential treatment or promotion of HQ nationals in companies espousing to be international can lead to resentment and frustration that can come out in international teams.

In one well-established European joint venture, people from the two European HQ cultures were subtly regarded as better educated and more experienced. As a result, people from South-East Asia and Africa would routinely get the 'do you understand what we are talking about?' treatment in response to potentially creative suggestions.

In a newly-established Pan-European marketing team in a large Anglo-

Dutch multinational, a German was appointed the leader because Germany had the largest sales volume and the other managers were ranked accordingly. The managers from the smaller national operations were afraid that they would not be listened to and that inappropriate procedures would be imposed.

While these are not cultural differences as such, they are organizational issues that affect the perceived status of different nationalities within the company. This, in turn, seems to increase or decrease the motivation, participation and expectations of team members. As such status is not always correlated to an individual's skills and knowledge about the task, the team can easily ignore good people and allow less competent people to dominate 'just because they come from HQ'.

F7: the geographic spread of team members

Geographic spread affects teams in a number of ways. Team members from different geographic locations can have very different levels of local management support for their work in the team, creating imbalances in possible involvement. If most, but not all, of the team is in one place, a subgroup may be created within the team unless there is a commitment continuously to involve those further away. Each team needs to create its own particular pattern between face-to-face meetings and working apart that keeps the team working closely. For instance, investing in compatible IT systems to communicate information across distances and leaving the 'hot stuff' for face-to-face meetings means that, whatever the geographic spread, meeting times are used effectively and no one person feels left out of the growing emotional bonding of the team.

Small and large Scandinavian companies, such as the Finnish company Mcgregor and the Swedish/Swiss giant ABB, have learnt to operate effectively with mobile headquarters and top executive teams dispersed across large geographic distances.

F8: differences between functional and professional 'cultures'

If the team members are all from the same technical discipline, it can cut a swath across national differences and allow a team to find strong common ground before branching out to profit from their different experiences and skills. However, even within the same technical disciplines and languages, teams may need to spend a long time understanding the national differences in professional and daily terminologies, for example, the USA 'trades' and the UK 'deals' in finance and the UK has 'critical success criteria' and the USA 'vivid descriptions' in setting objectives. In daily usage, the British 'car boot' is an American 'trunk', 'bonnets' are 'hoods', US 'verbiage' means 'words' as opposed to the derogatory sense of 'irrelevant excess' in the UK—to highlight a few of the many.

Outcomes from the interplay of these factors

The interplay of these eight factors creates the typical difficulties found in international teams. These can range from underestimating the initial time needed to agree on the task and how to do it, through failing to introduce each other properly, to not allowing for jet lag, airport delays, travelling logistics and food and beverage preferences. A common 'after meeting' phrase tends to be, 'I do no understand what these guys are up to, I thought we had agreed ...' as people wished they had taken detailed minutes. It is common in many cultures to use 'Yes' to show that you have heard, not that you have necessarily agreed; to clarify, one British manager suggested his Finnish colleagues say, 'Yes Yes' when they agreed to an action point. Often this lack of post-meeting congruence is the result of rushing into the task while wrongly assuming similarity—that 'things work the same over there'.

The seriousness of these misunderstandings can range from different interpretations of specific actions and timing to different interpretations of whole strategies or leadership roles, or differences in style. One American proposed 'redoing the team model' and produced a two-page fax with one- to three-word phrases such as 'process analysis periods', 'reformulations' and 'co-site facilitation'. In contrast, in one German subsidiary the resulting manual for filling in the travel expense forms was 120 pages long. Such things can happen anywhere.

Aside from these task outcomes, four common process outcomes of the interactions within international teams can be discerned (see Fig. 11.1):

- polite stand-off
- one subgroup dominating
- one or two people being excluded
- achieving interactive synergy where 'the sum of the parts is greater than the whole'

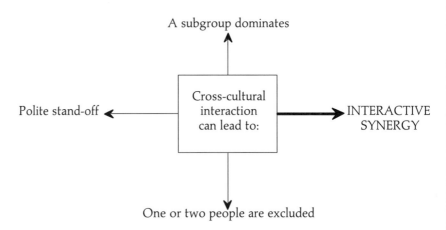

Figure 11.1 *Four common process outcomes of the interactions within international teams*

1 **Polite stand-off.**   Effective teams can only be polite for so long. If the team members do not bring their differences to the surface and rework them, the team will lose motivation and commitment. In one Paris-based consortium, two managing directors, one French and one German, had learned to accommodate each other's different managerial styles but had not delved deeply into the different vested interests of their parent companies. The vital consortium they headed fell apart.

2 **One sub-group dominates.**   This outcome is common when there is a large HQ national subgroup and if the mother tongue is the common language being used. In the case of an Italian acquisition of a US tractor firm, the heated debates at the main meetings would happen in fast idiomatic Italian and not English, the official common language. The gist would then be translated for the few Americans, who felt that they missed the important points and never quite knew what was going on.

A higher number of one nationality does not necessarily imply that the subgroup will dominate. In a weekly meeting in Hong Kong, the strict rotation of mainly Hong Kong Chinese speakers and the lack of interruptions meant that everyone had their say. In the UK, however, senior managers in one creative taskforce repeated one word or phrase louder and louder until they gained floor space. While they could argue that finishing each other's sentences and all talking at once was a sign of high energy, it was only manageable by fluent or mother tongue speakers who could handle the pattern and pace.

3 **One or two people are excluded.**   Lack of fluency in the common language is the most common cause of exclusion, but sometimes it happens through ignorance and prejudice. A Malaysian woman was working with six English, Dutch, Turkish and Nigerian men. When the men 'spontaneously' split into three pairs, it left her hanging over someone's shoulder. Yet she had the language ability, motivation and expertise to contribute and was asking pertinent questions which they ignored.

Sometimes exclusion happens unintentionally, such as not allowing time for long distance travellers to recover from jet lag. However, one Paris-based company purposefully started their meetings at 8.30 a.m. on Monday mornings so that their English colleague would always be late enough to be presented with a *fait accompli*.

4 **Interactive synergy.**   Synergy requires re-weaving the unique threads of cultural difference into coherent directions and ultimately, a cloth. A team may ignore, accommodate or only tolerate its inherent cultural differences instead of actively working to understand them. However, sooner or later these differences emerge, often creating havoc. Participants need to respect each others' expertise and different cultural backgrounds and create a pattern of interaction that involves everyone.

Some teams have attempted to resolve their differences by dipping all the threads in the same dye, i.e. weaving brown cloth from brown threads by saying something like: 'This is how things are done around here'. Such uniformly 'brown' teams can only respond to brown problems and tasks. However, cloth that looks brown from four feet away can also be woven from separate threads of bright yellow, green, red, blue, black and white threads. By allowing the colours to remain distinct, companies can create brown teams, grey teams, purple teams, turquoise teams, checked teams and flecked teams from the same pool of people.

Interactive synergy is characterized by the team being able to say that they fully utilized all the participants' different skills. The actual mechanics of how it is achieved in all cases is still a matter for in-depth research. On the interactive level of synergy, one team developed a seemingly unconscious pattern of leaving tiny pauses after every three sentences to check that the rest of the team was following. It may sound mechanical but it gave the space for people to come in without needed to interrupt, it flowed smoothly and kept everyone involved. Interactive synergy on a deeper level is possible when any hidden agendas have been cleared and 'strategic moments' worked through. When it is achieved, international teams get a real emotional high.

Strategic moments

While interactive synergy is a plausible goal, previous history and the reasons for the creation of the team often create uncomfortable situations in international teams—what Steve Mitchell, of Wellcome, calls 'strategic moments'. The frequency of them, the severity of discomfort and the implications of how they are handled by the leader or facilitator all seem to be far greater in international teams than national teams.

Imagine a British headquartered company with production facilities in both Korea and around Europe. The perception of the Korean production site is that the European site is given all the high quality work and that they would be shut down first if things got tight. They have, therefore, developed a competitive strategy of making sure they stay ahead of the European operations in R&D. This means they usually do not share what they are doing until it is a *fait accompli*. The UK-based company wants to be the first to market with three types of global receiver. A meeting is held with all the R&D heads from around the world.

Common goals and targets are soon agreed. However, when it comes to revealing how far each site has developed any of the three receivers, only the names of the top R&D executives world-wide are given. When it comes to developing an action plan, nobody from the Korean team is participating. The German R&D director gets up and walks out of the room, taking the British product management director with him. The team has reached a 'strategic moment'.

If the leader or facilitator knows the history, was expecting the stand-off and can lead the team through this moment, the likelihood is that old corporate patterns and years of antagonism and vested interests can be broken down. So while they may be extremely uncomfortable, strategic moments are also great opportunities for changing unworkable corporate habits. In fact, the team will be energized and enthused by the release of all the potential energy that was held in previous dysfunctional patterns. When cultural prejudices, ignorance and stereotyping are included in such a scenario, one can see why international teams tend to go through emotional and traumatic processes and key strategic moments before they start to benefit from their diversity. In a similar situation to the example above, pointing out that the German R&D director had probably walked out in frustration and asking what the team wanted to do about it—i.e. making the event conscious—triggered open admission of the internal competition and a team commitment to do something about it.

It is the leader's or facilitator's responsibility to get the team through such moments in the most creative way possible. The form of a strategic moment can vary from highly charged, 'over the top' emotional discharges to completely stony silences that are equally hard to work through. Courage, persistence, humour and, sometimes, temporary deviation are all useful strategies that leaders and facilitators can adopt. The strange combination of a personal thick skin and yet high sensitivity to what is going on is also very valuable. For instance, when being stonewalled by a Finnish group silence you can insist that, due to your cultural ignorance, you need to have the silence interpreted. Emotional outpourings and frustrations can be met by quiet acknowledgement and gentle feedback about someone's perspective and values. In response to an emotional outburst, one American facilitator suggested that if the group had not yet quite reached the creative conflict stage, they could ask the executive to take a walk and come back in 15 minutes when his contribution might fit in better.

Gaining knowledge of the eight cultural organizational factors, getting to know the history of teams' origins, and anticipating common task and process related difficulties and what any strategic moments may look like is the purpose of the extra 'three times one' preparation. By using effective procedures to manage the eight factors at each stage of the life cycle, the team leader stands a good chance of creating an interactive synergy from the diversity in the team and turning strategic moments into constructive breakthroughs. In listing these effective procedures, this final section will also identify which of the eight factors need to be attended to at each stage and whether each procedure affects, predominantly, the completion of the task or the interaction and involvement of the team members.

Managing team life cycles

The lives of some teams span decades and others only a few months. However, all teams will have a set-up phase, first meetings, a middle phase of activities and an ending (see Fig. 11.2). Team leaders will be there from the beginning and, in an ideal world, so should external facilitators. There are effective procedures that international teams can use at each stage of their life cycle. Eighteen procedures that can improve both the task and interactive processes are listed below.

For those beginning to work on international team process, the five most important ones, i.e. that can create the greatest improvement if they are not already being done, have been ranked as they appear in the life cycle. They are:

- **Rank 1** developing and agreeing the purpose of the team with the sponsors
- **Rank 2** clarifying the task
- **Rank 3** setting the process ground rules with the team
- **Rank 4** maintaining the involvement and passing on the learning to the rest of the organization
- **Rank 5** reviewing the learning within the team

These are the same basics as for any team, but made more essential by the complexity of cultural and organizational factors. For further clarity, each factor is marked indicating whether it improves the ability to complete the task directly or improves the interaction that the team needs in order to achieve high performance on the task.

Phase One: the start-up phase

Most of the preparation work before the first meeting will affect both the task and process. In particular it should give the team leader or facilitator an insight into where the team lies across all the eight factors and enable them to be prepared for potential difficulties.

- **Rank 1   Develop and agree the purpose of the team with the sponsors (mainly task related)**   The team leader and sponsors need to painstakingly clarify the mission, purpose, agenda, accountability, time frame, resources available and key stakeholders. The use of Metaplan (see Habershon, 1993) can be helpful in bringing out the different ways in which individuals understand the goal and task. Metaplan is a well structured and low technology group brainstorming and prioritizing technique that makes everyone's contributions visual and helps to prevent anyone dominating or being excluded from the process.
- **Establish and understand the reasoning behind the composition of the team (process related)**   The team composition could be based on complementary skills, similar functional background, certain positions within the company or political manœuvring. The leader can ascertain areas of similarity and differences, tension or cohesion from understanding the rationale behind the team's composition.

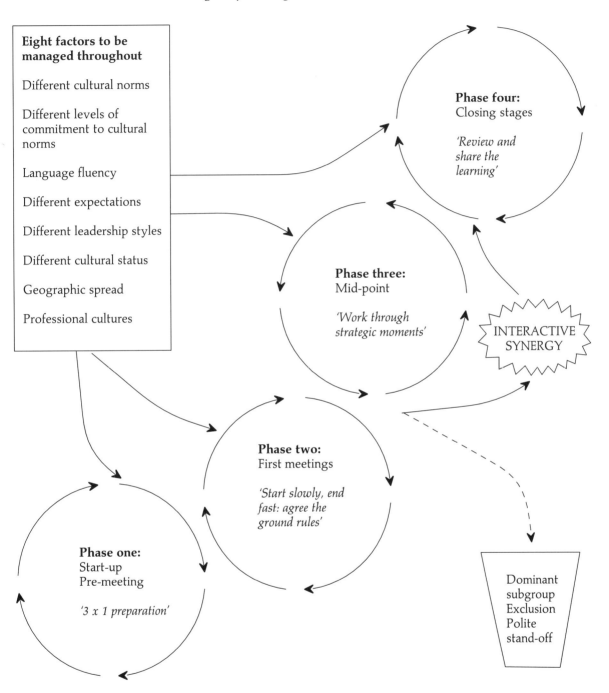

Eight factors to be managed throughout

Different cultural norms

Different levels of commitment to cultural norms

Language fluency

Different expectations

Different leadership styles

Different cultural status

Geographic spread

Professional cultures

Phase four: Closing stages

'Review and share the learning'

Phase three: Mid-point

'Work through strategic moments'

INTERACTIVE SYNERGY

Phase two: First meetings

'Start slowly, end fast: agree the ground rules'

Phase one: Start-up Pre-meeting

'3 x 1 preparation'

Dominant subgroup Exclusion Polite stand-off

Figure 11.2 *An international team's life cycle*

- **Interview the key players (mainly process related)**   Elicit participants' understanding of the task, their attitude towards each other and their level of commitment. Are all the members equally accountable for the outcome? It can be useful to send around a short questionnaire asking participants about their expectations about the task, the strengths and weaknesses, potential hot spots and their own contribution.
- Some leaders and facilitators find it useful to ask would-be team members to fill in personality tests or team roles questionnaires and to process these before the team first meets. Simplicity and cultural relevance is the key to the results actually being used creatively by an international team as a feedback tool to improve their own performance.
- **Decide if you need an external facilitator and contract with the sponsors and team, clarifying the boundaries of responsibility and the facilitator's role (process related)**   This is an opportunity to decided what level of facilitation skills is needed for that particular team and whether to use external or internal help. The key issues to look at when making that decision are as follows:

1 Are the team members coming with conflicting agendas where a neutral person would aid common agreement?
2 Does the team leader need to be heavily involved in technical detail of the task so that it will be difficult to also attend to process?
3 What is the level of experience and confidence of the team leader in managing an international team and with the particular nationalities involved?

Expense should not be a consideration. Good facilitators will pay for themselves many times over if the team would otherwise have difficulties. Many teams have rejected a facilitator only to have to start again when they have reached a stalemate. There is also no fixed role for a facilitator. A team leader may ask a facilitator to be there for the first one or two sessions just to observe and give feedback. It should be noted that, on the whole, the effectiveness of a facilitator depends on the level of clarity of the role, not on the content of role itself. Some companies suggest that facilitators should only participate if the team asks for help. This does not work. The facilitator who has no mandate to guide when the team hits a strategic moment will then be blamed for being ineffective.

Key team members, the leader and/or facilitator and key sponsors need to go through the agenda for the first meetings, checking to see that the proposed exercises will be new, culturally and organizationally relevant and pitched at the right level of experience. **Clarify the administrative support (process related)**   Collate and distribute necessary documentation, pre-reading and support facilities. View and book the venue, and the social and culinary arrangements.

It is impossible to stress enough that team leaders and external facilitators need to get this stage of the preparations right. The leader or facilitator is the easiest target for any frustration and anger. For instance, one colleague and I had feedback from a team saying 'the facilitators were seeking conflict'. We thought that the only message being put across was to develop the synergy between the two companies. Because only two key players had been interviewed before the meeting, we had not unearthed the waiting explosion of frustration and anger around confused organizational boundaries, loyalties and trust; I learned the need for extensive preparation the hard way

Phase two: the first meetings

In the first meetings, take the time to make sure that everybody is agreed and comfortable about the task, process, the context and organizational implications before heading into exclusively task related activities. This will avoid difficulties later on and save time. A useful adage is: 'start slowly and end fast; start fast and maybe not end at all' (see Fig. 11.3). Regarding the interactive process, if a subgroup is going to dominate or one or two people are going to be excluded, it is usually apparent from the beginning. Polite stand-offs cannot be seen clearly until the mid-phase, as some people take longer to be comfortable with the group and the group process. The building blocks for interactive synergy need to be set in place at this point, although the process itself will develop in the mid phase.

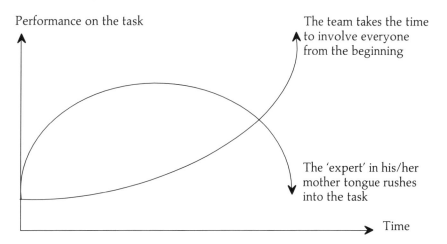

Performance on the task

The team takes the time to involve everyone from the beginning

The 'expert' in his/her mother tongue rushes into the task

Time

Figure 11.3 *Start slowly and end fast; start fast and maybe not end at all*

- **Rank 2   At the first set of meetings, work through identifying, prioritizing and agreeing the mission, purpose, objectives and key success criteria (task related working on factor 4)**   This is the what, why, how, and what it should look like when the team gets there. The focus is on accessing the fourth cultural factor of different expectations about how the team can work together effectively. It is important to use a process that brings out the different approaches and agendas that people have come with and that allows discussion and agreement. Metaplan (Habershon, 1993), Team net tools (Lipnack and Stamps, 1993), and Groupware (Johansen et al., 1991) are supporting tools that can help. All are brainstorming, prioritizing and goal setting processes: Metaplan uses cards and boards, Team net and Groupware use computer programmes that respectively structure the process and prioritize ideas.

- **Emphasize building the relationship within the team face to face in the these early stages (process related, working on factors 1 and 2)**   If the Anglo-Saxon rush off into the task, Latin and Middle Eastern team members may remain silent because the proper introductions have not yet been made. The Anglo-Saxons may be culturally informed and yet still come across as patronizing—saying, 'well, we had better introduce ourselves' while tapping the table with a pencil. The team may need two or three initial meetings with social activities in order to build working relationships.

- **Rank 3   Openly share the strengths and weaknesses of the team based on the balance or imbalance of the eight factors outlined in the first part of this chapter and any questionnaires that have been used (process related, working particularly on factors 1, 2, 5 and 8)**   One of the first tasks is to recognize the similarities or differences in professional cultures, discuss the leadership style and then specifically work to legitimize cultural similarities and differences and to introduce a common cultural framework. Putting in agreed and culturally appropriate modes of feedback will enable the team to work through any strategic moments caused by cultural differences in the mid-phase.

Both Hofstede's (1980) and Fons Trompenaars's (1993) frameworks of how different cultures vary across certain value dimensions are readily available as common frameworks. By adding in items such as preferred types of feedback, interruption patterns and ways of communicating pleasure and displeasure, they can cover most of the factors that will affect the team processes. One way to introduce these frameworks is to put each value dimension or communication style on a flip chart around the wall, colour code the nationalities and the organizational differences with stickers and assist the team members to plot themselves. It can be interesting to ask them to put how they would ideally *like it to be* as well as how they think *it is* in their organization. This gives an instantaneous visual picture which the team can then discuss in detail. For instance, if some people think that individuals should make final decisions and others prefer group consensus, a discussion of the reasons for the different preferences and a workable team approach can be forthcoming without either side feeling that theirs is the right or wrong approach. Sometimes the whole team prefers direct feedback but marks the organization as high on indirect feedback. The discrepancy can give rise to an interesting discussion about how the team will find out how it is performing.

These discussions form the basis of intercultural awareness and sensitivity within the team. If team leaders and members are sensitive to them, this one of the key skills that team members can develop on international teams that they cannot in national teams. Lack of these sensitivities, especially in the team leader, can result in some very upset members who become excluded by the dominant cultural norms.

Sensitive yet provocative team building exercises are also very helpful for creating some understanding and curiosity about each other's cultures. One UK manager, used to getting down to business straight away, was asked to role play a culture for whom social interaction was the primary basis for doing business. She was shocked to find that she could not imagine how to start the business negotiations and stay in role. This immediately started a dialogue. Becoming aware of these differences highlights the need to spend time agreeing a common way of working as well as the loss to the team if only one culture dictates the team norms.

A strategy for working with different levels of language fluency also needs to be established at this point so that, along with the differences in national status, it does not start creating subgroup dominance or exclusion of one or two people in the mid-phase of the team.

- **The final task of the team at this stage is to agree the first set of action plans (task and process related, working on factors 4 and 7)** The team needs to agree the what, who and when of tasks to be done before the next meeting and, most importantly, to agree a communication charter for how the team will exchange information when they are apart. This charter should specifically aim at how to manage the geographical spread. This often prompts companies to become serious about establishing global E-mail and standard software packages. Mike Brimm of Insead has noticed that, while seeming impersonal, imposing a more disciplined interaction into video conferences can in fact help teams to structure in their subsequent face-to-face meetings more effectively.

One team spent three 2-day sessions over 3 months completing this part of the cycle. It paid off 18 months later when they hit serious interpersonal problems. Although it seems counter-intuitive to action-orientated Americans, British and Scandinavians, teams that start slowly, speed up exponentially towards the end. The message again is: start slowly and end fast; start fast and maybe not end at all.

Phase three: mid-phase Keep reviewing what you are doing and align it to the task.

- **Rank 4   Make sure that everyone is involved and uses the feedback tools established at the beginning (task and process related, working on factors 3 and 6)**   Equal involvement does not have to equate with everyone speaking the same amount. It depends on individual feelings and whether the team is accessing and using the variety of skills available. Participation and involvement also needs to be carefully defined. Research in Hong Kong and Australian banks showed that although the Hong Kong Chinese employees would wait to be asked for their opinions, their language and criticism of their managers was more direct than the Australians. The Australian employees would volunteer suggestions, but they would use more disclaimers and 'hedges', while the managers used more loaded questions to bias the discussions towards the outcomes they wanted (see Lee, 1993).

  This is the time for the team leader to work hard to create an interactive synergy based on the positive process-related steps taken in the first meetings and to use them to guide the team through any difficulties. Preliminary research findings do suggest that in teams dominated by Anglo-Saxons, paying some attention to the process creates more even participation and higher levels of satisfaction. Given the different cultural styles of participation, the team leader will need to use a variety of strategies to balance the input into the group.

  Detailed observation and video feedback can highlight just how much one or two members are being excluded and the mechanisms by which older people are dominating the process. The leader needs to pay attention to the effects of different levels of language fluency, especially with differences in written and spoken English abilities, and also to the effect of different nationalities assuming different levels of status. As the team comes under pressure for action, the potential for strategic moments is greatly increased in this phase.

- **Keep a check on the timing, space the milestones and use the time apart to its full potential (task related)**   Teams tend to go through bursts of activity rather than producing a steady flow and so it is helpful to spread out the milestones and keep a check on the timing. It is sensible to put in process reviews in the lulls between bursts of activity on the task. Computer-generated realities and Groupware can allow the exchange and manipulation of data and reports in different time zones. Using the time apart for information exchange means that expensive time together can be devoted to resolving difficult decisions and interpersonal difficulties, although sometimes time apart may allow people to cool down and rethink their approaches.

- **It is important to communicate what is being achieved and to broadcast successes as they emerge (process related, working on factor 4)**   Teams need to think about whether their interim outputs are in the right format to be read and shared, i.e. not sending out a 40-page report without a summary. It may take some revisiting of the vision and objectives and fine tuning and adjustments. Communicating successes as they arise can maintain the interest and involvement of the sponsors. External inputs and different viewpoints can also help to prevent stagnation during this mature phase. Team leaders are advised to use anything (in good taste!) that will keep the motivation up at this point.

- **Introducing relevant task skills (task related)**   This stage can be a good time to introduce problem solving, decision making and creative conflict techniques, and to revisit these processes from different cultural perspectives.
- **Leaders sharing control and facilitators reducing their presence (process related)**   If it is culturally appropriate, by this time, leaders and particularly facilitators should be controlling events as little as necessary.

Figure 11.4 shows the possible relative levels of contribution of the team, team leader, sponsors and external facilitators. The role of external facilitators is to enable the team to enhance and develop its own performance, hence, after a lot of initial input, their presence should diminish. Currently many international teams call in facilitators as troubleshooters when they hit 'strategic moments' which does not foster the ongoing learning which would have occurred had they been there from the beginning. With or without facilitation help, after a lot of initial input, the team leader's control should be increasingly shared by the whole team, who all need to be accountable for the outcomes. The sponsors' main roles are to clarify the initial terms of reference and to give their feedback at the end.

Phase four: closing phase

- **Make sure everyone stays involved to the end (process related)**   There is a tendency to let team working collapse as the deadline presses, especially to decide that the cost of involving members from far away is too great. This can undo a lot of earlier team-building efforts and breed cynicism in those who feel suddenly excluded.
- **Rank 5   Review the learning within the team (process related)**   This is the most important part of wrapping up. Teams will only be able to work together better in the future if they can learn from their mistakes and can share their successes. One idea I have practised with other colleagues is asking each team to draw their process on large white boards with lots of coloured pens. Unlike the accepted linear pattern of forming, storming, norming and performing (Tuckman, 1965), the teams usually draw their processes with large ups and downs, circles and side branches. They often have light bulbs being suddenly switched on or suns emerging when one particular idea or helpful person broke through a thunderously dark cloud and clarified a direction. Rivers, boats and aeroplanes often

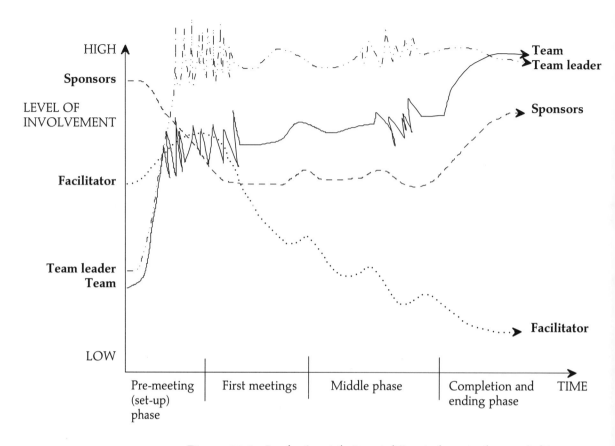

Figure 11.4   *Levels of contribution at different phases in the group's life*

figure, carrying the teams across the landscape, sea or sky. Sometimes the process has transformed a small confused grounded biplane into a sleek seven-seater jet fighter at 30 000 ft, or has built two sorry-looking meagre hamburgers and a hot dog into a triple layered big Mac.

The more serious in-depth part of the review should be formalized, revisiting each stage of both the task and the process within the life cycle. Written questionnaires and checklists can be helpful. After 4 months of project work, through answering a written questionnaire, a Finn was able to express his unhappiness with the team's interaction style. He had previously staged a protest by remaining silent for a whole meeting. Unfortunately nobody had noticed. So also using such questionnaires in the mid-phase can sometimes bring out unnoticed exclusion before it is too late.

Getting external feedback and evaluation on the outcome is also vital to benchmarking the team's performance. One team felt it had had a very difficult and turbulent time. However, when they got very positive feedback on their output from the board, they began to change to way they felt about their difficulties and see them more as bouts of constructive conflict.

- **Celebrate the success and plan for the future (task and process related)** This means laying out an action plan of how the results can be fully implemented and evaluated. It is one thing to celebrate within the team, another to creatively broadcast and celebrate the successes within the company. Reintegration of team members into other jobs is another critical task of this phase.

- **The team needs to pass on what it has learned to the rest of the organization (task and process related)** Herr Obermeier was a senior director in the Eurofighter consortium. He was involved in the project from its inception in 1976, lobbying the four governments as well as training a Spanish engineer how to use specific bits of German technology. He was multilingual and able to function at many levels. When asked what would happen after he leaves, he thought a moment and then said, 'When I leave, all my experience goes with me and when they start another project they often will make the same mistakes'. He thought again for a while and said, 'Maybe the universities could capture the learning and pass it back into the organization'. Clearly it is more cost-effective for companies to learn from themselves.

Consciously learning the skills needed to lead, facilitate and participate in these teams will enable any one of the team leaders to be effective leaders and facilitators in other teams. This systematic spreading of skill means that the effectiveness of international teams within the company becomes the line manager's responsibility rather than the responsibility of human resources departments (HR) or external facilitators. At the start of its drive to create high performance in its international teams, Wellcome formed a core HR team and extended network to co-ordinate requests from all over the company for international team facilitation. The aim is to keep the local relationship with particular trainers and to match the skills of the more experienced facilitators with the difficult teams, shadowed by less experienced facilitators; less experienced trainers and line managers will be allowed to learn on easier teams.

Conclusion

This chapter began by differentiating eight factors—five cultural and three organizational—that create the more complex dynamics that can occur in international teams rather than national teams. It then explored four common process outcomes from the greater complexity. The final section looked at useful procedures that can be adopted to manage these factors and to sculpt the complex interaction to achieve high performance and rich solutions on the task.

Alongside the discussion of the dynamics and useful procedures in international teams, there have been hints about the skills that successful leaders and facilitators will need. There is hot debate as to how effective cross-cultural training can be for all individuals. As Andrew Mayo of ICL suggested, some people seem to have a high level of curiosity and purposefully seek out people unlike themselves, while others seem to be much more comfortable with their own kind. Leaders need at least an open mind towards cultural differences and some ability to see the task and process from different points of view. They also need good interpersonal skills, an ability to motivate and include people in a number of different ways, an ability to identify problems appropriately, and a clear and persistent vision of where the team is going. If they are fully involved in the task, they need to understand the facilitator's role and delegate it appropriately. It can be delegated initially to an external person or there may be one or two experienced, or potentially suitable, people on the team.

Successful international facilitators need hands-on experience and many of the same qualities. It is a very active role, involving the capacity to sculpt the team's process to achieve the task as well as to anticipate and steer the team away from difficulties before they arise.

As mentioned at the beginning, many companies do not see themselves as organized into tight teams with clear life cycles. International 'standing' work groups, with expertise called in as needed, often operate loose networks. The tight framework should not put such companies off; the key messages remain the same. Three times one (3 × 1) preparation for meetings; recognizing and acknowledging differences; creating an open atmosphere where problems can be dealt with locally; using a variety of strategies to involve team members, especially temporary members; managing the geographical distance creatively; and finding creative strategies to pass on the learning to the rest of the organization.

Most international networks and teams are created to generate cross-border, cross-function organizational learning within the company or to achieve greater global efficiency. The dynamic interplay between global aims and local styles—similar goals but different ways of getting there—are the sources of the potential energy to be tapped within multinational, multi-ethnic, multi-company and multi-functional teams. The life cycle model only provides the loom. It is up to each team to weave their brightest colours into the finest fabric they can achieve.

Notes

1 The video analysis examined cultural processes in teams in Shell, including Shell Singapore, BP, ICI, Wellcome, Hong Kong Shanghai Bank, Hong Kong Telecom and Jardines as a doctoral research project at London Business School. In the second piece of research, 17 teams were interviewed and 50 more surveyed in companies such as Heineken, Fiat, Fuji Xerox, Alcatel, Wellcome, BP, IBM, Kone, British Airways as part of a research project on transnational teams for The International Consortium for

Executive Education and Research (ICEDR). Co-authors were C. Snow and S. Snell from Penn State University and D. Hambrick from Columbia. This study was completed in November 1993.

2 The life cycle model has emerged from working with teams over the last few years. Special acknowledgement is due to the Wellcome US/UK HR/ Training team who worked with it and enriched it in May 1994.

3 See H.C. Triandis, 'Cross Cultural Industrial and Organizational Psychology' in Triandis et al. (1994).

4 Triandis, op. cit.

5 See Example in Sue Canney Davison 'International teams; avoiding the pitfalls and creating a source of creative strategy' in Garratt (1995), p. 213.

6 See Richard Pascale. (1992) *The art of conflict*, BBC Training video.

7 For instance, Belbin's team roles and managerial grid can work for Anglo-Saxon groups but can be too involved for mixed groups, e.g. involving Asians who have very different managerial priorities and ways of seeing themselves. One such team very successfully used a three-colour learning style approach: red for action orientation, green for people orientation and blue for ideas orientation. They could lightheartedly ask each other to be 'less red and more green' without causing offence.

References and further reading

Canney Davison, S. (1994) 'Creating a high performance international team', *Journal of Management Development*, vol. 13, no. 2, pp. 81–90.

Garratt, R. (ed.) (1995) *Developing Strategic Thought*, McGraw-Hill, London.

Habershon, N. (1993) 'Metaplan: achieving two-ways communications', *Journal of European Industrial Training*, vol. 17, no. 7, pp. 8–13.

Hofstede, G. (1980) *Culture's Consequences*, Sage Publications, London.

Johansen, R., D. Sibbett, S. Benson, A. Martin, R. Mittman and P. Saffo (1991) *Leading Business Teams*, Addison-Wesley Publishing Company, Reading, Mass.

Lee, L.Y.N.T. (1993) 'Discourse modes in participative decision making in Hong Kong and Australian banking contexts'. Unpublished Phd thesis, MacQuarie University, Australia.

Lipnack, J. and J. Stamps (1993) *The TeamNet Factor*, Oliver Wright Publications, Vermont, USA.

Torbiorn, I. (1982) *Living Abroad: Personal adjustment and personnel policy in the overseas setting*, Wiley, London.

Triandis, H.C., M.D. Dunnette and L.M. Hough (eds) (1994) *Handbook of Industrial and Organizational Psychology*, 2nd edn, Vol. 4, Consulting Psychologists Press Inc., Palo Alto, CA.

Trompenaars, F. (1993) *Riding the waves of culture*, Economist Books, London.

Tuckman, B. (1965) 'Development sequences in small groups', *Psychological Bulletin*, vol. 63, pp. 384–99.

Introduction to Chapter 12

'Facilitation skills for cross-cultural team building', by Mel Berger focuses on the role of the trainer/consultant in helping people to develop cross-cultural awareness. The aim is to summarize some of the key facilitation issues which have been discussed in other chapters and to describe practical techniques. The chapter is organized in three sections.

The first section—by far the largest—explores the role of the facilitator in establishing a learning atmosphere.

The second section summarizes the advantages of a cross-cultural training team and also identifies some of the issues which must be faced and dealt with in order to achieve a collaborative partnership.

The third section describes three distinct learning methodologies: the didactic or lecture approach; the syndicate-based or discussion approach; and the experiential, 'here and now' focused approach. These approaches are shown to relate to cultural preferences.

The facilitator's skill and credibility will make or break most team-building events. Patience, preparation and experience will be the keys to unlocking success.

12 Facilitation skills for cross-cultural team building

Mel Berger

Competence in dealing with people from one's own national culture does not translate directly to effectiveness in a cross-cultural setting. A trainer or consultant, working with a mixed nationality group, may say things that unintentionally reinforce negative stereotypes or may push people to change in ways which run counter to their basic values and their home culture. This will probably result in 'polite' resistance to full participation. The learning process itself is a reflection of cultural norms and preferences. For example, whether emphasis is given to individual openness or team harmony is based on cultural values. Similarly, negotiation strategy can value 'consensus' building or competing.

Many single-culture training events aim at change or the learning of new skills. In contrast, cross-cultural training is more about recognizing and respecting the differences in others. It is about finding ways to utilize the strengths and preferences of people with different backgrounds in order to achieve collaborative solutions to problems or negotiations. It is not about changing deeply-held beliefs.

This chapter will concentre on the special abilities and attitudes that trainers and consultants need in order to promote cross-cultural teamwork. The first section explores the 'here and now' team and communication issues which are generally present when people from different cultures come together, and which can hinder cross-cultural learning. Often these process issues mirror the communication issues one hopes to address. For example, the group may be discussing the importance of listening and respecting the views of others. At the same time, members of one cultural group may be continually interrupting the members of another cultural background group whenever they try to express their views. If this obstacle to communication can be successfully addressed during the training, it will model how to do it in the real world.

This section will also consider the role of the trainer in creating a safe setting to discuss openly cultural differences. If the trainer describes his or her experiences, including difficulties and mistakes, this will make it easier for others to be open. Additionally, it may be easier for a trainer to comment about the behaviour of delegates from the same cultural background as his own. Similarly, it may be less inhibiting for a delegate to ask sensitive questions and trust the answers when the trainer is of the same background.

The second section considers the advantages of a mixed culture training team as a visible demonstration of cross-cultural team work. This section also examines potential difficulties of achieving team work, particularly in relation to different assumptions about how people learn.

The third section starts by examining three training methods didactic, experiential and syndicate-based. Each of these methods will relate to cultural preferences. It then describes different approaches to the design of cross-cultural events based on the cultural learning preferences of delegates.

Cross-cultural dynamics

Whenever people from different cultures meet, the *process* of how they struggle to communicate and understand each other will generally illustrate the most important points about the cross-cultural communication. This will happen both during formal sessions and while having a drink or meal together. Indeed, this 'for real' exploration of one another's opinions, habits and ways of thinking is a powerful source of learning. However, this learning about the international communication process will not happen automatically, simply through having contact, indeed, it is just as likely that culturally-based habits and defences may hinder understanding. The communication process must be carefully managed so that it becomes a source of learning and not a reinforcement of pre-existing biases. This section describes several common cross-cultural dynamics which can restrict learning, together with techniques for handling them. These dynamics include:

- Variable language skills
- Recognition of cultural differences without reinforcing stereotypes
- Different cultural norms about politeness and communication style such as interruption and argumentativeness
- Awareness of how perceived status differences between members of one culture and another can influence communication patterns
- Loyalty towards one's own cultural group

Dealing with these issues can involve the trainer making an input to alert people to the potential communication barrier, offering spontaneous coaching and feedback, structuring an exercise to highlight cross-cultural issues, and setting an example by modelling open communication.

Variable language skills

Where the delegates attending the training event have different native languages, a decision must be taken as to which language to use or whether to rely on interpreters. If they decide to work in a common language, that language is generally English, which immediately gives an advantage to the native English speakers. It will be easier for them to dominate the discussion—to communicate more fluently and to comprehend and respond more quickly. Those who are working in a non-native language will need to concentrate harder to understand and take part in the conversation. Their powers of focus may well expire every few hours, so that they will need more regular breaks to relax.

Communication will require patience and persistence by all parties; all groups must expect to work more slowly. Those with a higher level of language skill must exercise self control in giving those with lesser language skills more time to comprehend and formulate ideas. Conversely, those with less natural language fluency should be prepared to speak out and request clarification where necessary. Unfortunately, people are often too polite or too proud to admit to not understanding. Therefore, it is important to be a careful observer of non-verbal signs of confusion, involvement and disagreement.

The trainer's role in ensuring accurate communication

The trainer's role is to create a sufficiently informal discussion forum to work actively on the language barriers as they arise. The trainer must be aware of language difficulties and raise them to the surface. Listening must be rigorous to detect misunderstandings and to ensure that those with less developed language skills are given their say. This means acting as a referee to ensure fair play in the arena of communication.

This can be done through *coaching* dominant people to slow down their input of ideas and listen to the others. An issue which may surface is that the dominant talker types do not like silences and do not understand that some people are needing that silence to think. Even within the same culture, there are differences in people's speed of response. For example, some people typically 'think before they speak' while others 'jump in at the deep end', thinking as they talk. These differences become divisive where the dominant talkers judge the slow talkers as less intelligent or less prepared, and the slow talkers perceive the dominant talkers as intimidating, rude or unfocused in their presentation. This dynamic also can occur between people of different disciplines, for example the salesperson may accuse the engineer of trying to blind him or her with scientific jargon, while the engineer may label the salesperson as being evasive in his or her answers.

Conceptualizing the communication process

Issues related to language can also be addressed through an *input* which helps people to conceptualize and understand the process. The input can focus on differentiating the communication process where both parties have similar language skills from that used where one party has greater fluency than another in the common language (see Fig. 12.1).

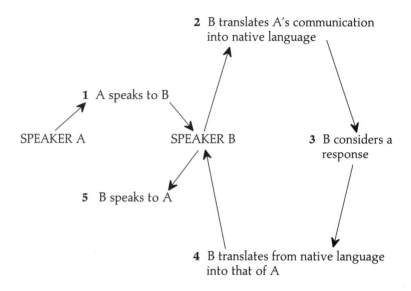

Figure 12.1 *Communication as a five-step process when A talks to B in A's native language*

When both parties are talking in their native language, they will speak and respond fairly quickly, sometimes automatically. In contrast, if you are not used to speaking in a given language you will hear the words, then translate them into your 'home' language, consider your reply, translate back into the language being spoken and, finally, make your reply. This can be a slow process depending on the complexity of and familiarity with what is being discussed. It will be further slowed down if a few of the words are unfamiliar or have more than one meaning.

Cultural differences and stereotyping

One of the most important learning goals of cross-cultural training is the development of awareness and respect for different cultural styles of behaviour and conducting business. In doing this, one must guard against reinforcing negative stereotypes and beware of believing that all members of a given culture will behave in the same way.

The trainer's role in identifying cultural difference

There are several ways of countering these unintended consequences. First, the trainer should *coach* people to describe other cultures in terms which are neutral and descriptive, taking care to avoid labels which can be perceived as judgemental and negative. For example, someone with an 'unemotional' style should not be labelled as uncaring and uninvolved. It is more helpful to characterize them as, say, in control of their emotions and feelings. Similarly, someone with an 'emotional' style should not be labelled as 'illogical' and 'out of control'. A more accurate characterization would be to describe them as someone who expresses personal attitudes and feelings openly.

Conceptualizing the process of stereotyping

There are many possible *inputs* about the process of stereotyping which can highlight the dangers of how people deal with others of a different culture. It is important to point out that stereotypes are, 'at best', averages, which means that there will be many people who are below the average and many who are above it. In fact, there may be very few people who actually conform to the average stereotype. 'At worst', stereotypes may have little basis in reality, being formed from a few bad experiences that happened many years ago, from second-hand gossip or from the media.

A second important point is to remind people that many 'cultural' differences, or stereotypes, can be identified within national borders. For example, people living in the north compared to the south of many countries, such as France, Britain, Germany and the USA, may have considerably different approaches to life. Similarly, we have talked at length about cultural differences based on age, technical discipline and type of organization (especially in relation to variables such as size, public versus private ownership and technology). These differences can be as powerful in influencing behaviour as national differences.

Cultural norms about communication

Different cultures have different norms concerning the communication process itself. Some cultures are formal and polite, with people speaking only when invited to comment by a high status person. Other cultures value a more individual style, where people are expected to interrupt and make points strongly. Individualist behaviour in the presence of people from a 'polite' culture would probably be labelled rude. For example, Americans are direct and open in making their argument, while people from many Far East countries are polite. When people from these cultures come together, the more individualistic group members will tend to assert their views, interrupt and dominate the conversation. The polite group members will be offended but not say so directly because they don't want to be rude and cause the other to lose face.

Cultures also have norms about the acceptable space, or silence, to be given between speakers. In many Latin countries, one can expect to be interrupted before completing one's point, while in many Asian countries people are expected to leave silences for thought and consideration before answering points. Continually breaking the silence can be seen as 'weakness' by Asians and as 'strength' by Latins! In the Anglo cultures, the second speaker often interjects at the precise moment that the first speaker finishes or, sometimes, when the former pauses for a long breath (Trompanaars, 1993). This means that to contribute to a group which includes Anglo cultures, you have to quickly enter the conversation with a loud voice.

It is notable that one's communication pattern may be different when using your home language and a second language. For example, the French can be very argumentative in the French language, but polite and needing pauses when speaking in English.

Ensuring participation   Trainers as *coaches* can point out these cultural differences and help to establish mutually acceptable ground rules for two-way communication. They can give an *input*, describing these three patterns of allowing space between speakers and offering ground rules such as:

- Listen with good attention and respect
- Allow a silence for understanding before putting across one's own points
- Do not interrupt others
- Summarize what the other has said before making your own point
- Ensure that all parties take turns in putting ideas across

Perceived status between cultures   Where people from two or more cultures meet, one of the cultures may be perceived to be of 'higher status' and, therefore, have the right to do most of the talking and to direct the action. Members of the 'low status' culture or cultures may expect to 'speak when spoken to'. Status is based on power or perceived power, including such factors as 'who owns who' and which country is seen to be the most powerful economically or militarily. For example, if a large German company has a subsidiary in a small, economically-poor third world company, then the Germans would be accorded high status in a cross-cultural meeting. This would be based on the power of company ownership and the perceived power of Germany as an economically strong country. The ascription of status is probably not conscious but would manifest in high status people taking more of the speaking time and interrupting or ignoring the comments of the others. Low status group members are sometimes said to be 'marginalized', or given a position at the 'edge' of the group. The same phenomenon can occur within the same country between men and women, old timers and young employees, and members of different ethnic background.

Working with status differences   The most difficult dilemma which this poses for the cross-cultural team trainer is that he or she is probably a member of the high status culture and is being paid by their head office. To point out status issues could be seen as a challenge to the authority structure. Members of the 'low status' culture may be equally unsupportive of these efforts to build equality. This is because they may feel insecure about their position and be grateful for a job which gives them security and high status in their home culture. Additionally, their model of authority may be one in which high status is not questioned. According to the Hofstede research (1980), most third world countries value 'high power distance'—an autocratic management style—and 'collectivism', that is, fulfilling one's position and maintaining harmonious group relations.

For all of these reasons, perceived status issues are difficult to work through. Cross-cultural trainers need to respect deeply-held values, even if they differ from their own. A constructive first step is to agree the objectives of the training within the context of the company vision.

In other words, does the company wish to promote a 'hierarchical' culture or a 'consultative' culture. If the company wishes to achieve a more democratic or consultative culture, it is important that some members of the training team are from the 'lower status' culture. In this way, the relationship between the trainers can set a model for delegates. Further, *coaching* people from the 'lower status' culture to be more participative will be much more credible coming from the lower status trainer. It will also be easier for delegates to question him or her, with confidence about the sincerity of creating a more equal culture.

Exercise to overcome status differences

A powerful way of initiating more open communication between cultures is to rely on syndicate exercises in which members of each culture examine the same issues and report back their conclusions. For example, each group could recommend ways of improving the cross-cultural teamwork or of solving a fictitious case study. In this way, communication about cultural differences is raised through representatives of each syndicate, which provides safety to the individual. A similar process can help build teamwork within a company by improving the information flow between senior managers and supervisors or between sales and manufacturing departments. For example, senior managers and supervisors may separately identify the key challenges and opportunities facing the company, and then share these opinions through representatives.

Loyalty to cultural group

When you are with people of your own culture it is often easier to discuss cross-cultural issues than it is when you are in the presence of people from other cultures. Openness in the latter situation can be seen as disloyalty to your home culture. Therefore, the tendency is to close ranks around a safe, polite level of conversation. For example, I might be concerned that if I describe my perception of another culture, it will be seen as rude by that culture. In addition, if I discuss my own culture, those of my cultural background may feel I am disloyal in raising sensitive issues. Because of this 'inter-group effect', a pure 'facilitation style' is unlikely to bring about openness and movement towards collaboration. In the cross-cultural situation, the trainer must be more direct in establishing norms of openness—he or she must become a role model.

The trainer's role in increasing openness

There are several techniques which trainers can employ in order to build greater openness across the cultural divide: they can use themselves as role models, design exercises which rely on safe structures, and establish supportive ground rules.

Using oneself as a role model is based on having personal experiences of living and working in different cultures. By sharing these experiences, others will be encouraged to offer their experience. By describing mistakes you have made, others are encouraged to say 'me too', which is a lot less risky than being the first to speak out. This sharing should be conveyed in a neutral or even self-deprecating manner, taking care to avoid the implication that people from the other culture are slow, inadequate or misinformed.

Structuring exercise to increase openness

Designing exercises with safe structures for sharing information is based on the assumption that it will be easier to be open among people of the same cultural background and easier to share that information, as a group view, through a representative. For example, you could ask the French to discuss and share their ideas about 'common difficulties and misunderstandings when they attend meetings with the British'. The British could similarly consider their views about the French. Ideas would be shared through representative spokespeople. This could help break the ice and lead on to a discussion of how to overcome the difficulties. A similar structure can be used when team building, say between the sales and manufacturing departments, in which case the topic might be to describe the 'common difficulties and misunderstandings which arise when attending meetings with the sales department'—and vice-versa.

A third approach, previously mentioned, is the introduction of guidelines and attention to the group process in reminding people to adhere to the guidelines.

Multicultural training teams

Cross-cultural training with a cross-cultural training team offers a highly credible model—practising what is being preached. Unless a lone trainer is very experienced in dealing with different cultures and can demonstrate a cultural empathy, he or she is unlikely to manage both the learning content and group dynamics.

Building an integrated cross-cultural training team, however, is neither quick nor easy. Cultural attitudes will undoubtedly be reflected in assumptions about 'how people learn' and, therefore, how to design a learning event. Additionally, subtle differences in language usage can make it difficult to describe one's training methods in sufficient detail jointly to plan a session.

Building a partnership

The author has built such a training partnership with a French colleague over the past four years. The start was slow as numerous meetings were needed in order to achieve a consensus about the course approach, objectives and methods. These meetings took place between two representatives of the client organization, one of whom was French and the other British, and the two trainers. Goals were agreed in a straightforward manner. The major cross-cultural difficulties began when discussing training methods. For example, frequent miscommunications arose while deciding how to use CCTV—close circuit television. We both used it to review group discussions and simulations but used it differently. To reach agreement on methods, it was essential to describe, in step-by-step detail, what we actually did and did not do.

There are critical elements of the training learning process where cultural attitudes will influence one's basic thinking and in which it will be necessary to find common ground. Reaching consensus is vital to designing a programme which is culturally integrated. If common ground cannot be achieved, the alternative is to agree course content and sessions, and then to assign full responsibility for each session to one trainer or the other. This can be workable but it models *détente* and not synergy.

Cultural differences in managing learning

There are at least two key dimensions of managing learning which must be agreed in order to build collaboration between trainers. These dimensions are equally important between trainers within the same culture. However, the cross-cultural difference means that the differences of approach are more likely to be deeply rooted in basic values about the educational process and, therefore, will be more difficult to resolve. This first dimension is the nature of the learning process and the second dimension is the management of time and agenda. Three distinct learning processes are described below.

Nature of the learning process

Didactic learning methods

The 'didactic' learning process is focused on the 'expert trainer' who inputs information and guidelines. The learner is expected to remember and apply the learning, which assumes that the learner has the basic skill and flexibility to implement the expert's solution.

Experiential learning methods

The 'experiential' learning process is focused on the trainee or manager who is expected to learn from 'experiences' which take place during the course, such as simulated negotiations and communication exercise. The trainer's role becomes one of designing relevant experiences and enabling people to learn from them. This method assumes that people will be prepared to be open with one another in sharing feedback about personal impressions and feelings and to 'play act' a role in a simulation exercise.

Syndicate-based learning methods

A third method is based on syndicate discussions in which learning derives from individuals sharing experiences or ideas about a case study, in small groups. This approach assumes that people will have relevant experiences to share and are open to sharing them.

Deciding which methods to use

While most learning events blend all of these methods, the proportion of time spent on each can vary considerably. This balance is dependent on what the trainer believes will lead to most learning and so may shift significantly between different trainers. As was mentioned previously, these methods will fit or conflict with different cultural value systems. The didactic approach values the 'authority' telling people what to do or not do. People and cultures that value two-way communication and open discussion between the authority and the student will not feel comfortable with this method. The approach requires trainers to have strong 'platform' or presentation skills. They will also need to have considerable cross-cultural experience—and to have read more books than the participants.

The experiential approach values individual openness and directness. People who look to the expert as the source of all learning will feel uncomfortable with this approach. The approach requires the trainer to have good skills of observation, feedback and facilitation of two-way discussion and relies heavily on the delegates being open in giving and receiving feedback. This is most acceptable to those from 'individualist cultures' and least so to those from 'collective' cultures. Using these methods, the trainer need not have more cross-cultural experience than the participants, though it is important that they have some experience on which to draw.

The syndicate-based approach relies on openness in sharing ideas but not in giving one another direct feedback. The approach requires the trainer to have good facilitation skills and the ability to design exercises which will elicit relevant learning points. Table 12.1 summarizes the differences between these methods.

Table 12.1 *Learning methods and cultural differences*

Learning method	Didactic	Syndicate-based	Experiential
Learning focus	• Information • Guidelines • Theory	• Case studies • Experience sharing	• Simulation of real situations • Direct feedback • Skills and technique
Relevant trainer skills	• Presentation • Organization of information and experience	• Facilitation of group dynamics	• Observation and feedback • Facilitation of group dynamics
Cultural values which support each given learning method	• Authorization leadership • Collectivism	• Consultative leadership • Learning by analysis	• Consultative leadership • Individualism • Directness

Cultural differences in managing time and structure

The second critical dimension is the management of time and structure. Many trainers prefer timetables to be drawn up and rigorously followed. In contrast, other trainers prefer to handle sessions flexibly, responding to the group's needs and inclinations. Overrunning stated time-scales are acceptable in the latter case. This dimension touches on cultural values relating to the need to structure or 'avoid uncertainty'. Clearly, if two trainers have different attitudes to time and structure, the training event will quickly become disorganized by being pulled in two conflicting directions.

If the training partnership can agree on the general approach and blend of methods, the lead role on specific sessions can be based on personal strengths and preferences. For example, my French colleague is strong on presentation skills and time management, while I am strong on observation and feedback skills. Our partnership works well because we recognize and value one another's strengths.

Other relevant dimensions which relate to cultural values include:

- Importance of theory versus practical guidelines
- Importance of practising skills and techniques versus discussing experiences

Conclusion

In working within a multicultural setting, there are new trainer/consultant competences to be learned. Personal flexibility and patience will be essential, both in the design and implementation of events. Knowing what is expected from a given culture is important, both the small things—for example, that yawning and burping is not necessarily rude—and the overall value system and educational preferences.

This chapter has summarized some of the cross-cultural issues to be faced and, hopefully, provides some 'hints and tips' for the globe-trotting facilitator.

Note

Thierry Hackett at Centor Idept, based in Paris.

References

Hofstede, G. (1980) *Cultures Consequence*, Sage Publications, London.
Trompenaars, F. (1993) *Riding the waves of Culture*, Economist Books, London.

Index

Further titles in the McGraw-Hill Training Series

WORKSHOPS THAT WORK
100 Ideas to Make Your Training Events More Effective
Tom Bourner, Vivien Martin, Phil Race
ISBN 0-07-707800-4

THE HANDBOOK FOR ORGANIZATIONAL CHANGE
Strategy and Skill for Trainers and Developers
Carol A. O'Connor
ISBN 0-07-707693-1

TRAINING FOR PROFIT
A Guide to the Integration of Training in an Organization's
Success
Philip Darling
ISBN 0-07-707786-5

TEAM BUILDING
A Practical Guide for Trainers
Neil Clark
ISBN 0-07-707846-2

DEVELOPING MANAGERS AS COACHES
A Trainer's Guide
Frank Salisbury
ISBN 0-07-707892-6

THE ASSERTIVE TRAINER
A Practical Guide for Trainers
Liz Willis and Jenny Daisley
ISBN 0-07-709077-2

MEETING MANAGEMENT
A Manual of Effective Training Material
Leslie Rae
ISBN 0-07-707782-2

LEARNING THROUGH SIMULATIONS
A Guide to the Design and Use of Simulations in Business and
Education
John Fripp
ISBN 0-07-707588-9 paperback
ISBN 0-07-707789-X Disk

IMAGINATIVE EVENTS Volumes I & II
A Sourcebook of Innovative Simulations, Exercises, Puzzles
and Games
Ken Jones
ISBN 0-07-707679-6 Volume I
ISBN 0-07-707680-X Volume II
ISBN 0-07-707681-8 Set Ringbinder

TRAINING TO MEET THE TECHNOLOGY CHALLENGE
Trevor Bentley
ISBN 0-07-707589-7

CLIENT-CENTRED CONSULTING
A Practical Guide for Internal Advisers and Trainers
Peter Cockman, Bill Evans and Peter Reynolds
ISBN 0-07-707685-0

TOTAL QUALITY TRAINING
The Quality Culture and Quality Trainer
Brian Thomas
ISBN 0-07-707472-6

CAREER DEVELOPMENT AND PLANNING
A Guide for Managers, Trainers and Personnel Staff
Malcolm Peel
ISBN 0-07-707554-4

DESIGNING AND ACHIEVING COMPETENCY
A Competency-based Approach to Developing People and
Organizations
Edited by Rosemary Boam and Paul Sparrow
ISBN 0-07-707572-2

SELF-DEVELOPMENT
A Facilitator's Guide
Mike Pedler and David Megginson
ISBN 0-07-707460-2

DEVELOPING WOMEN THROUGH TRAINING
A Practical Handbook
Liz Willis and Jenny Daisley
ISBN 0-07-707566-8

MAKING MANAGEMENT DEVELOPMENT WORK
Achieving Success in the Nineties
Charles Margerison
ISBN 0-07-707382-7

MANAGING PERSONAL LEARNING AND CHANGE
A Trainer's Guide
Neil Clark
ISBN 0-07-707344-4

THE BUSINESS OF TRAINING
Achieving Success in Changing World Markets
Trevor Bentley
ISBN 0-07-707328-2

RESOURCE-BASED LEARNING
Using Open and Flexible Resources for Continuous
Development
Julie Dorrell
ISBN 0-07-707692-3

All books are published by:

McGraw-Hill Publishing Company
Shoppenhangers Road, Maidenhead, Berkshire SL6 2QL, England
Tel: (01628) 23432   Fax: (01628) 770224